SCENE: THE EXECUTIVE DINING ROOM OF *LOOK* MAGAZINE, ONE OF THE GIANTS OF THE COMMUNICATIONS INDUSTRY

The intoxicating glow of the chandeliers casts a moneyed shadow upon the rosewood table. Seated there are men who make million-dollar decisions daily, who appear to have the inside information on government and international wheelings and dealings. Seated there also is Don Gussow. "I ate it up. Boy, oh, boy, I thought, this is really exciting stuff, this and the Kennedy/Manchester affair, and I was now part of it all. Quite different from publishing *Candy Industry,* my first baby, eh? Or working on the *Butcher's Advocate?*"

Different? You'd better believe. But in a way that Don Gussow never dreamed . . .

FROM BALLANTINE'S BUSINESSMAN'S LIBRARY

DIVORCE—
CORPORATE STYLE

Don Gussow

BALLANTINE BOOKS • NEW YORK
An Intext Publisher

For my wife, Betty, a fresh breath of air, becoming more refreshing and precious with the years—in the increasingly polluted world in which we live.

First Printing: May, 1972

Printed in the United States of America

Cover photo by Mort Engel

BALLANTINE BOOKS, INC.
101 Fifth Avenue, New York, N.Y. 10003

ACKNOWLEDGMENTS

While this book is based on my own personal experience, observations and research, I received valuable help and counsel from several sources. In particular, I wish to thank:

The handful of board members, executives and editors of Cowles Communications, Inc., who must remain unidentified, who were willing to talk freely and provide me with information that I could not have obtained in any other way.

My son, Mel, of *The New York Times*, who read my manuscript in its original, rough form and gave me unstinted but unswerving professional, constructive criticism.

My son, Alan, artist and conservationist, who interested Ian Ballantine in my book and who provided a special measure of encouragement.

Ian Ballantine, an unusual publisher and a still more rare human being who saw the potential in my manuscript from the start and whose enthusiasm was so much greater than that of the other two publishers who were interested in the book, each representing a much larger company, that my choice was an easy one.

Sam Kaylin, my editor, who brought to the task over twenty-five years of experience as one of the great business magazine editors of all time and thus a special appreciation of the content and purpose of my manuscript.

And, finally, my secretary, Nancy (Mrs. Louis) Picciola, who performed yeoman's service in a thousand and one areas, including checking and rechecking my research, particularly names, dates and figures, directing the typing and retyping (oh, how many times?) of the manuscript in its various forms (and doing some of it herself since only she had been able to read my handwritten notes), and most important of all, developed an enthusiasm that surpassed that of all others since she had lived through some of the experiences in it with me, Marvin Toben, our executive vice president, and others at Magazines For Industry, Inc., throughout the merger with Cowles, the time of the buy-back and the aftermath.

INTRODUCTION

When *Look* magazine folded in October, 1971, explanations for the disaster resounded throughout the communications community. They ranged from a simplistic effort to blame increased postal rates to complex analyses of social and economic trends affecting mass communications media.

Most of this book was written before *Look* gave up the ghost. The book started out to be, and still is, an account of how Gardner Cowles merged my trade paper business into his communications empire—whose key property was *Look*—and how I got out from under just in time.

Because I had a front row seat during most of the events leading up to the tragedy of *Look*'s suspension, my book goes a long way toward explaining how Cowles managed to preside over the destruction of a property he had spent a lifetime building.

Gardner Cowles is five years older than I am. When he was growing up as the son of a banker and newspaper publisher in Algona and Des Moines, Iowa, I was growing up as the son of an itinerant tailor in the Jewish ghetto of a small Lithuanian shtetel near the Latvian border. While Cowles was being educated in the best private schools, I was being kicked out of my homeland and was traveling in a boxcar to the Russian hinterlands. Cowles was attending Phillips Exeter Academy while I was scrabbling through Gomel, Vetka, Berdichev, Schlutzk, Warsaw and Danzig—under the Russian, Polish and German governments—during the years from 1914 through 1919.

After I arrived in New York in the rat-infested steerage of a converted troop ship in 1920, I compressed my grade school and high school education into five years and was ready to enter the Maxwell Training School for Teachers in Brooklyn, at about the time Cowles graduated from Harvard and was promoted from Associate Editor to Managing Editor of his family's *Des Moines Register and Tribune*. I started as an assistant editor of the *Butcher's Advocate* when Cowles was developing an expertise with picture stories that was soon to become important as a concept for both *Look* and *Life*. My subsequent career in trade paper editing and publishing, in the course of which I started my own stable of publications, had nothing to do with Cowles' subsequent career as the publisher of *Look, Family Circle, Flair, Venture* and other publications—until 1966, when our paths crossed.

I sold to Cowles Communications, Inc. the company I had developed—Magazines For Industry, Inc. I joined the board of directors of CCI. I looked forward to a long, happy association with one of the authentic publishing geniuses of our time.

Until the bubble burst.

This is the story of why and how that bubble burst . . . and how I avoided the explosion.

Contents

Contents

Begins

ONE:

Gifts in Strange Wrappings

At my first meeting of the board of directors of Cowles Communications, Inc., I wondered how I got there. I, a Jewish immigrant from Lithuania, the son of a Russian Jewish tailor and a Lithuanian Jewish housewife, neither of whom could read or write, among second, third, fourth and fifth generation native Americans, most of whom came from pioneer families of Iowa. I, public school educated—on the Lower East Side of Manhattan and Brooklyn—and the recipient of a normal school diploma, but minus any baccalaureate degree (despite four and one half years of university study at Maxwell Training School for Teachers, The College of the City of New York, New York University and the University of Vermont, where I received most of my education and which gave me my teacher's certificate), among the graduates of Harvard College, Harvard Business School and Harvard Law School. (The closest I got to the illustrious house of learning in Cambridge, Massachusetts, was to lunch in the alumni-club dining room.) I, who started a career in journal-

1

ism as an editorial assistant on a weekly trade paper called the *Butcher's Advocate,* with my beat the meat markets on West 14th Street and the slaughterhouses on the East Side, the prizefights and dinners with the butchers and meat packers—and my weekly gossip column about my experiences. Among these giants of communications—publishers and editors of *Look, Family Circle, Venture* and a string of newspapers, and executives of TV and radio stations and book publishing companies. How did I get to be the fourth largest stockholder and a director of such an illustrious communications empire, this "hot" publishing company, which some day would surely overtake Time, Inc. and McGraw-Hill, Inc., the only giants of publishing which were bigger? I was overwhelmingly awed. I followed every action of the board as if each routine resolution, "unanimously" approved by the sound of "aye"—a rhythmic chorus of ayes on the part of the sixteen board members—were a great matter of state.

How did I, the little Jewish lad from the ghetto of a tiny Lithuanian hamlet with elements of superstition and Chasidic tradition, who was kicked out of his homeland at the age of five and wandered throughout Russia and Poland during the next seven years before arriving in Paradise—the tumultuous, noisy, crowded East Side of New York (along with other immigrants, from Russia, Poland, Lithuania, Latvia, Ireland, Italy, Armenia and points east, north, south and west, but mostly east), how did I get here? To this awe inspiring, rosewood paneled board room on the richly carpeted executive floor of the Look building on Madison Avenue and East 51st Street, built on land originally owned by the Catholic Church?

Very few career experiences of my life until then—if, indeed, any at all—could compare with the thrill I felt attending my first meeting of the board of directors of Cowles Communications. While we were still putting the finishing touches on our deal and though our merger into Cowles would not be consummated until November 30, I was elected to the board at its quarterly meeting on November 20. Gardner Cowles invited me to attend the pre-board meeting luncheon at the executive dining room and to join the board at its meeting at 2:30 that afternoon. The first order of the board's business would be my election and that of several other new members. It would take only a few minutes, I was told.

I arrived at my office shortly after nine, but I might as well have stayed home since I could not concentrate on anything except the upcoming board meeting and the luncheon that preceded it. But then, there was not much point in staying home. I had awakened at four and could not sleep after that. As I was lying in our king-sized bed next to Betty, who was still asleep, I looked out of the window toward the west and 488 Madison Avenue. It was still dark and I could not see very much but I tried to envision what would await me on the sixteenth floor of the Look building. The friendly greetings. The spirited conversation during the pre-luncheon cocktail hour. The chitchat about the publishing business, with emphasis on business magazines, of course. The general camaraderie.

Luncheon was scheduled for 12:15. While I had the habit of arriving at meetings and appointments on time, I made sure not to be the first on this occasion. I walked briskly to the executive dining room where I had been on two previous occasions—at a luncheon with Gardner Cowles, Marvin Whatmore and Jack Harding to meet the Big Man, and a few weeks later at lunch with Whatmore, Harding and one of my lawyers, to finalize arrangements for my remuneration.

"Hi, Don, it is so good to see you . . . Come right in,"

was the cheerful greeting I received from Don Perkins as I entered the room. I had met Don about two months earlier and he was extremely friendly. He had a drink in his hand. "What will you have, Don?" he asked, as he led me to a bar with a mirror reaching to the ceiling.

"A Scotch on the rocks with a bit of water."

"Cutty Sark is our Scotch of the day."

"That's fine."

As Don was preparing my drink, Gil Maurer walked over. "Welcome, welcome," he said. "It's good to see you again, Don. How's the trade paper business?"

"Not bad," I said. "How's *Venture* and the educational publishing operation coming along?"

"Great!" was his immediate answer.

As Don handed me my drink and I took my first sip, I looked around and saw three men, whom I had not met, at the other end of the room. Don led me to them. "Fellows, I want you to meet Don Gussow, president of Magazines For Industry, our new, upcoming acquisition . . . Don, meet John Perry . . . Dave Kruidenier . . . and Vern Myers."

"It's nice to meet you—I've heard so much about you," Vern Myers said. I had not met him earlier but I had seen his picture. I was interested in meeting the fellow who at that time was vice president and publisher of *Look*.

"It's good to meet you, too. I've also heard a lot about you."

"I hope it was not all bad," he said.

"You have an interesting business, I hear," said John Perry, an important stockholder and an outside director.

"I think it's an exciting business, but quite different from the publishing of newspapers or general interest magazines," was my reply.

"Is it really that different?" Dave Kruidenier, who was vice president of the Des Moines Register and Tribune Company, asked me.

"It's not much different from a newspaper in that we also publish news and information," I said, "but it is quite different when you compare the type of news and information we publish with that of the daily newspaper. The news and information a good business magazine publishes—particularly the technological material—is of a professional nature. It's of special interest to a particular group of people, while the news and information normally published in a daily newspaper is of general interest to a lot of people. You have to have special expertise in an industry, or a number of industries, to be a good editor, writer or reporter for a trade paper. You must know as much about that business as the reader—or more."

As I was talking to Dave, the room began to fill up.

"You're Don Gussow, our new board-member-to-be? It's great to have you with us. I'm Larry Hanson." Larry's official title was Vice President, Corporate Advertising Sales; actually, he was *Look*'s chief salesman.

Shap Shapiro came over with a smile and a pat on the back. "Welcome aboard . . . it will be good to have another *landsman* with us, Don." Shap was a newsstand circulation specialist.

Then I saw the Big Man coming in. As he said, "Hi Vern, hi Gil," he came over to me, shook my hand warmly, and said: "It's so good to have you with us, Don."

Marvin Whatmore, president of Cowles Communications, entered briskly and jovially, followed by Jack Harding, executive vice president and general counsel. They carried folders with sheaves of papers.

"Hi," he said, waving to all in the room, then turning to Shap he said: "Great work, Shap. I hear that the advance sales of the *Look* issue that will carry the first installment of the Manchester book will set a new record."

"That's the way it looks, Marv," Shap said.

By now, most of the seats in the lounge section of the executive dining room were taken. I sat down next to Gil, with whom I felt more at ease than anyone else, with the exception of Marvin Whatmore, who was now whispering something to Gardner Cowles and Jack Harding.

As the room began to fill with laughter and increased noise from more spirited conversational banter, Gardner Cowles moved toward the rosewood oval table and said slowly, but fairly loudly: "Gentlemen, let us sit down for lunch. We have several items to consider here, and much more to take up at the board meeting. Take your drinks with you, please, gentlemen."

As we began to move to the table, Gardner Cowles said: "Don, won't you sit at my left, and John, [Fischer] you sit at my right."

Marvin Whatmore took his place at the other end of the table, facing Cowles. Moving to sit next to me was Lester Suhler, *Look*'s circulation director, who was dressed in a white wash-and-wear shirt (he commuted weekly between Des Moines and New York), a light grey suit and a long thin Scotch-plaid bow tie.

"May I sit next to the distinguished trade paper publisher?" he asked with a smile. I smiled back—and he sat down.

Others who took their seats around the table were: Palmer K. Leberman, board chairman of Cowles' *Family Circle* magazine, Carl J. Schaefer, *Family Circle*'s publisher, John Weinberg, an outside director, and Hoyt B. Wooten. Hoyt, who was chairman of the board of the broadcasting division, was a distinguished looking man in his seventies, with a big white moustache, a ruddy complexion, a deep Southern accent—a stereotype of the Kentucky Colonel. It was from him that Cowles bought the prestigious and highly profitable Memphis television and radio operation (WREC-TV and radio station WREC). A deal for the acquistion had been made and then called off. Then Wooten received an offer from another source—at a much higher price than that offered by Cowles. But the Southern gentleman felt that he had a commitment to sell his broadcasting properties to Cowles at the price originally agreed upon. He telephoned Gardner Cowles and told him of the new, much higher offer—and Cowles moved quickly to consummate the deal on the original terms.

As two neat middle-aged women began to serve the food, the board members continued to chat as they consumed consommé madrilene, barbecued chicken, caramel pudding with apricot sauce and demitasse.

Marvin Whatmore was ebullient about the upcoming publication in *Look* (in January) of abstracts from the Manchester book, *The Death of a President*.

"What did we have to pay for the privilege of publishing abstracts from the book?" John Weinberg asked. He was the board's not-too-forceful devil's advocate.

"Just under $700,000," Whatmore answered. "A high figure, but a bargain at that, considering the great PR we will be getting, and the sharp increase in newsstand sales."

"Marvin, tell the board members how we almost did not get the book—even at that price," Cowles said.

"That's quite a long, complicated story," Marvin said, his face brightening into a new smile. "Briefly, very briefly, this is what happened. Just about every major magazine was bidding for the publication rights of the book. Finally, when the price passed the half-million dollar mark, only *Life* and *Look* were in the running. Then, Manchester's agents began to use *Life* against *Look* and vice versa. Finally, we bid $600,000. The Manchester people insisted on pushing the price to $650,000 or higher, but we refused to budge. Their answer: 'We have to go to the *Life* management and tell them of your final offer. If *Life* outbids you, *Life* will get it.' We decided to stand pat—otherwise, the bidding could go to a million. Besides, the Kennedy family wanted us to get the magazine rights rather than Time, Inc.

"It was Friday and the top echelon of Time, Inc. had taken off on a yacht for a weekend cruise with some big advertisers. The Manchester people tried to reach them by telephone and radio but without success. Saturday was the deadline and $600,000 seemed like a good price. They reached me Saturday morning. 'If you will raise the ante to $665,000, the book is yours. Otherwise, we will wait until Monday for the *Life* management to return, although the deadline is today.' I telephoned Mike [Gardner Cowles] and Jack and we got together for a short meeting. We reasoned that $65,000 was too insignificant an amount to cause us to lose such an opportunity. Contracts were signed late Saturday evening. When the *Life* management returned to their offices on Monday, they were furious."

"Are we going to get any extra advertising as a result of the exclusive publication of this manuscript?" John Weinberg asked.

"Not in the issues that will carry chapters from the book," Marvin said. "Mike and Vern decided that as a matter of policy—and good taste—no sales presentation that used the book should be made to advertisers. But we will benefit from much increased newsstand sales, the great PR and, hopefully, increased advertiser interest in future issues."

"Gentlemen, we can talk about the Manchester book for hours on end and still fail to explain fully the great significance to us—to *Look* and to the corporation—of the publication of this unusual manuscript," Cowles said. "I want to assure you that in my opinion it was a great coup, one of the greatest in *Look*'s history. And we have had some unusual exclusives and scoops in the past. Now, let us turn to other matters before adjourning to the board room for our formal meeting. At my left is Don Gussow, whom most of you have met. He is president of Magazines For Industry, a prestigious business magazine publishing company, which we believe will form a significant nucleus of a much larger, highly profitable business and professional magazines division. He has some very ambitious but do-able plans. Don, tell the board something about your company and your plans for the future."

I was prepared. Briefly I told the story of MFI, its size, its standing in the industry (Number 23 of about 250 companies publishing about 2,500 periodicals), and then outlined some of my plans for growth in the next three to five years.

"Don, how did the merger come about?" Vernon Myers asked.

"Simply—I made a list of companies, most of them public, in the communications field, that were not engaged in business magazine publishing—but should be . . . and Cowles was on top of the list . . ."

"What were the other firms on your list?" Dave Kruidenier asked. Since this was a confidential meeting I could see no reason for not answering the question, although I did hesitate for a few seconds.

"My list included Cowles, CBS, IT&T and the Washington Star/Newsweek group," I said, "and in that order. But I did not have to go beyond Cowles."

Gardner Cowles smiled at that and continued with

the introductions. "John Fischer, the distinguished president of Teachers College of Columbia University, will also join our board. I have known and admired John for a long time. You know that I am a trustee of Teachers College . . . I have invited John to join our board because I know that he will be able to help us in reaching the goals of our educational book publishing division. John, who came to Teachers College from Baltimore where he was superintendent of schools, is recognized as both a scholar and an excellent administrator in the educational profession . . . and he is doing a fine job at Columbia. John, won't you say a few words, please?"

"Thank you, Mike. I feel most honored to join this distinguished board of publishing and broadcasting executives. I do not know what help I can give you gentlemen, since I have no experience in publishing or broadcasting . . . but I wish to assure you that I am willing. As time goes on, if there should be any questions pertaining to education, I will be most pleased to answer to the best of my ability. Thank you again, Mike, for inviting me to join this fine group of men."

By now, it was 2:15, and Gardner Cowles adjourned the luncheon meeting: "Gentlemen, let us convene in the board room—promptly at 2:30. . . . We have a lot of business to consider."

By the time Gardner Cowles arrived, at precisely 2:30, everyone had taken his place around the rosewood oval table. Cowles took the seat at the head of the table at the entrance. We were joined by William Attwood, editor-in-chief of the Cowles publications.

A young, bearded photographer, with one camera in his hand and another slung over his neck, and a pretty female assistant, also carrying a camera, entered. Cowles explained: "Before we start our meeting, the photographers will take pictures for a 24-page advertising supplement in an early issue of *Madison Avenue* magazine. Reprints will be made for additional promotional use. It will be called 'Inside Cowles Communications, Inc.' Why don't you converse among yourselves and try to be at ease? This won't take long."

The photographer and his assistant moved quickly around the table, standing on chairs and clicking away. In less than ten minutes, they were finished and left.

"Now, gentlemen, the next order of business will be to elect several new board members to serve on an interim basis until the annual stockholders' meeting in May," Cowles said. "As you know, John Cowles, Jr., my nephew, has already left the board. Dave Kruidenier and Hoyt Wooten will leave the board after today's meeting. Elected to serve until May, when their names will be presented to the stockholders along with the rest of the management slate, will be John Fischer, Don Gussow, Bill Attwood, Gil Maurer, John Perry, Tom Shephard and Merrill Clough. The board will be increased from fourteen to eighteen. I would like to ask the gentlemen who will be moved for election, as the first order of business, to leave the room. We will call them back, and it will not take long." We were called back within three minutes. Merrill Clough, who handled finances for Cowles, and Tom Shephard, soon to be publisher of *Look,* joined us as we returned to the board room.

Placed in front of each board member was a black loose leaf book, a pad of ruled paper and several pencils. I opened the book and saw that it contained a lot of figures.

"Gentlemen, let me welcome you officially to the board. Now, let us go on with the rest of the agenda," the chairman said. I leaned back in my Kroll chair and looked around. What I saw was an impressive group of men eager to participate in the next few hours in making decisions for a great and growing communications empire. The chairman read a motion to dispense with the reading of the minutes of the meeting of August 15. Larry Hanson moved the motion. It was seconded by Shap Shapiro. It was followed by "ayes" and the chairman then read the next resolution, which dealt with a number of resignations of minor officers, whose names meant nothing to me. Whatmore moved the motion. Perkins seconded it. Again, the "ayes." Everyone had a copy of the motions to be placed before the directors. The names of "the movers" and "the seconders" were indicated. I noticed that there were a lot of motions to be acted upon. But they were disposed of at a nice pace. Nothing much happened of importance until the chairman read the resolution to ratify an amendment of *The Death of a President* agreement with William Manchester. Harding moved the motion and I seconded it (as it was indicated for me to do).

"Before voting on the motion, are there any questions?" the chairman asked.

"I'd like to ask a question, Mike," P. K. Leberman said. "I understand that we are paying a record price for the magazine rights to this manuscript. What is our payoff?"

"That's a difficult question to answer, P.K.," Cowles said. "Let me ask Marvin to give us some details. He and Jack have been closer to the picture than I have been . . . Marvin, why don't you tell the directors the latest developments on the Manchester book?"

Now we were getting into something very exciting. The *New York Times* and the press around the country were full of stories on what had become a controversial matter—especially since the Kennedys, long time friends of the Cowleses, were now opposing the publication of the abstracts in *Look*. An especially strong position against the publication was being taken by Jackie and Bobby. I thought, now we will hear some inside details from the president of the company that publishes *Look,* and I perked up, trying not to miss a single word. The room was silent as the president began:

"Gentlemen, let me say for the record that the publication of *The Death of a President* is turning out to be the most exciting experience in the history of *Look* —and we have had some very exciting experiences, as some of you know. No book ever serialized in a magazine has received the kind of press we are getting with the Manchester manuscript, but then, no book serialization involved the assassination of a president in the modern history of the nation. It is most exciting stuff and we are getting the kind of PR in the daily press I never thought possible—day after day. It is tremendous, invaluable, priceless. *Look* is the talk of the century. It's on everyone's lips. It should mean a huge increase in newsstand sales of *Look.* And you know that this is something we need. Now, Jack has been involved in meetings with Jackie and Bobby, I'd like to have him tell you something of his experiences. With the chairman's permission, Jack, tell the board members . . ."

"Go ahead, Jack," Cowles said.

"I can make it brief. I don't need to repeat what you've read in the papers, every day, and you will be reading more. A full-scale story is being prepared for *Esquire.* I've been interviewed for it. The fellow who is writing it, a former *Times* man, seems to know quite a bit of the background, and he is digging for more stuff. It has been a traumatic experience for me, being flown in the Kennedy private plane to the Kennedy compound in Hyannis, and given a sales pitch by both Bobby and Jackie—the kind to which I had never been subjected before. It makes our presentation on *Look*

—the way Tom Shephard and his staff do it—appear pale by comparison. Jackie is quite a girl, I never expected her to behave the way she did. She is not at all the demure little girl the press has made her out to be. She comes on strong, very strong and tough . . . and she can show great anger. She tried it with me. I seemed to frustrate her because I refused to get angry in turn. I smiled as much as possible, and quietly stuck to our position—I was willing to listen, and compromise in some areas—but the manuscript would be published substantially as planned."

"Jack, for the benefit of the directors, do you believe that she will have much success with efforts for an injunction?" Cowles interjected.

"No, I don't think so . . . but I don't believe it will go that far. I feel confident that we can work this out without resorting to any kind of litigation."

Following a few more questions and answers, a vote was taken on the motion to amend the agreement and the "ayes" were loud and clear.

The next item on the agenda dealt with the impending acquisition of the Cambridge Book Company, a regional educational book publishing operation whose main line of products were high school and college test material. Following the reading of the motion to authorize the executive committee and/or one or more officers to continue negotiations and complete the deal, it was duly moved and seconded. At this point, Chairman Gardner Cowles called on John Fischer:

"John, for the benefit of the directors, please tell us what you know about Cambridge and how you feel this company will help our educational book division."

"I'm not too familiar with the Cambridge material, Mike," John Fischer said. "We did not use their testing texts in Baltimore since Cambridge distributes largely in the New York metropolitan area, and I have had no experience with their books at Teachers College. But I know the name and from what little I know about it, I believe the company has a good reputation. As to what Cambridge will do for the Cowles Educational Book Division, I would have to study the line of books and texts—both of Cambridge and Cowles— to give you a meaningful evaluation. I'm sorry, Mike, that I can't be of more help."

"Thank you, John."

A few questions relating to the Cambridge acquisitions followed. Marvin Whatmore and Gil Maurer, who were directly involved in the negotiations, provided some detailed answers.

Following the "ayes" on the Cambridge resolution, Chairman Gardner Cowles leaned back in his chair, took a long puff on his ever-present cigarette, and said:

"There will be no resolution on the next subject, but I would like to acquaint the directors with preliminary discussions that Marvin and I have had with some people in connection with our possible acquisition of a 35 percent interest in a group of English language newspapers in Bangkok."

Cowles then launched into a fairly long dissertation on a subject which seemed to have a full measure of international intrigue and which appeared to involve our State Department.

While the dollar and cents portion of the report appeared to be of minor significance, and while profit potentials received even less consideration, I ate it up. Boy, oh boy, I thought, this is really exciting stuff, this and the Kennedy/Manchester affair, and I was now part of it all. Quite different from publishing *Candy Industry,* my first baby, eh? Or working on the *Butcher's Advocate?*

My daydreaming was interrupted by John Weinberg, who asked:

"Why do we want to buy newspapers in Bangkok, of all places—especially when the profit potential seems to be so insignificant?"

"You're right, John, from the dollars and cents point of view there is not much in it for Cowles Communications," the chairman said, "but there is a lot more to it than that. I am not in a position to go into great detail now, but one thing this can do is to give us a foothold in the Far East where there will be plenty of growth in the next decade, and there is no telling what this can lead to. As I explained earlier, we can buy only a 35 percent interest. Thompson will acquire the same percentage and the rest will be held by Thailand natives. We already have a partnership with Thompson on *Family Circle* in Great Britain and in West Germany."

While none of the other board members expressed any particular enthusiasm for the Bangkok newspaper deal, Cowles said that he thought it would be a good idea for Marvin Whatmore to make a trip to Thailand and explore the situation firsthand and report on it at the February meeting.

"I think it is worthwhile to do it. The big problem we face is that the State Department does not want Thompson in the deal. They would rather have American ownership of the Bangkok English-language newspapers, but since Thompson brought the deal to us, we cannot buy it ourselves. At the same time, another American publishing company is bidding for the property and the State Department officials in Bangkok favor that company—only because it would put the newspapers in American hands. Thailand is considered strategically most important, most valuable to the United States, and the State Department does not want any possible interference from any source. It does not trust or like Thompson for some reason that has not been explained. I think Marvin will be able to deal with this subject when he gets to Bangkok. He will arrange to meet with the State Department officials in Bangkok and reassure them on Thompson—explain to them that we will be calling the shots. Bill Attwood believes that he will be able to set up the appointments for Marvin, and I know what kind of a job Marvin can do face to face with people in a situation of this kind. So, I hope the directors will not object to Marvin taking this trip. It could prove very valuable."

No one voiced any objections.

The next piece of business involved a report to the directors on the acquisition of land adjoining the San Juan Star building in San Juan, Puerto Rico. Per the script, Shap moved the motion and Larry Hanson seconded it. Cowles then explained the intrinsic value of the property and pointed out the fact that "we are getting a real bargain." There was no discussion and the "ayes" had it.

The final action of the afternoon was a report by Whatmore on the amount available for the third quarter dividend. Following his report, the chairman read the motion declaring a dividend of 12½ cents per common share. Dave Kruidenier moved the motion. Weinberg seconded it. There was no discussion and the "ayes" were loud and clear—louder and clearer than those voted on any other motion of the afternoon. It was four o'clock when the meeting was ended and by that time it was quite warm in the board room. I did not linger. I said goodbye to Whatmore and Cowles, and Cowles smiled and said: "It is so good to have you on our board, Don."

It was sunny and unusually warm on that fall afternoon in New York, but I felt cool and refreshed. The air on Madison Avenue was delightfully invigorating. How rewarding and exciting to be a director of this tremendous, growing communications company! And to be associated with interesting men of such stature and varied backgrounds! And to be involved in momentous matters, including the behind-the-scenes workings of the State Department! It was a delightful afternoon and the expectations of the months ahead seemed even more joyous. Briskly, I walked back to the office —as if on air.

Three board meetings later, no longer in great awe, I wondered how the rest of the eighteen-member board, the majority far above their level of competence (according to the Peter Principle), had gotten there.

For me, of course, this was not a quick, direct jump from the shtetel in Lithuania to the Madison Avenue publishing Big Time. Except for the first few months following my arrival in the United States at the age of twelve in 1920, I have not considered myself an immigrant. I became a citizen almost upon arrival through the citizenship of my father.

By the time I was graduated from elementary school, I had lost any trace of foreign accent. Seven and one half years later I passed the oral examination for a teacher's license in New York easily, despite the strictness and high standards set up by the board of examiners, who at that time would not tolerate any foreign accent. Apart from "basic Yiddish," I had no real roots in language, although I had a smattering of eight of them. I took to English quickly. It was almost instant assimilation, and New York became my beloved adopted homeland.

Rather than teach, I decided on a career in journalism. Unable to obtain a job on a New York City newspaper, I got into business paper writing and editing by default. Today, I cannot visualize greater fulfillment in any other work.

After thirteen years as a trade paper editor and publisher, I launched my own business in 1944 with a few thousand dollars, saved with much difficulty. Our first magazine, *Candy Industry,* became profitable with the first issue. By the time I merged my company into Cowles, we had a record of growth and profit in twenty-one of the twenty-two years we were in business. We published eight highly respected magazines covering various industries, four of which were the leaders in their fields, with the others coming up fast. We had the respect of our peers and our company was twenty-third among 250 business magazine operations. I was a self-made man and I was proud of my accomplishments. Nevertheless, I could not help being in awe of the great and exciting Cowles Communications establishment on Madison Avenue. And I was particularly taken with Gardner Cowles and Marvin Whatmore.

But, as time went on, I found myself asking again and again: How *did* this bunch of yes men (to the Great and Good Father—tall, stately but diffident Chairman Gardner Cowles) *get* there? And what was I doing there?

Who was Gardner Cowles? What manner of man was he? Who were the other sixteen? What situations brought them to their present points in their careers?

Obviously, my greatest interest was in Gardner Cowles. He was boss man. He was chairman of the board, chief executive officer and editorial chairman. Whatever he thought, whatever he did, whatever decisions he was going to make would determine (in the largest measure) the future of this business of which I now owned 101,000 shares, or three percent of the total shares issued. I kept telling my friends and associates that I did not *sell* my business to Cowles, but *bought into* this great and growing communications empire. That I was on the board of directors. That I was part of management. That I would help in its upcoming expansion, that I would share in this growth.

What about failure? Would I share in that too? I never gave much thought to anything but "growth" and "success." At least, not in my conscious mind. Cowles had a great, almost magnificent, ten-year record of growth. In 1956, its annual sales were $40,346,000. Its net profits were only $640,000. It owned and published only *Look* magazine, although the company by then had been in business for twenty years. In 1961, the company went public and consolidated revenues, net income and per share earnings increased each subsequent year. So that, in 1966, when I merged my company with Cowles, its annual sales were $146,313,000 and net profits after taxes amounted to $4,637,000, or $1.37 a share, and its stock was selling in a range from $13 to $15 a share, a low multiple (in comparison with other publishing companies) with much room to grow. Moreover, it had working capital of over $35,000,000, much charisma, great standing, both in the publishing and financial communities and a well designed plan for growth—largely through acquisition. Said Gardner Cowles in his prologue to the 1966 annual statement: "The next thirty years . . . We turn to a future which will offer one startling new gift after another. These gifts may not fit in old boxes. They may come in strange wrappings. They may frighten us by their unfamiliarity. Still, we welcome them and we anticipate the world of tomorrow as an adventure."

Prophetic? Only time would tell.

Who was Gardner Cowles, whom every member of the board, including me by now, called "Mike," a name

that seemed entirely out of place? This was not a
friendly, slap-on-the-back, easy-to-know "Mike." This
formal, dignified man was Mr. Gardner Cowles, no
matter what you called him. I could not even envision
his own wife calling him anything but Gardner, unless
she had her own private way of addressing him. It
was not Mike, I was sure.

Who was this person of many contradictions? This
basically shy, self-effacing and gentle man of few, well
chosen words? Was it possible that this extremely well
mannered sixty-four-year-old, who looked almost imposing in his dark blue suit, white shirt and blue butterfly bow tie, had gone through three marriages? And
that he was now working on his fourth and still re-
tained the loyalty of his long-time good friend and
private secretary?

I asked a friendly board member at lunch: "How
come nothing has been written about Mike—no in-
depth article, no book, no biography?"

His answer: "Nothing will be written about him until after he dies."

As I began to inquire, and as I observed him at
various conferences and at the quarterly board meetings, I learned a little more. While I could see little
evidence of it, I learned that Cowles, not unlike Henry
Luce, his counterpart at Time, Inc., and a friend of
long standing, had stuttered painfully almost through
his middle years. He spoke slowly and deliberately,
with more of an Iowa drawl than a Harvard accent.
He had a habit of smacking his lips and moving his
tongue to each side of his jaw as he spoke. This was
the way he learned to control his stammer. He spoke
in a monotone, never varying the pitch, sound or
speed. He never cracked a joke, he was totally serious
—and if he had a sense of humor, he showed no
evidence of it at these meetings.

Whether it was in his private luncheon room on the sixteenth floor or in the board room, he sat at the head of a rosewood oval table, chairing the meeting as if he were holding court. He would listen more than he would talk. Sometimes, he would not say a single word throughout a meeting except to call on various participants to comment on a particular subject under discussion. Then he would make his pronouncement. It was not long before I realized that this soft-spoken man who was slow and deliberate in his talk and reticent in appearance, made decisions—some involving millions of dollars—impulsively and arbitrarily.

As time went on, I was horrified to see the great man, a trustee of the Museum of Modern Art, a benefactor of the Philharmonic Society, the Metropolitan Opera and other cultural and charitable organizations, make mistake after mistake that resulted in millions of dollars of losses for Cowles Communications, and a steady decline in the price of its stock, during a time when the price of stocks of nearly all other communications operations continued to rise in the bull market of 1967–1968. Cowles behaved stubbornly, persisting in and compounding his errors. When the series of errors finally resulted in a huge loss and the end result meant dropping a particular property, the Great and Good Father, now looking more serious than ever, made his pronouncement in an almost priestly manner: "I am sorry, gentlemen, it was a mistake to do what we did— but I want you to know that I take full responsibility."

What did this "taking full responsibility" mean? Did it mean that the chairman of Cowles Communications intended to replenish the company's waning exchequer with his own funds, reputed to be substantial at that time? Nothing of the sort. He said he was sorry. What else could he say? Or do?

It was difficult to comprehend that this overly serious, highly impersonal man, bearing an impenetrable coat of arms was a "great lover," at one time the husband of the curiously attractive, noisy, bossy, flamboyant, flamingly colorful but brilliant and creative Fleur.

Fleur was wife Number Three. Entirely different in looks, background and temperament from wives Number One and Number Two. Wife Number One, whom he married in 1927, was Helen Curtis, the daughter of the Dean of Iowa State University at Ames. Helen was a charming young thing from the Iowa corn belt and she was as much infatuated with the tall and handsome young Gardner as he was with her. But the marriage didn't last. It was dissolved within the year.

It wasn't until five years later, in 1933, after Gardner had had his fling, that he married Lois Thornberg. Lois was a beautiful young graduate of the University of Iowa School of Journalism and her first newspaper job was with the *Des Moines Register and Tribune*. She was aware of the bright, young executive editor of the paper almost from the start. It wasn't long before Gardner became aware of her. The marriage, while the result of a typical office romance, was the big society wedding of the year in Des Moines. For a honeymoon, young Gardner took his bride on their first long-distance plane flight, piloting himself from Des Moines to New York. It was a good marriage and had the blessing of the Cowles family. The marriage produced four children, three daughters and one son, Pat, who was the youngest. One of the three daughters, a mongoloid, died in an institution at the age of eighteen.

The marriage began to fall apart shortly after Cowles started *Look* and during his involvement a few years later on the political scene and, particularly, when he became one of the top men in the Office of War Information in the early 1940s. His thirteen-year marriage to Lois was shattered by the time he met Fleur.

"We hated that bitch," a board member told me at lunch after a few martinis, "but those were our happiest days . . . Fleur ran great parties and we were always welcome at the Gardner (or should I say Fleur) Cowles brownstone off Park Avenue. None of us were ever invited to the Cowles' duplex apartment on Park Avenue or later to his very modern, spacious apartment on Fifth Avenue since his marriage to Mrs. Fancy" (Jan Streate, the former Mrs. James Cox, of the famous Cox newspaper family, whom he married in 1956).

"Fleur was a terror and many of us feared her and despised her," this board member continued. "She had the authority to hire and fire and she would exercise the authority whenever the mood struck her . . . She would call in an editor, curse him out in vile language and if he made any effort to defend himself—which many did—she would fire him on the spot, shouting: 'Clear the hell out of here—and clear out promptly . . . We don't need the likes of you here.' "

Gardner Cowles met Fleur at a party shortly after the war in 1945. Each was married at the time, Gardner to Lois Thornburg and Fleur to advertising man Atherton Pettingell. The Pettingells operated the Pettingell-Fenton Advertising Agency (Fleur's maiden name was Fenton), considered by many as the "hot" agency of the fashion field in that period. Fleur and Gardner were attracted to one another almost immediately and, before the party was over, they found themselves in a long, spirited and almost endless conversation. While they had not met before, they knew of each other, Gardner as the creator of *Look,* and Fleur as a newspaperwoman, copywriter and, later, an advertising agency executive. At first, they talked shop in an impersonal sort of way, but as the conversation progressed, they began to show special interest in each other. Fleur, strikingly dressed to bring out her fine body lines, looking taller than she was, and made up in the fashion of the day (and wearing her usual rose), did not have to try too hard to excite the up-and-coming magazine publisher and member of a famous newspaper family. But she did try a little. In his early forties, tall and handsome, Gardner made an impression on Fleur with his gentlemanly behavior and his quiet ways and gave her a feeling of romantic mystery. She wanted to know more about this man. Gardner told her that he had just left government service where he had had an important administrative spot with the War Power Administration and was now returning to the job of reviving his sick baby of seven years—*Look* magazine. During his absence, the once-growing news picture periodical had become a "girlie picture" rag. Cowles explained that he was both shocked and concerned to see what had happened to his creation during his absence.

"You should be," Fleur, who was not in the habit of mincing words, said. "But you can still save that little baby of yours."

"What would you do if you were editor of *Look?*" Gardner asked her.

For the next three hours, Fleur proceeded to tell him. What the magazine needed, she said, was style and character—personality. She told him that the magazine should be completely redesigned, with the newest in graphics and with an abundant use of color. Emphasis should be on fashion—not necessarily women's fashion, although that should be part of it—but "fashions of the day" in art, in books, in the home, in every form of life.

Gardner was very much interested in what this beautiful, eloquent thirty-five-year-old woman, seven years his junior, was telling him. Always a good listener, he absorbed what he heard. And he wanted to hear more of what Fleur had to say. They made a date for lunch for the following week. And then they began to see one another regularly. They learned they had a lot in common. Their romance began to bloom. In 1946 (on December 27), shortly after they divorced their respective spouses, they were married in a quiet civil ceremony.

A few months earlier, Fleur had joined *Look* as an editor. Dan Mich was executive editor, having returned to *Look* less than a year before Gardner had met Fleur.

Dan was one of the founding staff members of *Look*, coming to the magazine in 1937 from the managing editorship of the *Wisconsin State Journal*. Gardner Cowles favored hiring newspapermen for his new magazine and he liked Dan and was impressed with his newspaper record (all on the *Journal*) since he left the University of Wisconsin. During his early years with *Look*, Dan served in various capacities, moving up to the spot of managing editor before long, and then becoming executive editor. He helped perfect the magazine's picture story technique and later wrote a book, *The Technique of the Picture Story*, published by McGraw-Hill, which became a classic in the field and was used as a text in schools of journalism.

As an editor, Dan Mich believed in the philosophy that "nothing we have done in the past will ever be good enough again." He preached this credo to his writers, editors and photographers. And, as a motto for the corporation, this quotation was featured in large and bold type in the 1966 annual report of Cowles Communications, Inc. Dan was away from *Look* during the war years and returned in 1945 when Gardner Cowles rejoined the magazine after his government service.

While each had a professional respect for the other, Dan and Fleur did not get along well. Yet, together, the two were responsible for changing *Look* from a cheap "girlie picture" magazine to a respected, and soon-to-become profitable, high quality, general interest magazine. Fleur's contribution to *Look* was dignity, style and creativity. Dan brought a new excitement to *Look*. He also had the ability and the contacts to bring new men and women of talent to *Look*'s staff. It was he who saw the special editorial talent that a young, recently hired researcher had, and he was able to train Patrice Carbine to become one of *Look*'s most stable and most able editors. Carbine eventually became executive editor and second in command. Day-to-day editor, in fact.

The late forties and fifties were the most exciting years at *Look*. The magazine was becoming successful and soon earned the respect of advertisers and their agencies, as well as that of millions of readers. It began to prosper, and money became plentiful. Gardner Cowles was a good and generous boss. Nothing was too good for his growing and beautiful baby, *Look,* or his able staff members.

He found that he had one major problem. While he tried to give Dan a free hand, that free hand was bludgeoned by Cowles' exciting, hard working, fast moving wife, Fleur. Dan was a fine person. His interests were tremendously varied—travel, the theater, people—and baseball was his particular enthusiasm. While he was not as creative as Fleur, neither was he impetuous or compulsive, conditions which afflicted both Fleur and Gardner. Dan believed in deliberation, in examining an editorial problem slowly and carefully, sleeping on it and then taking the necessary action or abandoning a project that had seemed exciting at first but which appeared impractical after due consideration.

Fleur was different. If there was an idea that seemed exciting to her, she wanted to move on it immediately, even if it might not work out satisfactorily in the end. This could and did prove to be costly. But her record was good. A good many of her ideas were both creative and practical.

A break between the two was inevitable. And in 1950, it finally came. Mike could not talk Dan out of leaving although he had been successful in doing so on several previous occasions.

"I think you will be better off without me, Mike," Dan said, "*Look* is now a fine magazine. . . . It is going to grow and prosper . . ." Dan left to become editorial director of *McCall's*.

While *Look* did continue to grow and prosper, Dan Mich was missed. Now there was no one to put brakes on some of the wild, expensive, though interesting, ideas put forth by Fleur, who was now in full command, although several did try.

One of the more successful ones was Sam O. (Shap) Shapiro, vice president and circulation director of *Look*. A curmudgeon, if there ever was one, Shap was also a no-nonsense guy. And, if there was something he thought had to be done to promote the newsstand sales of *Look*, his favorite chore, he was not going to let anyone stop him—not even the boss's wife. Shap had several run-ins with Fleur but, for a while, each was able to contain the other. Shap was successful because he refused to take any "guff" from Fleur and he was able to tell her what he thought. In turn, Fleur always knew where Sam stood on a particular issue. Also, she found that she was able to use this old-time, extraordinarily promotion-minded circulation executive—one of the best in his business—who received his early training from Bernarr Macfadden and *True Story* magazine. So, while Fleur survived Dan Mich—at least, for a time—Shap Shapiro survived Fleur.

Fleur's great failing was her inability to work with people, particularly other creative editors, who began to come and go on the *Look* staff. So, while *Look* continued to grow and prosper, Fleur soon got in the habit of calling in an editor who did not follow her instructions to the letter, and bawling him out as a tough sergeant would an erring recruit. And she could, and did, use four-letter words in the manner of a trooper.

Her final downfall came after the failure of *Flair,* a most unusual magazine, that seemed to be very much ahead of its time. This proved to be a very costly fiasco and, to make matters worse, while she was spending thousands upon thousands of dollars on *Flair,* she began to neglect *Look. Flair* folded with its January 1951 issue—after eleven issues of publication—and Fleur once again gave her talents to *Look.* But things were not quite the same. The excitement of the forties was gone. The untimely, sudden death of *Flair* stunned, then saddened Fleur. And while all this happened, the romance with the boss man began to cool. In 1956, shortly before their ninth wedding anniversary, Gardner divorced Fleur who at the same time left her post at *Look.* The editorial chairman of *Look* sent a memo to *Look*'s executives announcing both the divorce and Fleur's separation from *Look.*

Shortly after her divorce from Cowles, Fleur met and married Tom Montague Meyer, one of the most affluent men in England, who had extensive lumber interests. Since their marriage, Fleur has lived in London and Sussex, writing and painting. I saw her show at the Hammer Gallery in New York last year, and found her paintings of tigers and flowers imaginative and colorful. Like her tamed, relaxed-looking tigers,

Fleur today has mellowed. She has adopted three children and her husband sponsors nineteen others.

But two and one half years before this (late in 1953), Dan Mich had returned to *Look*. He came back on the promise of Gardner Cowles that he would not be interfered with by Fleur. The chairman tried to keep his promise and, in her own way, Fleur tried too, but it did not work, resulting in much bickering between husband and wife and in quiet battles between Fleur and Dan. But redheaded Dan, whose hair by now was beginning to turn white, tried hard to keep his peace and go on with his work. He survived. But it was not until the departure of Fleur that a new prosperity and quietude returned to *Look,* and it soon attained new heights.

I knew how one, two or three members of the Cowles board of directors got there, but I continued to wonder about the rest. It was obvious how John Weinberg had become a board member. He was a member of the investment company which had been a long-time financial advisor to Cowles. I also knew how Dr. John H. Fischer got on the board. Gardner Cowles wanted some extra (non Harvard) window dressing from the Halls of Ivy—especially for his educational book division—and what better "education" window dressing than the president of Teachers College of Columbia University!

Since this was an "insider" board, most of the directors of Cowles Communications were employees who had come up from the ranks. Attaining board membership meant moving up almost to the pinnacle of success. Becoming a member of the executive committee—a very exclusive club—meant going to the very top of the mountain. Success at Cowles was attained in one of several ways: one, being born or raised in Iowa, preferably Des Moines, beginning an association with Gardner Cowles on the *Des Moines Register and Tribune* and then being invited by him to come to New York to work on *Look* from its beginning; two, being a member of the Cowles family or related to it in some way, or coming from a well-known "other" family, friendly and valuable to Cowles, and finally, three, being a respected, competent head of a company acquired by Cowles.

Most of the Cowles board members came from Category Number One, the second-largest group from Category Number Two, and a small minority from Category Number Three. The longest tenure was held by those in the prime category, the second longest in the second category. The tenure of Category Number Three rarely exceeded three years. Category Number One represented the majority on the executive committee, the minority came from Category Number Two. It was just about impossible for a Category Number Three board member to be invited to join The Club.

John F. Harding, by far the most competent and professional of Cowles' executives, came from Category Number One, but he arrived a bit too late to become president. He joined *Look* in 1944 as general counsel, coming from the prestigious New York law firm of Cravath, Swaine & Moore. When he was named to the executive committee in May, 1965, Jack was Executive Vice President—Administration (one of Cowles' two executive vice presidents), secretary and general counsel. But 1965 is a long time from 1944. By then, he was fifty-eight and still hard-working and vigorous. Iowa born and bred, Jack went to Harvard College and Harvard Law, and distinguished himself at both. Quiet and soft-spoken, of medium height and a bit paunchy, with a full head of grey hair, the wearer of a shy smile and a restrained but nervous laugher, his demeanor was misleading. Underneath his quiet, reserved and seemingly harmless manner, he was tough. Jack was a brilliant lawyer, a lawyer's lawyer. Everyone who knew him and worked with him quickly decided: "I'd rather have this lawyer on my side." It was Jack who successfully led the major battles in the famous Kennedy Clan Versus Cowles War, also known as the Manchester Case. It was he who had to confront all of the Kennedys, but particularly Bobby and Jacqueline, who were both tigers—very ferocious young tigers—at the time of the Manchester situation. Neither wanted the story of the John Kennedy assassination told to eight million readers in *Look* magazine in the manner planned. And all sorts of dire threats were made. It was a very strange situation, as the Kennedys and the Cowleses had enjoyed a unique friendship for a long period of time. It has been reported that the head of the Kennedy Clan, the late Joseph Kennedy, the father of the late president, was very helpful to young Gardner when he launched *Look* magazine. And Gardner never forgot that. When *Look* became a successful general interest magazine, Gardner made it his business to give the Kennedys every possible press break. And Gardner went all out when John ran for the presidency. Gardner was a Republican but he voted for FDR and campaigned for Kennedy, as he did in 1969 for Humphrey. But when the Manchester war began to heat up, Gardner seemed to be helpless in dealing with long-time friends. Jack Harding did the work and he did his job well. He had to take a lot of invective, shouting and threats from both Bobby and Jackie, but he took it all quietly and with his shy smile. But then his toughness came to the fore, still quietly but most forcefully, and he scored.

Socially, it was a real joy to be with Jack. He was

a listener. Jack and his explosively charming wife, Anita, complemented one another. Taller than Jack, blonde Anita always made Jack appear taller than herself. While they were different from each other in many ways, they blended beautifully and there were obviously great feelings of affection and appreciation between them. This was never shown more than when Anita contracted an illness that was soon diagnosed as stomach cancer. She was given six months to live. Anita decided to live every moment of those six months. She refused to keep her illness a secret or face the eventual consequences. She began to live for each day, now more than ever. And Jack behaved as if the new situation were "just normal." Six months passed, and then a year, and then another six months, but Anita continued to make the most of each day. By now, she was suffering from excruciating pain but it was her pain and she refused to impose her misfortune on others, including Jack. In turn, Jack was sharing her suffering, at the same time continuing to be his pleasant, matter-of-fact self.

While Jack was making $100,000 a year in salary and had 10,000 shares of Cowles stock, he often regretted leaving the large and prestigious law firm where he now would have been a senior partner, probably doing as well, if not much better, financially. Although his job was frustrating, he kept his feelings to himself. He had already suffered one heart attack. And while he was warned by his doctor to watch his diet and general regime of work, he paid little attention to this and continued to put in long days of intensive effort.

Don Perkins, executive vice president—sales, was a different breed of cat from Jack Harding. A natural extrovert, on the surface hail-fellow-well-met, Don was a more complicated personality than he appeared to be. A graduate of the University of Wisconsin (1932) and Harvard Business School (1934), Don joined Cowles as eastern advertising manager for *Look* in 1945, after some experience in advertising and publishing and following a stint in the Army. He came to *Look* at the beginning of its rebirth and he made a meaningful contribution to its growth. As a result, he won promotion after promotion, becoming *Look*'s advertising manager in 1947 and upped to advertising director in 1954, a post he held until 1964, all during *Look*'s greatest growth and the attainment of great stature in the general interest magazine field. In 1964, when Cowles began to expand rapidly, became a public company and soon moved to be listed on the New York Stock Exchange, Don was named to the board of directors and promoted to the post of Executive Vice President—Sales. Now making over $90,000 a year and beginning to acquire important stock holdings in the merging communications empire, Don had no specific assignment until 1966. While he gloried in his past performance record, he was unable to put his sharpened sales and marketing teeth into anything resembling a juicy steak. At the same time, a feeling of disappointment and frustration began to overtake him. Because of his great success in bringing *Look*'s advertising sales to new heights, Don had expected to get the Cowles presidency. But, in 1964, the nod went to Marvin Whatmore who from 1952 had served as vice president and general manager of the company. Gardner Cowles never explained it to anyone, and least of all to the board of directors who officially made the selection, but Cowles picked Marvin over Don for the top operating spot because: he could use Marvin better; Marvin was a more polished politician (Don was much more outspoken and frank, sometimes to an embarrassing degree); and, Marvin could sling figures around much faster and better than Don. Both men were heavy social drinkers, but Marvin handled his Scotch (or martinis) a bit better than Don. Marvin had suffered from an ulcer while Don had had a heart attack and, as a result, Marvin's general health had the edge over Don's. Finally, Gardner felt much more comfortable with Marvin than he did with Don.

In 1966, when *Family Circle,* Cowles' second biggest property, with an advertising volume close to $20,000,000 and profits before taxes of $2,000,000, began to flounder and move into the red, Don was made president of the women's magazine. During the year of his presidency, the fortunes of *Family Circle* went from bad to worse, finally clocking a loss of $2,000,000. Of course, Palmer K. Leberman, from whom Cowles bought the magazine, still continued as chairman and chief executive officer of Family Circle, Inc., and there are some who believed that P.K. held the reins of the Family Circle operations tightly, and never gave Don much of a chance to exercise his true ability. On the other hand, P.K. made no secret of his own feelings about Don. It was his belief that Don failed because "he could not or would not make decisions." At any rate, in 1967, just about one year later, Don was replaced in the Family Circle presidency by Gilbert C. Maurer, who had been president of both the Cowles Educational Book Division and *Venture* magazine. And once again, Don was now Executive Vice President—Sales, without portfolio, and more despondent than ever. Shortly thereafter, his charming wife Helen began to suffer from an ailment that seemed difficult to diagnose. After months of tests, it was finally determined that she had a rare, fatal disease and in 1969 she passed away. From outward appearances, Don appeared to take in stride the untimely death of

Helen, with whom he had had a close and loving relationship, but that was not the case. He was now despondent in his work and lonely in his personal life. He soon became a tragic figure, his one-time great talent in media selling now almost totally lost to Cowles Communications. He expressed himself very little in board meetings, knowing full well that it would be a waste of time and energy, and he took very little part at executive committee meetings, knowing that it was Gardner Cowles and Gardner Cowles alone who made all of the decisions well before the executive committee held its official meeting to vote on anything.

Vernon Myers, who beat out Don Perkins to the publisher spot and then to the presidency of the Look Division while Don was hoisted upwards to the executive vice presidency of the corporation, was described by some of his associates of the publishing community as "the gentleman publisher." Tall, stately, courteous and conservative, Vern looked and behaved more like a banker or merchant prince than a fast-moving, twentieth century magazine executive. But then, Vern, like Marvin Whatmore, came to *Look* by way of the *Des Moines Register and Tribune,* his first job after he was graduated from the University of Missouri in 1932. He remained with the *Register and Tribune* until 1938, doing various chores as he learned the newspaper publishing business.

In 1938, when young Gardner decided to launch *Look,* he invited Vern to join the charter team of the new magazine as Director of Visual Research. With that fancy title, he did yeoman's service in helping to find out what would "make" a picture magazine. When *Look* was off and running (though at a rather slow pace) in 1942, Gardner thought that he had had enough of "visual research." What *Look,* which continued to lose money, needed was advertising and he told Vern to go out and sell some space. He was space salesman in New York for a year or so and then went west to become *Look*'s first West Coast advertising manager. He remained there until 1947 when he returned to New York as *Look* promotion manager.

In 1947 *Look* was not only struggling, but had lost its course and direction. It was at this time that Gardner left his war effort chores in Washington and returned to his baby. Young and aggressive Don Perkins was now sales manager, Dan Mich and Fleur came to the fore and things began to really stir on the magazine. It was also the end of the war and the magazine business began to flourish. Television's competition was still far away.

Vern did not stay long in his spot as promotion manager. Gardner, who was president and editor-in-chief of *Look*, made Vern assistant to the president, a position he held from 1947 until 1951. In 1951, he was elected vice president of the corporation and named publisher of *Look*, and together with Don Perkins and other smart, up-and-coming self-assured salesmen, Vern did his full share in bringing in considerable advertising volume. By 1967, Vernon was a corporate vice president, a member of the board and was soon moved to the presidency of the *Look* Magazine Division.

In the wings now was Tom Shephard, Jr., who had succeeded Don Perkins as advertising director of *Look*. Tom took Vern's job as publisher of the Cowles' flagship property. From now on, and similarly to Don Perkins, Vernon Myers seemed to be at loose ends. He still presided over the *Look* or twelfth floor lunchroom, he made some "high level" advertising calls, he continued to preside at three *Look* luncheon presentations each year and tried to make himself "generally useful" in corporate affairs. But like Don Perkins, Vernon Myers had been moved upstairs and he had no specific day-to-day function. And like Don, he began to feel despondency and frustration, but with a difference. He became ultraconservative, like most of his neighbors in Darien, Connecticut, quietly discouraged about *Look*'s growth and potential and "unexplainably" (to himself) bitter about what was happening in the publishing and advertising communities of the late sixties—and to the country as a whole. With his wife ailing, Vernon was looking forward to retirement, perhaps an early one.

Enter Tom Shephard, Jr., the new vice president and publisher of *Look* and new member of the board in 1967. A typical Wasp magazine publisher, if there ever was one, Tom's modus operandi followed "the book"—the Madison Avenue book—definition of a magazine publisher, of the fifties. But with the advent of the sixties, particularly the late sixties, Tom could not adjust. Whereas the editorial staff of *Look* was modern and liberal, Publisher Tom—tall, pepper-gray and handsome—was old-fashioned and reactionary. While there were many long-haired staff members, Tom's hair was in the crew-cut style of the college freshman of the twenties. While most of the staff lived in New York and were urban-oriented, Tom resided in Darien in the most typical of Wasp neighborhoods, with the most typical Wasp life and outlook. *Look* writers and editors were writing and publishing features on today's scene—about the hippies, the Yippies and the drug generation. They wrote about the emerging race problems, the college campus race riots and the meaning behind the "revolution," the Black Panthers, the Young Lords, the new folk songs, the New Left and just about all forms of deviating life styles of the late sixties, while Publisher Tom from Darien was making front page headlines in *Advertising Age* and other media publications, as well as in the big city daily newspapers (in some instances, as a result of speeches before big meetings of the ad fraternity) in which he out-Nixoned President Dick and out-agonied the Vice President with "bunch of bums" and "don't you believe it" exhortations about the present generation. Example:

"Recently, *Advertising Age* reprinted a speech given by a prominent advertising man in which he had stated that we are involved 'in a revolution more swift and inevitable than any revolution we've had before—the Revolt of the Individual against the American systems of mass education, mass communication and mass conformity.' He urged his audience to put this revolution to use in their advertising or it could destroy them.

"Now, I read what he'd said and I saw what had happened. And what had happened to him is happening to many people in communications and advertising today. Their problem is that, by and large, they talk only to one another, they listen only to one another and pretty soon they have convinced one another that we are truly hell-bent for some wild new kind of society and some weird, offbeat culture.

"Worthy of special analysis in this revolution hysteria is the youth factor. We are constantly being told that our revolution is a revolution of the younger generation and that our young revolutionists are smarter, purer, more idealistic and just all around nicer than any other young people in history. Sheer nonsense! Smarter? Have you talked to any of our militant youth? The sophistry you get! The cockeyed syllogisms! The faulty reasoning! And the stupendous, monumental, earthshaking lack of information and basic knowledge!

"I had a young man in my office about two years ago who was looking for a job in our company, and he had the answers to all of the problems facing mankind, including a quick and easy solution to the racial unrest that was then gripping Detroit. What he did *not* know—as it subsequently developed in our conversation—was just exactly where Detroit was.

"Do you know the one big difference between today's kids and the kids of thirty years ago? It has nothing to do with the kids. The big difference is that today's youngsters are being listened to *seriously* by adults. When we were children, the adults were too smart to pay attention to us. I remember, as a teenager, spouting socialism and a few other isms to an indulgent high school teacher for hours on end, and I recall his quiet smile as he told me that some day I would grow up and learn that everything I had been saying was utter drivel. And he was right."

There were some who credited Big Tom's rise to his marriage to Gardner Cowles' niece, Nancy. Tom was neither Iowa stock nor Harvard trained. His college was Amherst (1940) which is a sort of Junior H. He started with *Look* as space salesman in 1946, after two years in marketing training with the Vick Chemical Company (1940–42) and a period in the Army. After selling space for *Look* for one year in New York, he became West Coast advertising manager in 1947, replacing Vern Myers in that spot. He remained in the West for two years, moving back to the New York headquarters in 1949. In quick succession, he became assistant manager, vice president and advertising director, and finally, publisher and member of the board of directors (as of May, 1967). Tom was pushing fifty, by now had four children, and he was getting more pessimistic and disenchanted with publishing and advertising as they developed in the late sixties. He wanted so badly to return "to the good old days of the golden fifties," knowing full well (or he should have known) that there was no return at all. His hobby was travel and his favorite "get away from it all" spot was Bermuda—especially in the month of May.

At board meetings, Big Tom just sat there, with his long legs stretched out, looking more bored and tired than ever, saying nothing except reciting a resolution that had been prepared for his reading, or seconding a motion that was indicated for him to second and saying: "aye", "aye" to the long series of resolutions moved by Chairman Gardner for approval. Once in a while, he was asked a question or prompted by the chairman to make a statement about the current position or prospects for *Look*. Reluctantly and looking particularly sad, like an aging Great Dane, Publisher Tom would slowly and deliberately enunciate the answer—and he would do it in an Iowa-cum-Amherst drawl. What he said did not make the other directors any happier for the hearing, or more knowledgeable about what was happening at *Look*. The magazines' revenue fluctuated, from a profit of $4,000,000 one year to a loss of $8,000,000 the next—but big Tom never deigned to explain why.

Handling the finances of Cowles Communications, Inc., was its vice president and controller, Merrill H. Clough, who was also a member of the executive committee. Merrill started with *Look* in 1948, after his graduation from the University of Texas, as a production accountant. In that capacity he trained to become a printing and paper estimator, and a printing and paper estimator he remained throughout his years with Cowles, even when he became vice president and chief financial officer in 1965, with the added title of Controller and the added honors as a member of the board of directors in 1967 and a member of the executive committee in 1968.

Tall, thin, lanky and a bit stooped, Merrill talked in

a strange Iowa-cum-Texas drawl, with a bit of Huntington, Long Island (where he lived with his wife and two children) thrown in. He enjoyed his Gibson martini or Scotch (more the former) but he knew his limit, and rarely went beyond that limit. He liked his job, which by 1967 paid him $65,000 a year. But while he knew his limit of imbibing spirits, he did not know, or he behaved as if he did not know, his limit in his job, and according to some of his associates, he had long passed the Peter Principle level of competence. In that league, he was the undeclared winner, the Numero Uno unchallenged, of all the members of the board of directors of Cowles Communications, Inc.

He could boast the smallest corporate controller's staff of any corporation the size of Cowles—or even half the size. And maybe even one tenth the size of Cowles. The staff ranged from two to four. With the exception of the two who seemed to have unusual staying power for some unexplained reason, the others kept coming and going. Some remained a month, a few hardy ones two months—some left within the first week.

Merrill's method of operation could best be described in one word—autonomy. He believed in autonomy. Some translated it as "don't bother me and I won't bother you." He also believed in "hear no evil, see no evil," but somehow forgot the rest of the famous saying. He offered no financial advice, or help of any kind to divisional (or subsidiary) managers, presidents or controllers. If such advice or help was sought, his stock answer was: "I am sorry, John, I don't have the staff." What he meant was: "Solve your own goddamn problems."

When problems did develop, Merrill and his two assistants insisted on getting an endless array of reports, expecting most of them "as of yesterday." As a result, most of the reports arrived on Merrill's desk (or those of his two assistants) long after the "due date." Merrill and his two overworked assistants never were able to quite "catch up."

And while all of this was happening or failing to happen, Merrill was busy with work estimating printing and paper. At the same time, he was also controller and chief financial officer for the Look Division. Why the Look Division, the corporation's biggest property (from the point of view of total revenue and cash flow) did not have its own controller and its own accounting department was never fully explained. Also, the mess and the continued, fruitless effort to "catch up" in the controller's office did not seem to bother the president very much—at least there was no particular evidence of it. But then, it did not matter much, since President Marvin Whatmore possessed the special gift of dealing with figures—and was faster than just about anyone else, without paper or pencil.

After all, Marvin was a financial man himself. Before he joined the *Des Moines Register and Tribune* as office manager in 1937, he was a financial officer of a bank (in Iowa, of course) and went through the ranks at R & T, Look and Cowles in various financial capacities. So, in reality, Marvin Whatmore operated as his own controller while Merrill went his merry way estimating printing and paper. Marvin Whatmore surely must have had his full share of hostilities. But generally they were repressed. Maybe that is why he had a stomach ulcer. Yet he was almost always genial, outwardly easygoing, friendly. He never raised his voice to anyone. With one exception.

The exception was Merrill Clough, whom he obviously considered his flunky. On a plane trip from Minneapolis to New York I kept hearing Marvin work over Merrill:

"Merrill, get me a glass of water . . . Merrill, get me a copy of that magazine . . . Merrill, please take away the tray . . . Merrill, please give me my coat. . . ." And gentle, quiet spoken Marvin Whatmore screamed at Merrill when the latter said or did something that displeased the president. Merrill Clough, financial vice president, controller and member of the executive committee, took it all without a whimper.

In turn, Merrill tried to take out his frustrations on his two assistants and, when the occasion arose, on a president or manager of a subsidiary or division. At board meetings, chain-smoking Merrill sat with his long legs stretched out, deeply inhaling one cigarette after another and saying nothing except when asked a question about figures in the black book before him. Then he would read the figures, in his Iowa/Texas accent, slowly, as if he were reading from Scripture. When it came to approving resolutions, Merrill's "aye" could be heard clearly and loudly.

Clarence S. (Larry) Hanson was easily the most amiable member of the board. Almost always smiling his sincere smile, Larry genuinely liked people and enjoyed being a part of the Cowles fraternity although he knew that he could never become a real insider. He was neither born nor bred in Iowa and he did not get his education at Harvard. He had not gone to college at all. But he was a great salesman, a salesman's salesman, and he had brought a lot of business to *Look* since he joined the magazine in 1950, after a stint as advertising manager of *Flair*. When that magazine died Larry was invited to become ad manager of *Look*. He was the only one who was successful in selling a sizable number of pages for *Flair*.

But then, Larry had had a lot of experience before he came to Cowles, and his record was the talk of

Madison Avenue. Before joining Cowles, he was advertising manager of the American Newspaper Advertising Network (1946–1949) and, before that, for a period of three years he was a vice president of the large and prestigious advertising agency of McCann-Erickson. He was an account executive and brought in a lot of business, making more friends as he went along. He had learned the magazine space selling business during a two-and-one-half year period on *Woman's Home Companion,* one of the leaders in the women's service magazine field, in the late thirties and early forties.

Larry was not only good in making presentations to advertising agencies and advertiser marketing executives, he was equally able in personal selling, including his famous three-hour luncheons. A good conversationalist and a fair listener, Larry became more talkative and "confidential" with each martini and he could match agency executives in martini consumption, even if an agency account man ordered his fifth, or seventh. By then, Larry still continued to smile his friendly smile but his conversation was a bit hard to follow. But, so was the advertising agency account man's. So it really didn't matter. Larry usually got his order. Even when selling advertising on *Look* became exceedingly difficult (as it did on *Life* and other mass circulation consumer magazines), Larry got his share of the dwindling ad pages. He was that likable. And helpful. Yet, when *Look* found it necessary to cut back sharply on its staff, reducing the editorial staff by more than half, and the ad sales organization by a third, Larry Hanson, a twenty-one-year veteran, was among the first to be "separated." But in 1967, Larry had already been on the board for seven years and was the high flyer of the *Look* sales-oriented executives, with the title of Vice President—Corporate Advertising Sales. Although "corporate" was part of his title, he devoted just about one hundred percent of his time and effort to *Look*. The "corporate" part was the safety catch for the corporation in its "easing out" program for executives who were being moved "upwards," while younger and potentially more capable and talented men were easing into their jobs. But Smiling and Friendly Larry's "easing out" was on the slow side. It took ten years and an advertising year on *Look* that was a real bomb. Larry was married, had three grown children. His hobby? People . . . he said it himself in his brief biography for the company's 1970 executive seminar. At board meetings, Larry sat, smiling his very friendly smile, thinking of the upcoming cocktail hour with the advertising account executives. And those refreshing martinis. He did not hesitate with his "ayes" to the various resolutions that needed approving. He was just bored. Still, he smiled his friendly smile.

William Attwood was both vice president and editor-in-chief of the corporation. But many of his associates were unable to say what functions he performed as vice president, and still more could not say what he did as editor-in-chief. The latter title and function had been held from the beginning by Gardner Cowles. In September of 1966, Cowles gave the title of honor to Attwood, and assumed instead the new title of Editorial Chairman. Regardless of title, Gardner Cowles continued to be editor-in-chief—mostly of *Look*, of course.

In a kind of halfhearted way, Bill Attwood tried to assume the role of editor-in-chief on some of the other Cowles properties. But there is no record of any special performance or major recommendation made by the editor-in-chief on any other Cowles property. Occasionally, he would visit with editors of various Cowles properties, but such visits were more courtesy appearances than anything else. He made one visit to the Modern Medicine offices in Minneapolis, and another to MFI offices in New York, but discussions in both instances were in the form of generalities. He made no suggestions of any kind and none were solicited from him.

In the case of *Education News,* published jointly by MFI and Cowles (but really the personal handiwork of Gardner Cowles), he served as one of three on the editorial committee. The other two were Marvin Toben, MFI's editorial director and David Whitney, the editor (and eventually president) of the Cowles Educational Book Division. I received regular and detailed reports of the *EN* editorial meetings. The meetings proved to be ineffectual because David Whitney always tried to dominate the agenda and discussions. Marvin Toben refused to let him get away with it. And through it all, Bill Attwood was extremely bored and could not wait until the meetings came to an end. He took no sides and made no meaningful recommendations.

Bill was a pleasant and outwardly easygoing fellow in his early forties, although he looked older and seemed more tired and weary than a forty-two-year-old man normally is. He did not seem to enjoy his association with Cowles—largely because he had no specific assignment, and if he ever thought of assuming one, there was no evidence of it. Some called him a "front man" and Bill did have some nice contacts, in Washington and in other parts of the world. A Princeton graduate (1941) he went into journalism after his war service. From 1949 until 1951 he was European editor for *Collier*'s magazine, then became *Look*'s foreign editor. He remained in that spot for ten years—probably too long a period. He left to become Ambassador to Guinea, serving until 1963 when he was made a special advisor to the United States United Nations Delegation,

for one year. Then he was moved to the Ambassador-
ship to Kenya (1964–66) after which he wrote a book
on Africa—naturally. It did not sell too well. And in
the same year he joined Cowles. A year later, he was
elected to the board of directors. And one year after
that he suffered a heart attack. This slowed him down
a little—for the next two years. He was married, had
three children and a home in Connecticut. His hobbies
were golf, bridge and reading, but not necessarily in
that order. During his tenure with Cowles he traveled
quite a bit, covering a good part of the world, writing
about his travels and visits with the famous for *Look.*
His interview with Egypt's strong man, Gamal Nasser,
in 1968, was thoughtful and penetrating. His report on
his visit to Cuba in 1969, a trip approved by the
United States State Department, was tepid. He did not
get an interview with Fidel Castro.

As Cowles was beginning to fall apart, Bill Attwood
became president and publisher of *Newsday,* which
covered Nassau and part of Suffolk Counties on Long
Island, and which had "beaten the pants off" Cowles'
Suffolk Sun several years earlier when Bill Attwood was
editor-in-chief of Cowles Communications, Inc., including the *Suffolk Sun.* He got his new job when the
Times-Mirror of Los Angeles bought control of the
very successful and highly profitable Long Island daily
for thirty million dollars, only twice as much as Cowles
lost on the *Suffolk Sun.* Instead of starting its own
paper to compete with it, Cowles should have bought
Newsday itself. As publisher of *Newsday,* Attwood succeeded Bill Moyers who was said to be "too liberal"
for the Chandlers of Los Angeles. However, one thing
Bill Attwood was not was a reactionary. Not even particularly conservative, except in dress. His salary at
Cowles was $70,000. His beginning annual stipend at
Newsday was $75,000.

At board meetings at Cowles he took little part, asking few questions and hardly being asked any. He read the resolutions indicated for him to read and seconded the resolutions placed before him to second —quietly. His "ayes" were even less audible. Not unlike Gardner Cowles, Ambassador William Attwood was a distinctly private man.

Sam O. Shapiro, or "Shap," as everybody calls him, was "the character" on the Cowles board. Also the clown and the comic relief to the boredom of most meetings. His anecdotes and stories were legendary. And some were really funny. A few had a sexual connotation and Shap seemed to enjoy talking about his own sexual prowess, particularly after his prostate operation and the paying of alimony. At this time in his life, he was happily married to a charming and intellectual woman, Tony, who continued to work as an agent to actors and writers. Shap, who retired (reluctantly, despite his protestations to the contrary) at the age of sixty-six in 1969 (one year after the "regular" retirement age requirement of the corporation), lived mostly in the past. And most of his anecdotes dealt with his experiences of days gone by.

Shap's title was Vice President and Look Circulation Director but his function generally involved newsstand sales. In this special field he was a past master. In all probability the best of his genre. Yet, of *Look*'s average circulation of 8,000,000 only 500,000 (and often less) represented newsstand sales, the rest coming from subscriptions, mostly direct mail, but a good part from high-pressure personal and telephone selling. *Look* was not doing any worse (and sometimes slightly better) than *Life* in the matter of newsstand sales but did not compare with a magazine like *Playboy,* whose newsstand sales amounted to over 3,000,000 of a total of 5,000,000. Sex—largely the "Playmate of the Month" spread—was the reason given (by Shap and others) for the willingness of readers of *Playboy* to fork over a dollar and a quarter ($1.50 for the big December issue) for a copy at newsstands, while only a handful bought a copy of *Look* at newsstands for 50 cents (or even 35 cents).

Shap started with *Look* from its beginning in 1938. But in 1941 he left to join Bernarr Macfadden. The next five years, during which Shap handled the newsstand sales, promotion and a number of other chores on *True Story* magazine and the other periodicals of the growing Macfadden stable, proved both exciting and erratic for young, fast-moving, colorful and devil-may-care Shap. But five years of the Macfadden shenanigans was enough even for Shap, so that, when Gardner Cowles, who had returned from his Washington war effort assignment to take over management of his baby, *Look,* invited Shap to return to the fold, Shap went back gladly. That was in 1946. The next ten years were golden for Shap, as they were for *Look.* Shap has enough funny stories of those days, particularly the anecdotes involving Fleur Cowles, various *Look* staff members and Shap's own publicity exploits, to make a book on its own.

In the launching of the *Suffolk Sun* and the two years that followed, during which Cowles lost about $5,000,000 a year, Shap was enlisted to help out. But even the great Shap was unable to do what he set out to do—to build the *Sun*'s paid circulation to 150,000. When the figure touched 70,000, the *Sun*'s circulation began to level off and it soon became clear that merely to maintain a paid figure of 70,000 would be too costly, if not a downright impossibility. The failure was not due to Shap's lack of ability or effort, but to the many things that were wrong on the *Sun* to begin with.

Shap pointed out the inefficiencies of the *Sun* that doomed it to failure—the poor editorial quality of the paper, the absence of local news and sports coverage, the incompetence of many of the staff members and on and on—but unfortunately needed remedial actions were never taken or were too little and too late. And shortly thereafter, Shap retired or was retired.

While he would have liked to take part as a good board member should, Shap knew that if he did take issue with some of the resolutions offered for ayes that should have been voted nay (and vice versa), his tenure on the board would be cut forthwith. So, not unlike the rest of the board members, he said very little but most of his "ayes" were not particularly audible. And he eased some of the frustrations—his and those of other board members—with his wry humor and the telling of an often repeated anecdote that never failed to bring at least a chuckle from even the most downhearted board members. In the months after his retirement he was sorely missed.

Lester Suhler, vice president and Look circulation director, was another member of the board who appeared to be a throwback to another age, another time. This tall and thin, blue-eyed, smiling, friendly man from Kansas looked like a circus barker of the twenties or thirties. Dressed in a flashy, colorful suit with a narrow, long snap-on bow tie, he headed a direct mail circulation department that had changed very little from the operation it was in the thirties. The computer and just about every conceivable automatic electronic hardware (and software) had long been available to modernize mass circulation fulfillment and direct mail. But Lester Suhler's operation in Des Moines was no more modern than it was when it started in the thirties. Over 2,000 men and women (mostly women) did the best they could with old, broken-down Speedomat machines. They had to promote and to fulfill more than 8,000,000 entries every two weeks. They had to process millions more entries in subscription selling via direct mail. And they had to deal with a long list of subscription agencies. It was not until 1968 that Cowles finally decided to buy the services of a computer and to set up a department to handle this phase of the work. And when it did that, it went to the other extreme—buying one of the most expensive services of its kind. Naturally, the determination to computerize the circulation department was a top level management decision, since it involved a capital investment of three to five million dollars, but there is no record that Old Timer Suhler ever asked for, or developed a plan for, the automation of the decrepit, aged, long-outdated circulation and direct mail setup in Des Moines. Lester had long since moved his offices from Des Moines to 488 Madison Avenue but he shuttled between New York and Iowa, and when he was in New York he was in daily (and sometimes hourly) telephone contact with his assistants in Des Moines.

Lester Suhler later became the sacrificial lamb, when the Rooney (Congressman Fred Rooney, Pennsylvania) investigation of subscription selling practices hit Cowles the hardest of all major mass circulation magazine publishers. Time, Inc., Hearst, Readers Digest and others felt Representative Rooney's sharp axe, honed on invective. Charges flew of odoriferous, high-handed subscription selling practices, known in the trade as PDS's (paid during service). And Circus Barker Lester Suhler was blamed by the great and growing Cowles Communications empire.

Lester soon suffered a stroke, and after his recovery was no longer the same hearty, smiling person of a few months earlier. Very shortly thereafter, Chairman Gardner Cowles announced at a board meeting that Circulation Director Lester Suhler "at his request, and after long and dedicated service," was taking early retirement at age sixty-two—"beginning immediately." And the proper resolution was read, seconded and passed without a dissenting vote or quiver.

Of course, the ex-circulation director was not expected to suffer too much, despite the loss of his $68,-000 annual salary. He could now sell his several thousand shares in Cowles Communications and retire to his Westchester farm estate where he was raising several hundred prize heifers. Which was just what he did, and the latest report from Lester Suhler is that his health has improved and he is smiling his old smile once again.

Palmer K. Leberman, chairman of the board of The Family Circle, Inc., and publisher of *Family Circle* magazine, was one of the most distinguished-looking members of the board. Tall, stately and with a full grey head of hair, P.K. appeared strong, opinionated and dogmatic. While he was not the founder of *Family Circle,* he was so closely identified with this unique women's magazine concept that just about everybody in the field (and in Cowles) thought that he was. Actually, *Family Circle* was established by the Safeway stores at about the time that its principal competitor, *Woman's Day,* was founded by the A & P stores—each as a vehicle for the promotion of the many products sold by these two chains. The magazines were sold only in the stores of these two chains, at a nickel a copy. And soon, manufacturers who sold to these chains (or wanted to sell to them) flocked to the magazines with their advertising pages and cam-

paigns. The other women's magazines and a few manufacturers shouted, "Foul," and before long, an agency
of the federal government (the FTC) told the chains
to "cease and desist."

At that point, P.K. and several associates took over
the ownership of *Family Circle* for a minor consideration, while Fawcett Publications acquired *Woman's
Day*. P.K. continued the same concept for *Family
Circle*—selling it only through supermarkets—but
rather than confine its distribution to Safeway (which,
at this point, dropped selling it altogether), he moved
to sell it to almost all supermarket chains that wanted
to handle it, including, eventually, A & P and Safeway.
P.K. did well with *Family Circle* and in 1964, he sold
it to Cowles Communications for $4,000,000—half in
cash and the other half in stock—resulting in a nice
capital gain for himself and his associates. Additionally,
P.K. got for himself a five-year contract (at $68,000
per year) to run *Family Circle* and to serve on the
Cowles board ($500 a year extra for that). The first
two years were great. *Family Circle* prospered and by
1966, the magazine reached a paid circulation of more
than 7,000,000 in individual copy sales in supermarkets and recorded earnings (before taxes) of $2,-
000,000. The cover price of the magazine was now 15
cents a copy. And *Family Circle* was way ahead of
Woman's Day in advertising revenue and substantially
ahead, also, in circulation. P.K. was much admired by
Chairman Gardner Cowles and the other board members.

But in 1967 the picture began to change. For at least
two reasons. The management of *Woman's Day* decided to declare war on *Family Circle* with the aim of
replacing it as the top women's magazine in this special
field. *Woman's Day* was improved substantially, more

space salesmen were hired, a new, smart publisher was brought in and a powerful promotional campaign was put behind the property.

It was not known whether P.K. was aware of what was happening. But very little, if anything, was done to face up to the new Fawcett challenge. And, as a result, it was the beginning of the end for *Family Circle* leadership—and for P.K.'s own happy days at Cowles. As *Woman's Day* began to gain both in circulation and advertising, *Family Circle* started to lose ground. Within one year, the $2,000,000 profit turned into a $2,000,000 loss. Don Perkins replaced P.K. as president. P.K. was pushed upstairs to the chairmanship. Then, Don was replaced by Gilbert Maurer, who also assumed the chief executive office. Shortly thereafter, P.K. was eased out, collecting his salary until the end of his contract in 1970.

Carl J. Schaefer, P.K.'s first assistant, also came along with the deal as publisher and vice chairman of *Family Circle*. Whereas P.K. was tall, dignified, impressive and the kind of fellow who made his presence known wherever he went and whatever he did, Carl was the opposite. Of average height, average appearance, quiet and self-effacing, he would have gone entirely unnoticed at board meetings except for the fact that he had the habit of dozing off and had to be awakened to read the resolution assigned to him. When awakened, he would read in a whisper and then fall back into slumber. He never seemed to be embarrassed. Since he made no trouble, doing little and never complaining, he was permitted to remain with Cowles and collect his salary ($60,000 a year) until his contract expired in 1969. After his tenure with Cowles, he became a consultant to publishers.

Gilbert Maurer was the bright light of the Cowles board of directors. The youngest member of the board at age forty, and with fifteen years of tenure with the company, Gil was looked upon as a real comer and some thought of him as the heir apparent to President Marvin Whatmore. While he was slow in getting started, he gained speed about midway in his career with Cowles, and at the third length he was sprinting. Soon, however, he was huffing and puffing. Amiable and personable, blond, pale-faced and on the short side (5′ 7½″) but trying to look taller, Gil almost always seemed to be standing on his toes, ready to leap, eager to get into the race and run, full speed ahead. The trouble was that he was moving (or being moved) at too fast a pace—from one Cowles job or function to another.

A Harvard Business School graduate (1952) having done his undergraduate work at St. Lawrence University, he joined Cowles after a short period of work in radio broadcasting. His initial assignment at Cowles in 1952 was as space salesman on *Look*. In five years in this spot he did extremely well. Both Gardner Cowles and Marvin Whatmore, especially the latter, began to like him a lot. In 1957, he was promoted to the post of assistant to *Look*'s advertising director and two years later was made *Look*'s regional advertising manager. He did well in each job. When Cowles decided to form a book publishing company in 1962, Gil was picked to head up the new business. That was probably a mistake—for Gil as well as for Cowles.

During five years as vice president of the Cowles Book Company, Gil made little progress in its special field, the educational book area. Not that Gil did not try. The trouble was that he knew nothing about book publishing, though no more or less than anyone else at Cowles, and even less about running an educational book publishing company, a highly specialized volatile field rife with problems. To make matters worse—at a time when he needed to do his spadework (and plenty of learning) in the book company—he was also enlisted to head up the new Cowles magazine, *Venture, the Traveler's World*. Gil had experience in selling space and knew a little about magazine management, but he had yet to learn the new language and ways of a travel magazine. However, Gil was given the additional office and function of corporate vice president and soon was made a director. Within one year, he became a member of the executive committee. All this, before he was forty-one. Who said Cowles officers and executives were a bunch of old fogies? And, in 1968, when *Family Circle* was in trouble and ready to strike out, Pinch Hitter Gil Maurer was called to bat as president and chief executive officer of Family Circle, Inc.

In the meantime, what happened to Cowles Book Company and *Venture?* A genius by the name of David Whitney, whom Gil hired as editor, succeeded his young boss as president. He lasted a few months and it was soon discovered that the Cowles Book Company's budget and projection figures had been ballooned to unexpected proportions, and worse still, the Great Editor had amassed a book inventory that was so heavy that it could not be moved. The full realization of these accomplishments did not become crystal clear until Bill Buckley, a hard hitting, no-nonsense book man took over the reins. By this time, young Gil, getting older by the minute (and looking more weary by the hour), had been made Vice President of Corporate Planning, a new post. It was not spelled out what kind of corporate planning Gil would be doing, especially since the corporation was losing money and had very little capital left to carry out any expansion plans. And while this was being considered, Gil began to take on chore after chore that was thrown at him by President Marvin Whatmore.

The sad part of it was that Gil was bright, could analyze a situation well, and was able to handle figures speedily and creatively. Given the right job and the proper direction, he could have become an excellent publishing executive. I liked Gil. We met for lunch now and then and had lengthy and spirited conversations about the frustrations at Cowles. On one such occasion, I asked Gil:

"What in the world are you doing at Cowles? What makes you stay?"

His answer: "I believe that I will be able to make a lot of money with Cowles." I was distressed with his answer. In my opinion, Gil remained with Cowles because he liked Marvin Whatmore, liked his $52,000 salary and liked the prestige of being a vice president, member of the board and member of the executive committee—which meant being a real Cowles insider. Gil lived in Westport, had a nice wife and five children, the older ones now teenagers. While Gil knew what Cowles should be doing and was not reluctant to voice his opinion at luncheons with me (and perhaps with others), he took no position at board meetings. What position he took or did not take at executive committee meetings I do not know. One thing I did know. Gil could not, and would not, do anything contrary to the wishes of President Marvin Whatmore whom he admired much and liked even more. And just as Marvin was beholden to Gardner Cowles, Gil was beholden to his "benefactor." As a result, neither could move progressively or aggressively.

The three outside directors (those who were not employees of the corporation) were: Dr. John H. Fischer, president of Teachers College, Columbia University; John H. Perry, originally chairman of the board and president of Perry Publications, Inc., and later president of Perry Oceanographics, Inc., of Riviera Beach, Florida; and John L. Weinberg, partner, Goldman, Sachs & Co.

Of the three, John Weinberg was the only one who actually behaved like an outside director, and that only up to a point. John was the board's official devil's advocate. He asked pointed, pragmatic financial questions. Examples: "Why are we buying and what can we expect from the acquisition of Cambridge Book Company?"; "What can we do to improve our cash flow?"; "What will the Alioto case cost us—provided we do not lose it?"; and "Should we continue to pay dividends in view of our worsening cash position in the face of losses?" Once his questions were answered, he did not press any more. After all, Goldman, Sachs had been the investment bankers and financial advisers to Cowles for a long time, and to insist on complete, definitive answers to embarrassing questions would be out of place. He felt that he was doing his job by merely asking important, timely questions. If Cowles did not choose to answer those questions except in a cursory way, well then, "that was Cowles' problem." He had done his duty. Of medium height, leaning toward a middle-age girth (he was in his middle forties), with a full head of greying black curly hair, John made his presence felt at the board. He talked in a loud voice. My only objection to John Weinberg was his continual smoking of a big, smelly cigar which seemed to give off more smoke than any cigar smoked by anyone in my experience. I always tried to avoid sitting next to him. He really stunk up the place— especially on a hot summer afternoon, when the air conditioning couldn't contend with all the carbon dioxide in the room. More than half of the directors were smokers and John was not the only cigar smoker (Larry Hanson smoked cigars, Marvin Whatmore shifted from cigarettes to little cigars and several others had cigars in their mouths), but none of the others smoked such big cigars or gave off so much smoke so furiously.

Within a period of two years, John had two deaths in his family—first his mother, then his father—the famous Mr. Wall Street—the great Sidney Weinberg. But neither death prevented John from attending the Cowles board meeting. He rarely missed one. John was a practical man. He never mixed his private life with business. And at board meetings he was strictly "business."

Of the three outside directors, John Fischer participated least, by far. I do not recall John Fischer asking a single question at any meeting. And unlike John Weinberg, he attended very few meetings. Often he would appear at the pre-board meeting luncheon and then leave after lunch. John was not my idea of a president of a large, prestigious big-city college, a division of an Ivy League university. He looked and talked more like a school teacher, which he once was. He came to his post at Columbia from the superintendency of the Maryland school system. He did not appear to be an intellectual. And, if he had any knowledge of business, the board members did not find out.

John Perry was probably the strangest member of the board. He was the only one who did not take a drink. He had two great hangups: health—particularly sexual health and delaying the aging process—and miniature submarines. In his mid-forties, he went to Switzerland and had one of those famous youth rejuvenation operations. When he returned to his home in Palm Beach, he divorced his wife and shortly there-

after married "a young one." He told me this the very
first time we had a chance to talk at one of my earlier
pre-board meeting, pre-luncheon cocktail hours. I wondered why he did not take a drink and I asked him.
Then I heard the "story of his life."

He inherited the Perry chain of twenty-two newspapers (dailies and weeklies, all in Florida) from his
father. Plus a television station (WESH, in the Orlando
area). Plus a monthly magazine, *Palm Beach Life*. He
did not particularly like this business. What he liked
was fiddling around with miniature submarines. In
1966, he sold WESH to Cowles for $1,000,000 in
cash and 228,500 shares of Cowles stock, part of which
he shared with his mother and a brother. That was
when he was put on the Cowles board. In 1969, he
decided to sell off his newspaper chain and the magazine. Since the chain as a group could not boast particularly high profits, a newspaper broker advised him to
sell the Perry newspapers and the magazine piecemeal.
By the end of 1969, all of the Perry newspapers had
been sold and Perry did very well indeed, coming out
with about $60,000,000 in cash and stock, some of
which went to the other members of his family. Cowles
bought the *Ocala Star Banner* for a whopping 348,937
shares of Cowles stock—at roughly 55 times earnings.
Gardner Cowles felt so conscience-stricken about the
deal that before the board meeting called to approve
the acquisition, he invited some of the board members,
including me, to his office to "explain" what a wonderful buy this was—potentially.

By this time, John Perry owned and/or controlled
577,437 shares of Cowles stock, making him the second largest stockholder—next to and not far away
from Stockholder Number One, Chairman Gardner
Cowles. And while John continued to come to board
meetings regularly, he began to devote most of his

working time to his submarine venture in Riviera Beach. In fact, he spent a great deal of his time under water. He was allergic to the sun.

Just as I had been at the beginning, John was very much in awe of Gardner Cowles. Now fifty years of age, or seventeen years younger than the chairman, John had met Gardner Cowles when he was still a youngster in school. John's father, the upcoming newspaperman of Florida, was on friendly terms with Gardner Cowles, the great and legendary newspaperman from Iowa. And John's father always talked to him about Gardner Cowles. But when the Cowles stock began to plunge downward, moving from $13 a share when the *Ocala Star Banner* deal was completed, to $7 and then to $3.25, John Perry was no longer in awe of the Cowles Chairman.

TWO:

The Stuff that Dreams Are Made of
—Or Are They?

As I barely whispered "aye" to an inconsequential resolution, read by Gardner Cowles, moved by Donald Perkins and seconded by William Attwood, I wondered not only how the rest of the Cowles board members got there, but what the hell I was doing there, especially on that sunny, warm, humid afternoon in August when I could have been relaxing at our summer home on Monhegan Island in Maine.

But how different I had felt, how thrilled I had been on August 15, 1966, just one year previously, when my dreams of heading a division and becoming a member of the board of directors of the great publishing empire of Cowles Communications, Inc., began to loom as a possibility. Marvin Whatmore, president of Cowles, was my guest at lunch at the Marco Polo Club at the Waldorf where we explored a possible deal.

While this was the first time we met, it was "Marvin" and "Don" right away. Unlike Gardner Cowles, Marvin

Whatmore was friendly, warm, extroverted, easy to be with.

The luncheon meeting was my idea and it came about after a year of thinking, dreaming and planning. The Whatmores lived in the same apartment house as we, on Sutton Place South. As a matter of fact, they occupied a similar apartment on another floor.

"Do you know whom I met in the art class at the Museum of Modern Art?" Betty asked me at our usual cocktail hour one evening.

"I have no idea. Tell me."

"The wife of a publisher who lives in our building— the same apartment we have, on the tenth floor."

"That's nice, what's her name?"

"Lois Whatmore."

"The wife of Marvin Whatmore?"

"Who is he?"

"Who is he? He is the president of the great Cowles Communications, the publishers of *Look,* the magazine that is bigger than *Life* . . ."

"Is there anyone you don't know?"

"I don't know him. I know of him. Who in publishing has *not* heard of Marvin Whatmore? But I would *like* to *know* him."

In the months ahead, we talked about inviting the Whatmores down to our apartment for cocktails, but nothing happened, although Betty and Lois continued their friendship. By that time, my desire to meet the Whatmores had developed a more practical objective than just getting acquainted with the president of a famous, up-and-coming, fast-moving, "growth" communications house. I had been thinking about the idea of merging our company, Magazines For Industry, Inc., publishers of eight business magazines, into a firm such as Cowles. I liked Cowles and I was sure that it would prove to be an ideal business marriage.

I had been toying with the idea of merger for some time. We had been approached by several public and private companies, both within and without the business press community, including the Cahners operation, which was on an acquisition binge in an effort to become Mr. Big in business publishing.

Ten or even five years earlier, merging our company with one of the giants in publishing was something I would not consider. Conversely, we weren't big enough for any of the more important public publishing corporations to be interested in us. What I wanted to do then was to continue to build our small but growing trade paper publishing company and then go public— so that I would have a capital gain and also money or stock to buy other, smaller (or even bigger) publishing companies. As a matter of fact, we tried to do just that—in 1961. But it proved to be the wrong time and wrong for our little company. We were not ready, and Wall Street was not ready for us. Nevertheless, we made a good try and came close to success. Of course, we had to settle for a third line underwriter and had to go through the pains and complexities of drawing up the "red herring" and filing with the Securities and Exchange Commission.

Underwriters who handle new stock issues come in a range from the largest investment bankers with capital in multimillions (which includes such prestigious firms as Lehman Bros.; Merrill Lynch; White, Weld; Goldman, Sachs; Paine, Webber; Kidder Peabody; Smith, Barney; Dillon, Read, and Kuhn, Loeb, who manage issues that involve the obtaining of millions of dollars—), to a smaller but still solid group of financial companies with seats on the New York Stock Exchange and other markets—down to small, sometimes fly-by-night companies that will underwrite new, start up and untried firms, marginally profitable and some with huge losses.

Many of these "underwriters" have little capital and less experience. They usually spring up during a period of an onrush of new issues and more often than not go out of business when the new issue market dries up or settles down to normal. This is just what happened in 1961 and again in 1969 and 1970.

A "red herring" is a preliminary prospectus which is supposed to include complete and full disclosure about a company planning to go public. Details, including copies of the prospectus, are filed with the Securities and Exchange Commission for registration. It is called a red herring because some of the printed matter on the front page appear in red, explaining that is a preliminary prospectus and that the registration statement had not yet become effective. Red herrings are distributed to brokers in advance of registration so that they will be alerted of potential new issues to come to the market.

It so happened that 1961 was The Year of the Merger, the first of the avalanche to follow during the rest of the sixties, and every little company under the sun was trying to sell to some Big Fish or "go public." When an underwriter came to us to sell us on the advantages of going public, we reacted enthusiastically to the idea. Unfortunately, we started late, the SEC was overworked and took months to get out from under the piles of "red herrings." By the time it reached the MFI prospectus, it was too late. Wall Street had had a bellyfull of inconsequential public offerings and the buying of stocks at inflated prices. The 1961 "crash" was on and the new-issue market died a sudden death. The cost to us of the abortive effort to go public was $35,000 and the months of time that we could have utilized better in promoting and operating our magazines. But the experience did have some value. We were a little more cynical about the machinations of going public and a bit more sophisticated about matters pertaining to our great and wise financial community. Was the experience worth $35,000? Maybe. Anyway, we went to work and our little company began to prosper and grow at a faster pace.

But then 1966 saw the beginning of The Great Merger Surge, with the big public companies gobbling up almost everything in sight—medium and smaller companies—whose private owners, largely entrepreneurs of family-owned enterprises, wanted a piece of the action provided by the fast-swinging stock on the New York Stock Exchange. They were buying these companies not with hard cash but with common stock, or so-called Chinese Money, in the form of debentures. And many were paying high prices in relation to earnings. Competition for acquisitions was keen. It was a seller's market.

So, here I was in this type of environment, with offers and temptations to merge coming from many directions. Not only from publishing companies but also from outfits that did not know the difference between business paper and consumer magazine publishing. Or did not particularly care. An offer came from a company that printed bank notes, another from one that produced greeting cards and a third from a premium stamp business. These were in addition to offers from publishers, of course.

Merge or not to merge? That was the big question. I was fifty-eight and enjoying good health. More important, I liked what I was doing but I was beginning to get a little bored. I felt I needed some new, bigger challenges, new excitement in the world of publishing and business. I wanted to be in stream with the times. But completely. I reasoned that it took me twenty-two years to build a business of eight small but respected business magazines, four undisputed leaders in their respective fields, with a volume of $2,500,000 and a modest profit. I had started six magazines from scratch, sold off one and had acquired three from the Reuben H. Donnelley Corporation, a division of Dun & Bradstreet. I owned 80 percent of my company's stock. My salary was $53,000 a year (plus another $10,000 in deferred compensation for pension purposes). Not bad—for Chaim Dovid Yankel from Pumpyan. But not great. Others were doing better, some much better. Look at Norman Cahners.

Norman Cahners started with one magazine in 1946 —two years after I did—and in 1966 published over twenty magazines, with a volume of about $25,000,000. Moreover, he had sold a 40 percent interest in his company to the International Publishing Company of London for $13,000,000—or one million dollars more than it cost him to build his empire. Which means he got his money back, with a profit, still controlled his company, and was ready for a much more ambitious growth program through acquisitions. At this writing, Cahners, with some thirty-five magazines and sales in excess of $50,000,000, is Number Two and the very aggressive challenger of Number One in business magazine publishing—McGraw-Hill. Of course, Cahners' chairman, Norman—a very fine and able gentleman, assisted by an equally able, hard-hitting first assistant, President Saul Goldweitz—did not start with simply an idea and zero capital as I did. They had the backing of the Rabb supermarket (Stop 'N Shop) millions, plus more millions from the conglomerate giant, Nate Cummings. No matter, Norman Cahners and others were doing better than I was. And Norman was several years younger than I.

True, at fifty-eight, most businessmen think of easing up and some plan for their retirement. I could have sold to Cahners for a million-plus in cash (Cahners, not being a public company, bought for cash) and begin to ease up and think of retirement at sixty-five. After all, a million in cash invested in tax-exempt bonds would provide a handsome income. And financial security. But that was not for me. To me, retirement meant death. Since I was in excellent health, with exciting interests, and enthusiasm in the field of communications and business generally, retirement or even "easing off" was something I could not even contemplate.

Most important of all, I had a yen to build and operate a much bigger business than MFI as it was structured in 1966. I reasoned that if I continued to grow at our normal past pace, ten years hence I would not be running a much bigger business. From a practical point of view, the best I could look for was a business with a volume of five million dollars. That would mean doubling our present business, or a growth rate of seven percent a year—good but not great. No, what I wanted to run was a fifty-, twenty-five-, or at least fifteen-million-dollar business in trade paper publishing, and I wanted to do it in the foreseeable future— say, the next three to five years. Even going public with MFI (and going public was not yet the "in" thing in 1966—that was to come a year later, reaching avalanche proportions in 1968) would not bring our company enough capital to build this kind of business in three, or even five years. So, the answer was merger— merging with a large public company, in the communications field, whose stock was traded on the New York Stock Exchange, a company that had a good track record in respect to growth, reputation and people. I made one other specific criterion. The company with which I would merge should be in various areas of communications, the more the better, but not in the business magazine field. My plan was to sell this company on the idea of entering my phase of communications by the acquisition of MFI as a nucleus to build a large and substantial business and professional magazine division which I would head as president and chief operating manager. I would take stock in such a corporation and I wanted a seat on the board of directors.

My next step was to make a little list. I quickly eliminated Time, Inc., because I felt that this great, prestigious giant of the communications fraternity had "had it." It was a fully mature company, rich, and in many ways, self-satisfied. Besides, Time, Inc. had made stabs at the business paper publishing field (with *Architectural Forum* and attempts at several others) and had failed because it tried to run its business magazine division in the manner it operated its consumer publication business. While both publish magazines, they are in different worlds. Time, Inc. did not realize this, or did not listen if the matter had indeed been brought up. Time, Inc. was not for me. I started with a dozen names and my final list narrowed to three public companies in the communications field whose stock was traded (and doing well) on the Big Board. Plus one that was poised to go public. Cowles Communications, Inc. was on top of my list. While smaller than each of the other three, and listed on the New York Stock Exchange for only a short time, it seemed to be the ideal company for a merger with MFI and for carrying out my growth plan in the business magazine industry. For one thing, Cowles was the only major public company engaged in every area of communications except business paper publishing. It published a great consumer magazine, *Look*. It also had two interesting specialized consumer magazines—*Family Circle,* the leader in the important women's service field, and *Venture,* known as The Traveler's World, in the burgeoning travel field. Cowles published successful, profitable newspapers in growing Florida markets and in San Juan, Puerto Rico. It owned and operated growing, profitable television and radio stations in excellent markets. It owned valuable real estate property, had started a book publishing company specializing in the important education field, and was interested in developing other communications properties. It had a long and great heritage in publishing, especially in the newspaper and consumer magazine areas, was well financed and had the "gung ho" and charisma needed to build a great and profitable diversified communications empire. It was not a conglomerate spreading out its corporate tentacles in all directions with unrelated businesses. Cowles was a congeneric operation, specializing in the large, growing and exciting communications field, with a competent, knowledgeable manager heading up each separate or special division such as consumer magazines, book publishing, television and radio, and newspapers. This is the way the company appeared to me after investigation and research. Additionally, its most recent annual report showed an enviable record of growth, both in sales and earnings.

This, then, was the company for me. It was my job to sell the Cowles management on the ideas of buying MFI as a nucleus to be used for the development of a major business magazine complex and giving me the challenge and opportunity to build this division. At fifty-eight, I had at least seven productive years ahead to do this job. And I set the following goals: Phase One, to reach a volume of $15,000,000 and a minimum pre-tax profit of $2,000,000 in three years; to be followed by Phase Two, to attain sales of $50,000,000 and pre-tax profits of $8,000,000. I would do this largely through acquisitions, and the fields that I would pursue would be medicine, education, plastics and computer technology.

The next step on my action calendar was to meet with Marvin Whatmore and explore the potential steps that I had in mind—leading to a merger with Cowles. The approach must be made on a direct, business basis and what I needed was a third party to handle it. I had such a man in mind. Frank McGehee was a consultant who specialized in the communications field and he had a fairly good track record in the areas of mergers and acquisitions. I had used his services in buying three magazines from the Reuben H. Donnelly Corporation. Besides, I remembered that Frank had done some work for Cowles some years back.

At lunch with Frank one day, I outlined my plan to him. I listed the four companies that appeared to be logical partners for my business magazine growth program. I told him that Cowles was on the top of my list. He was very excited about the idea and he fully agreed that Cowles was the most desirable company to approach first. We quickly agreed on terms and he wasted no time in setting a date with Marvin Whatmore for the very next morning.

At eleven that morning, Frank McGehee called. He was so excited and out of breath that he could hardly talk: "Don," he finally began, "Marvin Whatmore is not only interested in seeing you, he is very excited about the whole idea . . . I think you can make a deal —and make it quickly."

When I met Marvin Whatmore for lunch at the Marco Polo Club later that week it became obvious that Cowles would buy my dream. I liked Marvin from the start. The chemistry was right, he was a listener and he seemed the kind of a man with whom I could enjoy working. At the conclusion of the luncheon meeting, he asked me to provide him with MFI operational figures of the past five years, a five-year projection, short biographies of each of our key executives, recent copies of each of our publications and a brief description of the markets covered and the position of each magazine in its field. He also asked me to indicate what price I had in mind for MFI.

When I left the Marco Polo Club, I was flying. I had had only one Scotch-on-the-rocks at lunch but I might as well have drunk a full fifth. A dream that I dreamt so many times was now unfolding, giving vent to the most extreme fantasies that my mind could grasp, visualize and elaborate. The prospect of merging with Cowles really appeared to be the stuff that dreams are made of.

Immediately upon my return to the office, I went to work gathering and preparing the material requested by Marvin Whatmore. Before the day was over, everything was ready, and early next morning, a sealed packet of papers and magazines marked "confidential" was placed on the desk of the president of Cowles Communications. Since it was vital that the preliminary negotiations be conducted on a "classified" basis, I swore my secretary to secrecy.

Betty, the only other person who shared my secret at this point, also shared my excitement and enthusiasm. But she also had some trepidation! "Everything you say sounds just great. . . . We'll become millionaires, with marketable securities. But, you will be building a bigger business, perhaps a much bigger business—for somebody else. It won't be your business. . . . Now, what you have is yours, all yours, you can do what you want, you call all the shots, you make all the major decisions, you have no one to report to, no one looking over your shoulder. . . . Darling, how are you going to feel working for someone else—at this stage of the game?"

I agreed with her about building a much bigger business "for somebody else," but I pointed out that we would be major stockholders of the corporation, that we would own a part of that "bigger business" and that, in turn, we would also share in the future growth of this great and growing company. Of course, I could not argue that my posture would not be different after the merger.

"Obviously, I will have someone looking over my shoulder and I will have to make periodic, regular reports to the president and/or the chairman of the board of directors of Cowles," I said. "I will have to make an adjustment and it may not be easy, but there are many compensating advantages. For the first time in our lives, we will be financially independent, and while our stock in Cowles at the outset may be worth about a million-and-a-half or two million dollars, there is every reason to believe that in several years, the stock will have a market value of three to five million dollars. Besides, I will head up a division in communications about which no one in Cowles knows anything. They'll need me more than I'll need them. I will be their business magazine expert, and, having met Marvin Whatmore, I feel he is the kind of a man who appreciates management talent as well as the special expertise I have in the business magazine field." I went on and on, citing advantage after advantage of a merger with the great Cowles company.

"I hope you are right, darling . . . but I can't help feeling a little uneasy. . . . You have been so happy building and running your own business. . . ."

I was not to be deterred. Betty realized this. And she went along with my decision to merge our company into Cowles. She continued to have reservations, but I was able to answer just about all her questions and to reassure her that what I was doing was right and good for us.

Our attorney, David Regosin of Regosin, Edwards, and Freeman, also agreed that a merger with Cowles would be in our interest. He took this position despite the fact that he could not continue as corporate counsel, for which he received an annual retainer. In addition to Dave, I called in Edwin McMahon Singer as special counsel to work with us on the merger. Ed had had experience in the field and had just completed a similar merger in the business magazine industry. I had known Ed for some time, as friend and attorney to Jack Mulligan—my sidekick on the candy magazine going back to the days I trained him as a space salesman in 1936, when I was editor of *International Confectioner*.

Dave Regosin thought that the merger with Cowles made sense from a business point of view, but Ed was even more enthusiastic about the deal and, by the time he met Marvin Whatmore, he became ecstatic about the upcoming relationship with the great Cowles empire.

Within a week, after he received the MFI statements and my projections, Marvin called me and said that Cowles was ready to go ahead with the merger. August 15 was set for a meeting in the offices of Goldman, Sachs and Company, Cowles' financial advisers. We met at two in the afternoon in the office of John L. Weinberg, a Goldman, Sachs partner, and a Cowles director. Joining us were my financial adviser, Chandler (Bus) Hovey, Jr., partner of White, Weld and Company, with whom I had been working on a number of situations for about ten years, and one of his associates. The purpose of the meeting was to agree on a price for MFI in terms of Cowles common stock. I had asked $2,500,000 for our company and Marvin did not argue about the figure.

"If you say $2,500,000 is a fair price for your business," he said, "I will accept this. However, our stock, now selling at around $15 a share, is underpriced. Realistically, I believe it is worth about $20 a share. I am prepared to give you your asking price of $2,500,000 on the basis of pegging a value on Cowles stock at $20 a share." He explained that they had made just such a deal in an earlier acquisition.

My advisors felt that this would be too low a price for MFI and suggested putting a value of $17.50 on Cowles stock. After considerable discussion, Marvin revised his offer, basing it on the value of Cowles stock at $18.50 a share, adding:

"On the basis of earnings of the past few years, the price we are willing to pay for MFI is a bit high, but considering that I am putting a value of one million dollars on the services of Don Gussow, I think it is a good deal."

Bus Hovey's associate, looking at the situation from a completely objective point of view, thought that we should insist on the basis of $17.50 a share. However, Bus and I looked at one another and we agreed that $18.50 a share would be a satisfactory basis. The "million dollar" remark by Marvin proved to be worth (to Cowles) $106,177.50, or 7,722 additional shares at the closing price of $13.75 per share. (When the deal was consummated on November 29, 1966, the price of Cowles stock was $13.75, which meant that we received about $2 a share less than the price of the stock on the day—August 15—we agreed on the deal.)

At any rate, I accepted Marvin's offer and John quickly figured out that at a price of $2,500,000, on the basis of $18.50 a share, MFI stockholders would receive a total of 135,135 Cowles shares. Since I owned about 80 percent of MFI stock, I would be receiving about 101,000 shares of Cowles stock. We shook hands on the deal. Marv asked John to check on the price of Cowles stock at that moment. It was three o'clock, the market had closed and Cowles stock sold at the closing for $15⅞ per share. This meant that the actual price for all of MFI was just over $2,000,000 and my share of it would be $1,600,000. Of course, the actual price would depend on the quotation of the Cowles stock on the day of the closing. And the actual cash I would receive would depend on the price of the stock at the time of a secondary offering.

Of course, if I sold any or all of the shares, I would have to pay a capital gains tax, which was 25 percent at that time and was increased substantially in the next few years.

Inasmuch as my original investment in the company was minor, I would probably have to pay the full capital gain tax—or very close to it. In other words, assuming the price of stock would not go beyond $13.75 per share, my net proceeds in cash would be slightly over one million dollars. However, the expectations were that the stock would advance substantially in the years ahead. As an insider, I could sell very few of my shares until there was a secondary offering. I was restricted by both the SEC rules for insiders, which stated that I could not sell more than one percent of the stock traded during any one month, and that I could not sell stock more than once in six months. Additionally, I required the approval of Cowles before selling any stock.

However, it was understood that a subsequent "secondary" offering would be made to a group of underwriters (probably headed by Goldman, Sachs and Company), at which time I could sell any part or all of my shares. This situation was predicated on the stock moving up to higher levels—say $25 per share or higher. Such an eventuality would depend, of course, on the continued growth and increased profitability of CCI.

The stock to be issued to my associates and me would come from additional authorized but, at that time, non-issued stock. Approval of issuance of additional stock would come from the New York Stock Exchange. All of these items were to be clearly spelled out in the contract to be drawn up in the weeks ahead.

Although, that evening, Betty and I toasted one another, "To the millionaires," Betty continued to have some reservations about the transaction.

"You've enjoyed building and running your own company, especially during the past few years when everything has been going just right," she said. "How are you going to feel working for as large a company as Cowles?"

"I will not be working *for* Cowles. I will head an important, profitable, growing division of Cowles. I have been promised complete autonomy. That is why I picked Cowles rather than a company like Cahners. Merging with Cahners or with another company currently holding an important position in the business magazine field could result in my becoming a mere 'cog in the wheel'. Not so with Cowles. Cowles is a large, potentially great communications company, involved in *every* phase of communication—except business magazines. No one at Cowles knows anything about business magazines. This means that they will have to look to me for the expertise and the direction in this field. They will need me more than I will need them. . . ." I was beginning to repeat myself.

The days and weeks ahead were among the most exciting—and also among the most tense and apprehensive—of my career. My fantasies during the day were loaded with grandeur. I envisioned the stock going to $50 a share, even $100. I remembered the stock of Time, Inc. selling at $12 a share—only several years ago, when it was traded over the counter—and now it was approaching $100. And I felt that Cowles (based on the growth of the past ten years and the general feeling in the publishing and financial communities) was the emerging giant in communications that could surpass Time, Inc. in growth and even in size in the next five to ten years. At $50 a share, our 100,000-plus shares would be worth $5,000,000. And that would make me a multimillionaire and give me the kind of financial security I had wanted and hoped for so much.

And what would I do with the four million dollars in capital gains resulting from the five million dollar value of Cowles stock? Since I had no plans to retire in the foreseeable future, answers to this question did not seem important. Total financial security for Betty, our younger son Paul and myself seemed to be the most dominating element of my daytime fantasy in this area. Also, generous incomes for our older sons, Alan and Mel. A Rolls-Royce, a winter home in the tropics, traveling to the far corners of the earth were only fleeting thoughts. I had no interest in them. The excitement was in work—in building a fifteen-million, fifty-million, even a hundred-million dollar business magazine company, perhaps the biggest business magazine operation in the United States. The United States? The world! My new areas of interest in the business magazine field would include medicine, education and some of the new emerging fields such as ecology, oceanography and new forms of computer technology. And perhaps even a magazine that would compete with *Business Week* and *Fortune*. Why not? I had the ideas, the expertise and the needed contacts and approaches. And Cowles had the stock and the millions. From an immediate and pragmatic point of view, I had my eye

on one company that published medical magazines—
among the most prestigious, largest and foremost in the
field—and on another company that published some of
the best periodicals in the area of education as well as
a general business magazine that could become a major
challenger to *Business Week*. I had wanted to buy
these companies for some time. I had refrained from
approaching them because of the fear of rejection. After
all, MFI was much smaller than either of these companies. Oh, so many times I had thought of making an
approach to one or the other but after an unsuccessful
and painful experience in 1958, trying to buy Breskin
Publications (publishers of *Modern Packaging* and
Modern Plastics) I had decided against such a move.
In 1958, Breskin was five to six times bigger than my
small company, then called Don Gussow Publications,
Inc. We were then publishing only two magazines and
an annual—*Candy Industry, Bottling Industry* and the
Candy Industry Catalog and Formula Book.

Interestingly enough, as small as we were, we came
close to buying Breskin. It all started with a telephone
call. The caller was Burt Gussow, my cousin once
removed, who, for the past fourteen years had been a
space salesman for Breskin.

"How would you like to buy Breskin?" were Burt's
first words when he called one morning in December
of 1958.

"You must be kidding," I replied, "Breskin is many
times bigger than we are. He runs two of the greatest
magazines. He practically 'owns' the plastics and packaging fields from a publication point of view. How
could we buy Breskin? Why would he even consider selling to us? And where would we get the
money?"

"As far-fetched as it may sound, it is possible . . . and

I can arrange a date for you with Charlie Breskin to talk about it."

At lunch, Burt breathlessly explained:

"Charlie Breskin had a deal going with McGraw-Hill, whereby Mr. Big in publishing would acquire Breskin Publications for $2,700,000 in McGraw-Hill stock. After months of negotiations, all that was needed was the signatures of the parties—"

"So, what happened?"

"Before formalizing the deal, Charlie was called in for a conference with Nelson Bond, president of the publishing division of McGraw-Hill. Not only did Charlie wait in the reception room for over half an hour, but when Nelson Bond finally saw him he did not even show him the common courtesy of apologizing for or explaining the excessively long delay. Breskin had been punctual, arriving within three minutes of the appointed hour.

" 'That goddamned bastard,' Charlie shouted as he barged into Allan Cole's office (Cole was president of Breskin Publications and Breskin's right hand man for over thirty years). To make the story short, Charlie was mad enough to call the deal off. 'To hell with him, I don't need McGraw-Hill and I don't need to take this kind of crap,' Charlie said, as he dictated a curt note to Nelson Bond, calling off the merger."

"So—what makes you think Charlie will want to talk to me? To consider selling his business to us?"

"You have to know Charlie. Now he would like nothing better than to sell his business to a much smaller company than McGraw-Hill—and especially to a Jewish-owned company—as long as the price was right, say, at least $100,000 more than the McGraw-Hill deal. As a matter of fact, I have a date for you with Charlie for four this afternoon . . ."

That was just like Burt, all right. The boy of action. He had not waited to learn whether I would be interested in seeing Breskin. He presumed, and correctly, that I could not say no to such a meeting. Nor was Burt concerned about my ability to obtain the $2,800,000 needed to buy Breskin Publications. Somehow he had confidence enough that I could raise this kind of capital. He was also enough of an egotist to feel that if I could not obtain this huge amount of capital, he would find a way for me to obtain the money and/or the backing.

It was a sunny, brisk December day when I left my office at 18 East 49th Street at 3:45 to walk to the offices of Breskin Publications at 475 Madison Avenue on the corner of 56th Street. Compared to our plebian, crowded offices which had no reception room at all, the Breskin offices seemed spacious, lush and inviting. Promptly at four, I was ushered into Charlie Breskin's office, a large, square, amply furnished room, with a fluffy sofa, comfortable chairs and abstract paintings on the walls. It was a bit on the gaudy, garish side and not to my taste, but not entirely unattractive. Charlie Breskin was sitting behind a huge desk facing the door. He literally jumped from his chair and greeted me warmly:

"Sit down, sit down. . . . I have heard so much about you . . . from Burt and Allan Cole . . . It's nice to meet you, sit down, have a cigar. . . ."

The meeting, which lasted only half an hour, went well. Yes, he would consider selling me the business. It would have to be all cash and the price was $2,800,000.

"Can you raise the money?" he asked.

"Of course, no problem at all."

"Then go to it."—and with that, he handed me a batch of financial statements and the most recent copies of the Breskin magazines and promotional material. No word about McGraw-Hill was mentioned, and of course I did not let on what I knew.

"Naturally, it is vital that we keep all this in the strictest of confidence," he said. I assured him that this would be the case; it would be in my interest as much as his.

When I returned to the office, I could think of nothing except, "How do I get $2,800,000, and get it before the little, ebullient, unpredictable Charlie Breskin changes his mind?" Suddenly I had an idea.

I had been buying a small amount of stock through the large prestigious investment banking firm of White, Weld and Company. Chandler Hovey, Jr., a White, Weld partner, was a gracious, Harvard educated Boston Brahmin in his early forties. He listened to my story and was sympathetic to what I was attempting to do. After several meetings with him and several of his associates, following a study of the figures that I presented on the Breskin and MFI operations, he concluded that this was too small a proposition to be handled by White, Weld. Their required minimum for a public offering was $10,000,000 in annual sales and $1,000,000 in profits before taxes. Even when the Breskin business was combined with ours, the pro forma sales amounted to less than $5,000,000 and profits before taxes were only $250,000. Nevertheless, Hovey (known as "Bus") felt that the deal was do-able and offered to introduce me to a smaller investment banking/underwriting firm that might be interested in handling it.

After several days, he found a company that would be interested in moving with the Breskin acquisition. The company was Shearson, Hammill, smaller than White, Weld but also prestigious and very active in the new-issue market. At the next meeting at the White,

Weld offices, I met Stan Cruzen, head of Shearson's underwriting division, and several of his associates.

Following a series of meetings and completion of the needed research, Shearson developed a plan which would include the merger of Breskin and MFI and then take the combined operation public. Breskin would receive his desired $2,800,00 in cash and I would wind up with an ownership of about 20 to 25 percent of the combined public company, giving me sufficient working control of the business. Shearson, with possible help from White, Weld, would then work with me to build a larger public company in the business magazine field.

We started talking to the Shearson group early in January and by the time the plan was ready for formulation, it was May. In the meantime, I met with Breskin on numerous occasions. Also with Allan Cole. And during this time, I had an opportunity to become fully acquainted with the *Modern Packaging* and *Modern Plastics* operations. I also covered the annual AMA Packaging Show, held that year in April in Chicago, with Charlie Breskin. Working with him, seeing him in action with top packaging executives, proved to be a show in itself. The man was absolutely wild, moving speedily from man to man and group to group, like a cat on a hot tin roof. And the way he entertained his advertiser friends in the packaging field! He had one of the largest, gaudiest suites on the top floor of the then new Executive House. An elaborate bar was set up, hostesses and waiters were serving drinks and a great variety of tidbits as if there were no tomorrow. A four-piece jazz combo kept playing throughout the evening and throughout the night. Every once in a while, Charlie would take one man or a group for a private, hush-hush conference in one of the many bedrooms of the suite, for some wheeling and dealing, or the passing on of some "very private" intelligence about something "really exciting" in the packaging business. At least once, he brought me into one of these "secret sessions." Charlie Breskin worked at these conventions in manic fashion. By midnight, I was worn out, completely spent. Charlie was still going at full speed.

When we met again in his office in the middle of April, Charlie began to become a little impatient with the "slowness" of our buying his business.

"Look, here, Don, this can't go on much longer. I have exposed my self and my business to you. . . . I have given you plenty of time. Now, come through with the cash—all of the $2,800,000 of it—or the deal is off."

I tried to explain to him that everything was moving along nicely, that I had been assured by Stan Cruzen and his associates at Shearson that the offering would be put forth without a hitch.

"But what guarantee do I have that everything you say will take place and that I will get my $2,800,000 before long?"

"You have the assurance of one of the most reliable investment banking firms."

"That's not enough. . . . Anything could go wrong. In the meantime, I have wasted a lot of time and I've taken the risk of exposing my operation to you—a possible competitor."

He was right. And I knew better than to argue with him. So, I just remained silent.

"I'll tell you what I'll do. . . . You get me a check for $280,000 in earnest money—ten percent of the deal —and I will give you two months to complete the deal. . . . Win or lose, I keep the $280,000. If for *any* reason, the deal is called off, the deal does not meet with my understanding of it or you are unsuccessful in completing it within the allotted two month period, all bets are off and I keep the $280,000."

"Isn't this a bit unreasonable?" I asked.

"I don't think so. So far, I have gambled everything. . . . I have lost time, I stand naked before you . . . and you have lost nothing—"

"This is not really so. I have spent four months working on the proposition, investing a lot of time and energy—"

"That's not enough. Get the $280,000 or the deal is off. . . . I am sorry—My patience is at an end."

"How much time do I have to get you the $280,-000?"

"Two weeks from today."

Since I knew that Charlie Breskin meant business, I met with Stan Cruzen that afternoon and relayed to him Charlie's ultimatum.

"I believe Mr. Breskin is most unreasonable," Stan said. "This is not the way we do business. Besides, neither you nor we can gamble on forfeiting $280,000 'for any reason'."

"But what guarantee does Breskin have that the underwriting will take place, that it will be successful, that he will get his $2,800,000 in cash in a reasonable time?"

"Guarantee, no, but the assurance, yes. . . . If he insists, it will be up to you to provide the money and then gamble on it. . . . As an investment banking company, we cannot take this kind of gamble. We have to continue with the merger and the underwriting in the usual, routine, accepted, conservative fashion."

I followed my meeting with Stan Cruzen with visits to my bank, the Irving Trust Company, and my attorney, Dave Regosin. Both thought that Stan Cruzen was right in his attitude and Breskin "unfair" and "unreasonable." At any rate, neither the bank nor my attorney advised me to gamble $280,000, an amount which I did not have but could raise. My surplus in our business at that time was $175,000, an accumulation of fifteen years of work. I had sufficient bank credit to borrow another $150,000. But to give Breskin $280,000 under such circumstances meant putting my business and most of my resources on the line. While there was every reason to believe that the underwriting would be successful and that it could be completed within two months, there was always the possibility that something could go wrong or that the timetable would not be met. My own judgment and instinct said, "Go to it," but all of my advisors said, "Don't dare, it's too risky."

As a result, I spent the next ten days trying to obtain venture capital from various sources, including private, speculative investors, at least two of whom were famous Hollywood personalities. No go. The price they asked proved to be prohibitive. They wanted too much equity in the business. Instead of winding up with working control of 20 to 25 percent, all I would have would be about 10 percent. It was just too high a price to pay.

I still wanted to gamble my business and my resources because I felt that the Breskin business, at $2,800,000, was a bargain. Besides, I knew what I could do with this kind of a nucleus in a public company. But no one would go along with me, and I felt that I could not make this kind of decision against all of the professional advice.

The result of almost five months of work was inevitable. I finally induced Charlie Breskin to meet with me and Stan Cruzen in the latter's office and at least to listen to what the investment banker had to say.

"OK, I'll meet you there . . . but unless you'll be ready to hand me a check for $280,000, I'll call off the deal."

The meeting in the large, formal board room of Shearson, Hammill did not last long—just a few minutes. Stan began to explain the normal procedures that must be followed in a successful public offering. Charlie hardly listened.

"What you say may be right. But what guarantees do I have that the underwriting will take place or that I will get my $2,800,000?"

"Of course, we cannot give you any guarantees. But, for the record, we have been successful with each of our public offerings of the past year—not a single failure to date . . ."

"Well, this might just be the first one. Market conditions, our economy could change—"

"That is always possible . . . but not likely." Stan tried to be reassuring.

"In the meantime, I will have to expose my entire operation to other underwriters and brokers. When the 'red herring' is printed and made available to brokers, everybody will know my business."

"But this is the usual procedure. We have to file with the SEC. We have to invite other underwriters and brokers to participate . . ."

"Well, I talked this over with my lawyer and my nephew who works for Becker and Company in Chicago, a well-known and well-rated underwriting company, as you know, and I was told that I could go public myself. Becker would be the underwriter. . . . Sorry, gentlemen—unless you are willing to put up earnest money now, right now, the deal is off."

That was it. Charlie and I returned uptown in a taxi together . . . but we did not talk very much. When the taxi reached Breskin's office, he turned to me and said:

"Don, why don't you merge with us?"

I laughed.

"Why do you laugh? We're bigger than you are. I like you . . . I think we could work together."

"Thank you Charlie . . . but I'm not interested."
"Think about it."

Apprehension came at bedtime or in the early hours of the morning. I never had a problem with sleep. I could fall asleep almost at will. For example, before going out for an evening, especially to an industry dinner—which meant moving around during the cocktail hour and table-hopping during the dinner itself—I made it a habit to come home half an hour earlier than usual and sit down with a paper or a book for five or ten minutes. I soon found myself getting a little drowsy, then looked at my watch and closed my eyes. Within seconds, I would be asleep, sleeping soundly for about fifteen minutes and waking up at the time planned, refreshed and ready for a big evening's activity. My usual bedtime was eleven thirty, and as I almost always read in bed for half an hour or a bit longer, I would not turn off the lights until midnight, and off I would go to a sound sleep until about seven in the morning. Following the deal I made with Cowles' President Marvin Whatmore in the offices of John Weinberg of Goldman, Sachs, I found myself remaining awake on several occasions past the midnight hour—and sometimes until one, two or three in the morning. At other times, I would fall asleep promptly at midnight as usual, but I would find myself waking up at about four thirty and could sleep no more. And it was during these wakeful hours that apprehension would set in.

Why do I want to merge with Cowles—or any other company? I'm doing well, I'm free to do as I please. I make my own decisions and I have no one looking over my shoulder. The only boss I have is the Internal Revenue Service.

No matter how I view it, merging with Cowles would mean that for the first time in twenty-two years

I would become an employee once again. Once the acquisition took place, I would become exposed, naked in the eyes of Marvin Whatmore, Gardner Cowles and other Cowles executives. Whatever I did, whatever results I attained, whatever successes or failures were mine would be on view, fully and openly. Do I really want this? No, I really do not want it. I cherish my freedom, freedom of action, freedom to make my own decisions, freedom to gain from my successes and freedom to pay for my failures. Without exposure to anyone.

Why, then, am I merging with Cowles? I have been promised autonomy of operation. But does it really mean full and complete freedom? Obviously, it does not and cannot. Cowles is a public company whose stock is traded on the New York Stock Exchange and is owned by some four to five thousand stockholders throughout the country. Thus, and rightly so, Cowles has an obligation to its stockholders to operate as a large, public company should. Autonomy or not, this means that each division must be watched and watched carefully. No, I could not possibly expect to have the same freedom as head of a division of Cowles that I have had as an independent businessman.

If so, why do I want to merge? Because I want the opportunity to run a bigger, much bigger company than I have been operating by myself. Because I want to become financially independent—at last—with marketable stock. Because I want new business excitement, new associations. Because I want to be part of a much bigger business league.

But is all this worth it? Will I be able to stand someone constantly looking over my shoulder? Reporting to a president, chairman, two executive vice presidents and others—all strangers, all part of a large, sophisticated communications empire? Do I really want this? Is this for me?

Then came the great day. The meeting with the giant of the newspaper and consumer magazine field—Gardner Cowles. Marvin Whatmore telephoned me about a week after our meeting in the Goldman, Sachs offices. "Are you free for lunch next Tuesday?" I did have a luncheon date, but I was ready to postpone any appointment to meet Gardner Cowles. This was to be the decisive step.

At 12:15, I left my office for the historic meeting, walking at my usual fast pace, and by the time I reached 488 Madison Avenue, it was four minutes before 12:30. I wanted to be there on time—but not too early. So, I walked around the block. I entered the Look building a very proud man—didn't everyone in sight know that I was going to meet the mighty Gardner Cowles?—at 12:29. I pressed the button for the sixteenth floor in the elevator. At precisely 12:30, the elevator doors to the sixteenth floor opened to a beige-carpeted, brightly lit hall. As I opened a heavy glass door, I was greeted by a smiling receptionist who sat behind a very large, attractive, modern rosewood desk. I told her that I had a date with Marvin Whatmore and Gardner Cowles.

"Yes, Mr. Gussow, they are expecting you," she said with a very bright smile and then went to an inner office to announce my arrival. She returned promptly with the message: "Mr. Whatmore is on the telephone . . . he will see you in a few minutes."

As I sat down in a stylish upholstered chair, my eyes took in the long and wide reception room. Behind the receptionist's rosewood desk was a wall of beautifully paneled rosewood. A door in the paneled wall was slightly ajar, and I could see a large conference or board room. On one papered wall were covers and pages from current issues of *Look,* the corporation's flagship property. On large, low, glass-covered tables were current copies of various Cowles magazines and newspapers. I picked up copies of *Look* and *Family Circle,* but I do not remember what I saw except for the names of the publications. I could not concentrate on anything except my upcoming meeting.

After a long five minutes, Marvin Whatmore came out of his office to greet me warmly. But then, Marvin Whatmore was a great charmer from 'way back. Charm was definitely one of the major assets of the president and chief operating officer of Cowles Communications. A man in his late fifties, of medium height, although he was trim in build, smartly dressed in grey and quick of gait, Marvin did not look particularly impressive. Most certainly, he did not have the bearing of a publishing tycoon. He had a small face, thinning grey hair over a big forehead, with slightly bulging eyes and a small mouth which seemed to remain open, giving the picture of a jolly, friendly, playful dolphin.

"It's good to see you, Don. Let's go to the dining room. Mike will join us soon. . . . He is so anxious to meet you."

I followed him into *the* executive dining room. (There were three others, I learned later—one for *Look*, one for *Family Circle* and one for second-line executives.) It was a large, modern and beautifully furnished room. At the far end there was a sitting-room area set up for the pre-lunch cocktail hour.

"What is your pleasure?" Marvin asked me as he went to the amply stocked bar.

"Sctoch-on-the-rocks with some water. . . ." I was going to ask for my special brand of Scotch, but I noticed that one particular brand of Scotch and one brand of bourbon were placed near the ice bucket and the glasses.

"We serve a different Scotch and a different bourbon every day so that we will not offend any of our advertisers. Liquor advertising is an important category in our magazines and newspapers, and just about every brand uses some space."

Just as Marvin handed me my drink, the door opened and into the room slowly walked a tall, conservatively dressed man, wearing a dark blue vested suit and a solid blue butterfly bow tie.

Not waiting for any introduction, he walked over to me: "I am Mike . . . It is so good to meet you, Don. Marvin has told me so much about you."

At last I had met the Great Man himself. The creator of *Look,* the only real threat to *Life.* I was practically speechless. All I could say was, "It is good to meet you."

When we sat down with our drinks, Marvin said to me: "Don, why don't you tell Mike a little about your company, your magazines and your plans for the future —just as you told me at lunch the other day?"

My God, I thought, the Big Man actually wants me to tell him about our business, about our magazines— and about my plans for the future!

As briefly as I could, and making a strong effort to refrain from displaying the slightest degree of immodesty, I reviewed the history of MFI, and how and when I started, stressing the fact that I was basically an editor, that our first magazine, *Candy Industry,* made a profit with the first issue and wound up the first year in the black—which was something of a record for a new magazine and a new publishing venture. However, I quickly added: "But how different it was when we launched our second magazine, *Bottling Industry,* two years later. It took four years to break even and it drained every cent of the profits from *Candy Industry,* plus outside investment. I learned an interesting lesson from this experience. It takes knowledge of a field and contacts to assure the success of a new business magazine. When I started *Candy Industry,* I had been the editor of two candy magazines for almost fifteen years and during those years I fortunately had built followings among both readers and advertisers. But it was different with *Bottling Industry.* While I used the same formula, the same format and the same news approach, I knew almost nothing about the soft drink industry or its people. Nor did I know anyone in the field. And no one knew me. It took the first two years just to get acquainted, to learn something about the industry. The lesson was never to start a magazine without bringing in people who are thoroughly knowledgeable about the particular industry, people who have both the expertise and the contacts in the field to be covered by the new magazine. It became an inviolable rule for me."

The Great Man listened and I felt he was impressed. More importantly, I noticed that Marvin liked what I said and the manner in which I said it. Obviously, he wanted me to make a good impression on the Great Man—to win instant approval of his recommendation to acquire our company.

I continued with my review of the history of MFI, briefly explaining how we acquired the other properties, giving us nine business magazines covering several industries. It was now time for lunch.

"Now, Don, tell us something about your plans for the future—what you would like to do after the merger."

Gardner Cowles called me by my first name, now, I suppose I should address him as Mike, I thought, as I proceeded to outline some of my plans "for the future" ... "after the merger" with the great Cowles empire.

"What we have in MFI is a small but good nucleus for the development of an important business magazine operation. I would like to build MFI from its present $2,500,000 in annual sales and modest profits into a $15,000,000 business magazine company, with profits of $2,000,000 before taxes—this to be done in about three to four years after the merger. My long-range goal is a little more ambitious: to expand the business magazine division of Cowles into a $50,000,000 unit, with annual pre-tax profits in excess of $5,000,000 and hopefully as much as $10,000,000."

"How would you move to accomplish your goals? Would you buy or start magazines?" Cowles asked me, in a quiet and slow, relaxed, friendly voice.

"Both ways—but largely through acquisitions. While it costs less to start a new trade paper than to buy one, the risk is much greater. Using Cowles stock, traded on the New York Stock Exchange and hopefully continuing to appreciate in value, we will be in a position to acquire good, profitable business magazines with growth potential."

"What fields will you be considering at the outset?" Cowles asked me.

"My priorities are medicine, education and plastics. I know the companies that I want to buy in the medical and education fields. And in the case of plastics, we may be better off by starting our own magazine, since it is close enough to the packaging industry already covered by two of our magazines, and the man who heads up these publications knows the plastics industry almost as well as he knows the packaging field."

"I don't know much about plastics, but obviously it is an important, growing field. . . . It sounds fine. . . . But I am particularly pleased that you would plan to

enter the medical and educational areas. These interest
me very, very much," Cowles said. "I would like to
hear more about your plans in these fields . . . not
now, when we meet again, when the merger plans have
been fully worked out . . ."

When lunch was over and the three of us stood up,
Cowles shook my hand and said: "Don, I'm so pleased
that you will be joining our company. Your plans for
the future sound just fine. . . . In addition to running
the business magazine division, we would like you to
assist us in the management of the entire corporation."

Did I hear him right, I wondered as I walked out of
the office and floated down the elevator. He wants me
to be on the board of directors of the company? Of
course, I had intended to ask for a seat on the board
. . . but I did not have to ask. He offered it to me. The
Big Man wants me to assist him in the management of
his business—the great and growing Cowles empire!

THREE:

The View from North Salem

The months ahead were exciting but they were not without a degree of frustration. The first thing I had to do was to call a meeting of MFI's officers and principal stockholders and tell them of the impending merger. This had to be done before Cowles mailed out the official release announcing the "agreement in principle" to acquire our company. As a public company, it had no choice but to make such an announcement since it was required under the SEC's rule of full disclosure.

Attending the MFI meeting were: Burt Gussow, Jack Mulligan, Jerry Stevens and Art Yohalem—four of our six vice presidents, who together owned about thirteen percent of the stock in MFI, acquired through options, almost all prior to our aborted effort to go public in 1960–1961.

I opened the meeting with: "I have something very important to tell you. We are merging our company . . . and I want you to be the first to know."

"I'm not surprised. I can guess with whom," Burt said, typically interrupting me.

"Go ahead, tell us with whom," I said.

"Crowell-Collier."

"Not quite," I said. "We are merging with a company in publishing all right, but one that is not presently in the trade paper field, although in everything else in communications. It is a growing, prestigious company whose stock is traded on the New York Stock Exchange. It is Cowles Communications—the publishers of *Look* and *Family Circle*."

There were gasps from all except Burt, who said: "That's whom I meant—I knew it all the time . . ."

I spent the next few minutes giving them details of the deal and answering a number of questions. They seemed to be pleased.

Except for a two- or three-month restriction, each could sell his stock at will and if they did, each would come out with $80,000 to $100,000 in capital gain. Not bad, since their investment was only several thousand dollars apiece, going back to 1960. I was in a different position. As an "insider" with major holdings in Cowles, I could not sell any stock at the outset and only a very minute percentage every six months or once a year—and even this small amount with the approval of Cowles.

My associates would also have an opportunity to share in the growth of a communications empire—not in stock options (since Cowles did not have a stock option plan) but in job improvement, salary increases and a bigger share in "contribution to overhead" or profits before general and administrative costs. No wonder the news was received with such enthusiasm. At the close of the meeting, Art Yohalem shook my hand and said: "Don, I want to congratulate you on making such a fine deal—and with such an excellent company."

Only Jack Mulligan was not entirely excited about the upcoming merger, although he accepted it graciously. "I suppose what you are doing is all right, but I have an uneasy feeling about the whole thing. It just will not be the same . . . not the same old crowd anymore. We've been so happy working with you, as an independent, that I can't see how things can improve. I hope that everything will work out as you hope and say it will . . . I'll pray for you."

Meetings with lawyers, drawing up contracts and completing details of our negotiations were to take up a good deal of the time in the weeks and months ahead. David Regosin and Ed Singer went to work with Ezra Eisen, our controller, who was also an attorney, to prepare needed material. The contract would be drawn by the Cowles legal department.

I was delighted to see Ed Singer work so well with Dave. I had been concerned about it since Dave had been my personal attorney and friend for many years and his company was legal counsel to MFI. But I had called in Ed because of his experience in the merger of a publishing company. I had known Ed casually, having met him at several parties at Jack Mulligan's house. Several months earlier, however, Ed had called me to discuss an idea he had. At lunch, he told me he had been called in by the Chase Manhattan Bank to handle the legal work for Ed Williams in the merger of the Williams Publishing Company into Cahners. Ed Williams, whom I had known for about twenty years, was publisher and owner of *Quick Frozen Foods,* the leading magazine covering this industry.

"Ed made a fantastic all-cash deal with Cahners and the Cahners people have been awfully nice to work with. They're first class. So I thought maybe you would be interested in talking to them . . ."

Cahners had been interested in our company for over a year. One day during the previous summer, Fulton Cahners, Norman Cahners' younger brother, dropped in to say "Hello." Before our twenty-minute chat was at an end, he said that Cahners would be interested in talking about a merger with me at some future date, if I had any interest in pursuing it. I did not express great enthusiasm, but did indicate that I might be interested in talking about it—at a future date. Fulton followed through with some correspondence, telephone calls and one more visit. But a few months later, he passed away suddenly. He had been operated on for an aneurism by Dr. Michael DeBakey in Houston, Texas. The operation was "successful" but he died about ten days later—at forty-eight years of age. Some time later, Saul Goldweitz, the president of Cahners, picked up the "negotiations" by telephoning to make a date to see me. But no date was set, as I had plans to go to Europe in the spring, and Saul was involved in a number of trips himself. We agreed to get together after returning from our respective trips.

I told all this to Ed at lunch, explaining that, while we had had no really serious negotiations, there was little question that Cahners was interested in our company. Because of his satisfactory experience with Cahners, we agreed that it might be a good idea to pursue discussions further with enthusiasm.

I did not see Ed again after that until after I had made the deal with Cowles. When Ed heard the terms, his face lit up and he said: "This sounds like a marvelous deal. Cowles is a fine company, and putting you on the board shows how they feel about you. It's just great—much better than anything you could have gotten from Cahners, although a deal with Cahners would not have been bad . . . Go to it, Don, and may God be with you."

About a week later, Marvin Whatmore invited Betty and me to join him, his wife, and several officers and executives of Cowles and their wives at brunch at his country place in North Salem in Westchester.

North Salem is only an hour's drive from Manhattan —and an enjoyable drive on that sunny Sunday morning in late August. But in the hours that followed, Betty and I were transported to a world we had dreamt of but did not think we could ever reach. The Whatmore country place turned out to be a beautiful 150-acre estate on a delightful hill surrounded by mountains. It looked more like a place in Vermont or Colorado than in suburban New York. The main house itself was large. Constructed of wood and stone, it was the kind of spacious home you found in the fine old New England towns. Alongside a large pool area were tennis courts. The estate was only a fraction of a mile from a country club that boasted one of the best golf courses of the area. (Marvin, I learned, was an avid golfer, playing on that course every weekend.) The estate also maintained two hundred of the best breed of cattle. And a unique feature of the estate was an observation tower that looked like a miniature Eiffel Tower. After our second drink and just before brunch was served, Marvin, Jack Harding and I walked up the one hundred or so steps to the tower to enjoy the spectacular view. Marvin explained that you could see points in at least three states—New York, Connecticut and New Jersey. If you had particularly good eyesight and/or a better than average imagination (and perhaps a third drink), you could also see Pennsylvania, Massachussets and perhaps even Vermont.

When Betty and I entered the living room a few minutes before noon, Lois Whatmore introduced us to Lester Suhler, the Cowles circulation director, and his wife, Don Perkins, the executive vice president of sales, and his wife, and the Hardings. Joining the group within the next half hour were: the Gilbert Maurers, the Shap Shapiros, the Dave Whitneys, the Merrill Cloughs, the Palmer Lebermans and several others.

It was obvious that the purpose of the brunch was to have Betty and me meet most of the Cowles bigwigs and, in turn, for them to take a look at us. While there was a certain amount of inside banter, the atmosphere was generally relaxed and we did not feel particularly uncomfortable. We commented on two interesting modern paintings in the living and dining rooms and Marvin Whatmore explained that the paintings were recent acquisitions from an obscure French painter whose work he liked very much.

"My interest in art is of very recent vintage. As a matter of fact, I am just beginning to learn something about it," he said.

Betty mentioned our son, who paints. Marvin showed much interest and promised to visit Alan's next show.

While everybody tried to be very courteous and receptive, I found the friendliest (and most talkative) to be Don Perkins. He and his wife, Helen, a charming woman, sat with Betty and me during brunch. Don soon disclosed that shortly before we started negotiations with Cowles they had called off an impending merger deal with Cahners. Don then volunteered that it was he who had "killed the deal." He said he felt that Cahners would have become the largest Cowles stockholder (with the possible exception of Mike Cowles in combination with the holdings in Cowles by the *Des Moines Register and Tribune,* the Cowles old family newspaper). That, he felt, would be dangerous. He also believed that the price "was too high."

"I like your company and I'm very glad that you're coming along with us," Don said.

Gardner Cowles was not there, but just about everyone else among the top echelon of the Cowles organization joined the Whatmores for the special Sunday brunch, which was served in style. Everyone was "charming" and it gave Betty and me an opportunity to take the measure of some of the men I would be working with.

At four o'clock we left, explaining that we were on our way to attend a dairy and ice cream convention. New York, New Jersey and Pennsylvania dairy groups were meeting at Grossinger's in the Catskills. It was the first time that we had been to the famous Grossinger resort and we didn't like it at all. Most of the guests seemed rather old and they were sitting around most of the time. It gave me the impression of an old folks' nursing home rather than a swinging Jewish resort. It was the first time that I had attended this particular convention in over twenty years and I knew only a handful of the people. However, Howard Grant, publisher of our *Ice Cream Field and Trade Journal,* who was there with his wife Selma, knew just about everybody and introduced us to a lot of delegates with whose names and companies I was familiar.

Attending this gathering reminded me of my coverage of my first ice cream convention many, many years before—in 1930 or 1931, when I was about twenty-two. I was assistant editor of *Confectionery–Ice Cream World.* The convention (only New York State operators at that time) was held in a resort on Lake George. I was the only representative of my publication and I had been associated with it for less than a year. I did not know a single person. What a strange and uncomfortable feeling—walking through the public rooms filled with hundreds of ice cream men and their wives and their suppliers and not knowing any of them.

"I am Don Gussow of *Confectionery–Ice Cream World,*" was the way I tried to start a conversation with a likely, friendly-looking stranger. But it didn't work. No one wanted to talk to the nervous kid from that weekly gossip sheet in New York. Or so it appeared. I walked from public hall to public hall, then outside through the beautiful grounds, then back again inside, sat down for a minute to rest, then resumed my walk, tried to meet a person or two once again—with little success. It was a terrifying experience.

How different that experience was from future conventions, particularly those of the candy industry. Only a few years later, I couldn't enter the lobby of a convention hotel without being greeted: "Hi, Don," again and again, now knowing hundreds of people, many of whom had become close friends of mine (and Betty's too, for by that time, I had begun to take Betty along to all conventions). The friendly greetings of so many were sweet music to my ears. But I never forgot the loneliness and the frustration of my first convention.

Following the Whatmore Sunday brunch, I had expected that the merger plans would move along fast. We had agreed on terms. The chemistry seemed satisfactory. All that was needed now was for the Cowles legal department, after consultation with my attorneys, to draw up a preliminary draft of a contract. Inasmuch as our merger was not the first for Cowles, drawing up the draft should not have required a great deal of time. All that was necessary was to fill in the details of our arrangement in the usual basic, standard contract to buy assets for stock. However, days and then weeks passed and nothing happened. When I telephoned Ed Singer and inquired whether he had received a copy of the first draft, he said that "they are still working on it."

While I wanted action, I hesitated to call Whatmore to inquire about the contract lest I appear to be overly anxious. But after several weeks had passed and there was still no word, I decided to make the call. When I reached Whatmore on the telephone, he was most charming and friendly. I made it a point to merely inquire about the status of the contract, explaining in a matter-of-fact style that the reason for my inquiry was to establish some sort of timetable so that we could proceed with our anticipated plans in an organized manner.

At first, Whatmore seemed surprised that we had not received the draft, then he explained that delay might have been caused by the legal department's involvement in the Manchester–Kennedy affair—which began to occupy columns and columns of newspaper space—and the additional legal work required in the launching of the *Suffolk Sun,* a new Cowles property. The first issue of the *Suffolk Sun* was scheduled for some time in November. It was obvious that Whatmore understood that we had a firm deal. . . . If details were not worked out this week or this month, it didn't matter. . . . Next week or next month would do. . . . In the meantime, why could we not proceed on the basis that the completion of the deal was merely a routine matter?

"Incidentally, Don," Marvin Whatmore said, "Mike and I would like to have lunch with you once again to discuss an idea that has been brought to us for the launching of a weekly newspaper in the education field."

"Is this, by chance, the Dean and Levine plan for *Education Week,* brought in by McGehee?" I asked.

"It is."

"It's an interesting concept. It was proposed to me two years ago. I turned it down, because I felt it would have required at least a million dollars' investment to put it across. It was just too big for us."

"That's very interesting. Obviously, you're familiar with it. Can we meet for lunch next Tuesday?"

While we still had not received the first draft of a contract, the lunch the following Tuesday was the first working meeting with Cowles, as the discussion centered around the possibility of launching a newspaper for the education market, to be called *Education News*. It turned out to be a crucial meeting, although I was not aware of its importance at that time.

Once again we met at the executive lunchroom on the sixteenth floor. And once again, I reveled in the experience.

Whatmore, Cowles and I were joined by Gil Maurer, president of the Cowles Education Corporation, and head of *Venture* magazine, and David Whitney, editor-in-chief of the Cowles education properties. Since I had met both Gil and Dave at the Whatmore Sunday brunch, I found myself fairly comfortable with the entire group although I could not help being aware of the fact that I continued to be the focus of interest at the luncheon, as I had been at the brunch.

I had taken a dislike to Dave Whitney from the moment I met him and I found myself liking him even less. He had a supercilious way of discussing a subject. He behaved as if he were the final authority on the issue in question and, at the same time, he questioned the ability of the others to deal with a matter about which they knew so little. While he had a fairly extensive vocabulary and verbalized well, he made minor speechlets each time he spoke instead of joining in a natural, normal conversation.

I became particularly annoyed with his pretense to expertise in a speechlet on business magazines, a subject with which he was not familiar.

"You supercilious ass," I wanted to say, but I quickly repressed my impulse. But I had his number, and then and there, I made up my mind to keep an eye on him.

Apparently Gardner Cowles thought well of him. As did Marvin Whatmore. Before long, I learned that both looked on him as a great editorial genius in the educational market, with the added capabilities of being a sound business man and administrator. As I was in awe of Gardner Cowles and considered Marvin Whatmore one of the brightest of publishing executives, I tried very hard to buy what David Whitney had to sell —his unusual talents and expertise in the education field—but I continued to doubt. However, I was willing to be charitable and follow a wait-and-see policy. It may well have been a mistake.

Whitney had been with Cowles for less than two years. He was not an officer of the company nor of a division. Yet he was one of the very few who seemed to have been accepted as "insiders," and was consulted and listened to with great respect on matters dealing with educational publishing. Months later, I discovered that he was the only one at Cowles who had an educational publishing background. He came to Cowles from Field Enterprises where he had been editor-in-chief of the educational publishing division of the famed Chicago-based newspaper and educational publishing company. Before that, he had been with Grolier. He was from Kansas and was a graduate of the University of Kansas.

Gil Maurer was a different breed of cat. He was friendly, he was humble, he was bright. He was also a listener, and appeared to be a concerned, up-and-coming member of the Cowles team. We were to become good friends in the months ahead. Gil, at thirty-eight, was the youngest of the top Cowles executives. He was liked by both Gardner and Marvin, and it appeared that he had a great future ahead of him in the company. He was a Harvard Business School graduate and had been with Cowles for about thirteen years—practically his entire business career to date.

As we moved to the luncheon table, Gardner Cowles asked me to sit at his right and motioned to Dave to sit at his left. Marvin faced Cowles at the other end of the oval while Gil sat next to Dave.

The business of the meeting started immediately we sat down to lunch. "What we want to do today is to explore our possible involvement in publishing a weekly newspaper for the scholastic community," Cowles said. "In particular, I want to show you the presentation and a dummy issue for such a magazine brought to our attention recently. I understand that Don Gussow is familiar with this proposal, since his company had been among several offered the opportunity to publish the new magazine . . . Don, what are your comments?"

"As I explained to Marvin the other day, Frank McGehee, the publication broker and consultant with whom we have been working for several years, brought the *Education Week* proposal to us about two years ago. I agreed that it was an interesting concept, but I felt that it required a minimum of a million dollar investment, much more than we had to invest in such a project. . . . I must also say that there is nothing particularly unique about the idea. As a matter of fact, MFI had long been interested in starting a business paper in the education field. There is very little in this proposal that is original or that is much different from our own thoughts and plans."

"Could you elaborate?" Marvin asked.

"In the first place, I believe that a biweekly frequency could prove to be more practical and economical than weekly. Additionally—and this is most important—*Education Week,* as proposed by Dean and Levine [Sidney Dean and Leon Levine were two entre-

preneurs who visualized and presented an idea for a
weekly newspaper, with a circulation of over 1,000,000,
covering the entire scholastic field from teacher to principal and administrator] is a consumer-oriented publication covering the entire spectrum of the education
field, from the secondary school to the university, and
aimed at the school administrator as well as the teacher.
This is much too broad an approach, much too wide
a coverage. Besides, I believe that what the field needs
is a trade paper—a business-oriented publication for
the school and/or college executive . . ."

Dave Whitney looked at me as if I had uttered a
terribly dirty word. "Did you say a trade paper for
the educator? The educator will never countenance, he
will never support a trade paper. . . . What he wants—
and I know what he wants—is a real, honest newspaper—his own, his very own newspaper, that deals
with the broad spectrum of the present and future
problems of the educational community at its various
levels and components . . ."

He went on and on: "The educator does not care
one bit about what kind of brooms are used to clean
the school johns—the kind of stuff you would expect
to find in a trade paper. What he wants to read about
are the vital, serious educational problems he has to
face every day he comes to his office."

"You don't think he wants to read about new types
of curricula, about new school construction, major personnel changes, the new technology in teaching aids
and methods, and the long list of new products for the
school room and plant?" I asked.

"I doubt it," he said. "He gets all this information
from the literature and throwaways of the suppliers."

I decided that I would not let Whitney bother me,
or cause me to change my mind about the upcoming
deal with Cowles. He is not an officer of Cowles, I

reasoned. He is not part of the inner circle. He has been with the company less than two years. I should have no serious problem in handling him. I could ignore him if I chose to. I was not going to let him spoil the wonderful dream that was soon to become a reality for me.

What should have concerned, or at least surprised me, was that none of the others took much part in the conversation which before long became a sort of debate between Dave Whitney and me. Instead of being participants in a discussion, they behaved like auditors or observers. While I was not consciously concerned, I did not like the turn of the discussion and I made an attempt to change the direction of the meeting.

"My experience has been totally in trade papers or in the 'business press,' as it is now called," I said. "Insofar as the consumer publishing field is concerned, my knowledge is limited to that of a reader or, at best, a concerned observer. If we are going to start a trade paper, I can bring the needed expertise and experience to the project . . . If we are going to launch a consumer or even a quasi-consumer periodical, I can offer very little assistance. Besides, I believe that it is better, more economical, to buy an existing magazine than to start one."

"Do you have in mind any particular magazine in the education field that you believe we can and should buy?" Cowles asked.

"Yes, just as I know exactly what medical magazine group I want to approach, I know a specific company that publishes periodicals in the school and education field that I have watched and would like to buy."

"What company is it?" Gil Maurer asked.

"It is the Management Publishing Company of Greenwich, Connecticut, publishers of *School Management,* the leading publication in the education field, and several other periodicals. I have a feeling we could—"

Before I could finish the sentence, Marvin broke in: "Don, I'm sorry. We can't buy that company. I am not in a position to discuss it, but this is not for us—for a very good reason . . ."

I was shocked, and wanted to know why . . . So, I did pursue it: "Don't go into detail, Marvin, but could you tell me the basic reason why we shouldn't buy this company?"

"It's a matter of personality compatability. We just could not possibly work with one of the principals of the company. You know, Don, the one thing we look for most when we consider acquiring a company is the man or men with whom we'll work on a day-to-day basis. We are in a 'people' business, and the person I have in mind is not for us . . . so, we'd better forget about him and this particular company."

"And Don, I believe that we may be better off starting our own education publication," Gardner Cowles said. "In this way, we could develop the kind of newspaper or magazine that the educator needs and will support. Which gives me an idea. Marvin, why don't we consider doing a survey—using the Louis Harris organization—a survey similar to the one Harris did for us in connection with the launching of the *Suffolk Sun?*"

"Yes, Mike, Louis Harris did a fine job for us in studying and determining the market for the *Suffolk Sun.* It pointed to an overwhelming need for such a newspaper, and even delineated the direction such a newspaper should take. Yes, I'll call Louis Harris and talk about it. Then we'll meet with him and listen to his proposal."

I was impressed. Imagine a survey by Louis Harris! Not only would we have some very valuable information, it should also prove tremendously helpful in the marketing, promotional and space selling efforts, I thought. But I made no comment.

Of course, in launching each of the six MFI magazines—from *Candy Industry* to *Food and Drug Packaging*—I never used any surveys to determine the need for these magazines. I just felt, I just knew, that there was a need for each of the magazines that we started and in each case I was right. What's more, five of the six magazines I launched proved to be successful. The one exception was not the result of a lack of need, but rather timing and money. But even this magazine, I was able to sell and came out whole from the experience.

Nevertheless, the idea of having a study by Louis Harris intrigued me. It could and should provide some meaningful information that could shorten our lead time in the launching of a publication in the education field, I thought. It seemed obvious that, as part of Cowles Communications, I would soon find myself playing the publishing game in a different league— very definitely in the "majors." With surveys and all!

"Don, I like your idea of a biweekly rather than a weekly," Cowles said. "However, let the Louis Harris study come back with some answers with regard to frequency. It would be interesting to see how prospective readers feel about a weekly versus a biweekly —or even a monthly."

Who could argue with such a proposal?

So, the meeting ended with everyone agreeing that a survey by Louis Harris would be of great help in determining whether we should start a publication in the education field, what form such a publication should take and what its frequency should be.

It was not until several weeks later that the first draft of the MFI purchase agreement arrived. Cowles had

not been stalling. On the contrary, both Marvin Whatmore and Gardner Cowles were anxious to complete the
deal with me as quickly as possible—largely because of
their interest and excitement generated by the various
proposals I had made for growth. The delay was
caused by the inability of the overworked four-man
legal department to handle the unusual amount of work
that had piled up in the Manchester–Kennedy case and
the upcoming launching of the *Suffolk Sun*.

The daily papers were full of the Manchester–
Kennedy affair. In meetings with Marvin Whatmore
and occasionally with Jack Harding, behind-the-scenes
tidbits about the fantastic case involving Jackie Kennedy were revealed. Jack Harding, Cowles' executive
vice president and head of its legal department, was
directly involved in the negotiations with Mrs. Kennedy and Bobby, then a senator from New York. Harding was flown in the private Kennedy plane to the Kennedy Cape Cod compound for a confrontation with
Jackie in connection with the proposed publication of
extracts in *Look* magazine from the Manchester book
on the Kennedy assassination.

Jack did his homework, he knew his law and, in his
own quiet way, he knew how to put a point across at
the right moment. He was a man of few words, but
convincing when he had something specific and important to say.

Marvin Whatmore was quite different. He loved to
gossip. He enjoyed taking you behind scenes. It was he
who passed on to me some of the interesting tidbits
about The Case and Jackie. And I ate them up. I
"replayed" some of these to Betty and to some of my
close friends. I knew bits and pieces about The Case
before they became available to newspaper reporters
and some of the tidbits I received from Marvin were
not made public until months later. The one item that

shocked me more than anything else was the report by Marvin about the meeting of Jack Harding with the Kennedys at the Kennedy compound. Jackie was evidently very angry at *Look* for considering publishing those excerpts of the book that she had not and did not want to approve. In her anger, she shouted at Jack Harding, using four-letter words freely. Jack Harding blushed all over, according to Marvin Whatmore. Eventually, of course—and after all sorts of dire threats —The Case was settled amicably. *Look* carried the story and the book was finally published (by Harpers, which was controlled by John Cowles, Sr., and John Cowles, Jr., brother and nephew of Gardner). As an "insider," familiar with the intricacies of The Case, I had felt that this would be the result despite protestations to the contrary from so many sources.

I was terribly, terribly impressed with the whole thing. I was taken behind the scenes of such an important, historic incident in American politics and magazine publishing. And the company I would join before long was a household word with millions of Americans. Just about everybody who was anybody was now aware of *Look* magazine, as well as Cowles Communications.

The contract was a massive document, consisting of seventy-eight pages. Since MFI was being sold on the basis of assets for stock, all of the MFI assets had to be listed. Also, all existing contracts and every possible detail involving the transference of such assets. In addition to the contract, the deal also called for the drawing up of an employment agreement for me, the details of which were quickly agreed upon. I was to receive a seven-year contract together with a three-year option (by Cowles) for renewal of the contract. I would be president and chief executive officer of the new Magazines For Industry, Inc., which would become a wholly owned subsidiary of Cowles Communications, Inc., and would be incorporated in Delaware (the old MFI was a New York State corporation). Additionally, I would be named president and general manager of the bigger Cowles Business and Professional Magazine Division and Technical Book Division. I would be elected a member of the board of directors of Cowles and I would become part of the Cowles profit sharing program and would share in all other fringe benefits, giving up at the same time my future benefits in the MFI pension trust. With Cowles having an excellent ten-year growth record—both in sales and earnings—being part of the Cowles executive profit sharing program seemed like a very attractive plus and appeared more advantageous than continuing on the MFI pension program, as good as that program was (and it was very good). At any rate, I was so taken with the idea that I would be on the Cowles profit sharing plan immediately upon closing the deal that I did not bother to analyze the potentials and/or limitations of this program in relation to the MFI pension plan, nor did my attorneys. That proved to be a costly mistake.

The only element in my contract that remained open was my salary. I had been drawing $53,000 per year and I felt that I should be earning more as head of the Cowles Business-and Professional Magazine Division. A luncheon meeting was set by Marvin Whatmore to include Ed Singer, my attorney of record. The three of us met in the 16th floor executive dining room shortly after Labor Day. Ed Singer was so taken with Whatmore and with how Cowles felt about me, and their excitement about the upcoming acquisition of MFI, that I felt embarrassed. I wanted to call him aside and say: "Cut it, Ed, you are overdoing it."

When coffee was served, Marvin Whatmore got down to cases.

"What is your present salary, Don?" Marvin asked.

"It's $53,000 . . . but I would like $65,000 or at least $60,000 under our pending contract arrangement."

"Don, I would appreciate it very much if your salary remained at $53,000. . . . We have other ways of compensating our top people, and I can assure you that you will be doing very well. Besides, you will be getting dividends on your Cowles stock—about $50,000 a year—so please, Don, stay at your present salary."

I tried to argue, but not much. After all, I would not be earning $53,000 but $103,000, including the dividends from Cowles stock. Besides, I heard this fine, wonderful man saying: "We have other ways of compensating and you will be doing very well . . ."

I looked at Ed who seemed to be on Planet 9. "Don, I believe you can trust Marvin. He and his associates think so well of you, you have nothing to worry about."

And so I accepted "the same salary arrangement," not even asking the president of Cowles Communications to spell out or identify "the other ways of compensating" in addition to being part of the CCI profit sharing program. The way Marvin Whatmore talked and the way Ed Singer reacted, I felt foolish, if not downright pushy, to insist on a higher salary or a spelling out of "the other ways of compensating." This also proved to be a costly mistake.

To discuss the details of the purchase agreement, my attorneys and I met the following Saturday morning at Ed Singer's offices at 500 Fifth Avenue. In addition to Ed and myself, participating at the meeting were David Regosin and Ed Vogel, whom Ed Singer had called in to assist him. I had no idea that Ed Singer would bring in another attorney and I did not like being surprised. And, as Ed Vogel began to ask some penetrating questions and attempted to "dot the i's," I began to resent him.

"Who needs this character?" I thought. "Lawyers often ruin a deal and the way he's going about the various details in the contract, he is bound to ruin the Cowles deal."

Obviously, I wanted the merger with Cowles so much that I could not countenance any possible threat to it—even if this attorney was trying to help me. My mind and eyes were closed. I could not see what Ed Vogel was trying to do—behaving like a down-to-earth, independent, no-nonsense lawyer, trying to get the most for his client. Unlike Ed Singer, he was not impressed with Cowles Communications, Gardner Cowles, Marvin Whatmore or Jack Harding. Or if he had been impressed, he was not saying. He was looking at a contract and he wanted to make sure that the final contract brought for my signature was by far the best that could be written—from my point of view.

Instead of seeing this and appreciating it, I resented him, and even tried to show it at first. Then I decided to be patient and find out what he had in mind. It became clear what he had in mind when he met with me in my office several days later. I tried to avoid this meeting, but when Ed Singer and Dave Regosin called asking me to give Ed Vogel the courtesy of such a meeting, saying that he had something very special to talk about with me, I agreed.

"Don, from what Ed Singer and Dave Regosin tell me, the subject that I am going to discuss is anathema to you," Ed began. "I know that you do not want to talk about it, but as an attorney who has had experience in such matters, I believe I must make a recommendation. . . . I just couldn't sleep, I just couldn't live with myself if I didn't make an attempt."

"What do you have in mind?" I asked rudely, by

this time having an idea of what he had in mind, what he planned to discuss.

"Don, please hear me out . . . I would like you to consider taking cash rather than stock for your company—"

"I don't want to hear any more about it."

"Don, please, do me the personal favor of listening . . . then you can decide any way you like. The decision is yours."

I decided to listen. "All right, go ahead."

"Your share of the proceeds of the sale of MFI to Cowles will be approximately $1,500,000 in stock. Of course, you do not have to pay any capital gains tax until you sell any part or all of the stock. On the other hand, if you take cash, you must pay the 25 percent capital gain tax immediately. However, the tax on $1,500,000 is $375,000, leaving you net proceeds of $1,125,000. My suggestion is that you take cash, pay the tax, then invest $1,000,000 of the proceeds in tax-exempt bonds, giving you at least $40,000 a year in tax-exempt income, or the equivalent of $80,000 in income before taxes. At the same time, you will have $125,000 in cash to do what you want . . ."

I listened, but did not actually hear what Ed was saying. I just did not want to take cash.

"Ed, you don't understand . . . I am not selling my company. I'm buying into Cowles Communications. I have been offered a seat on the Cowles board, and a part in the overall management of the company. That is what I want. One of the first questions Mr. Gardner Cowles asked me at our first meeting was: 'Don, when you make the deal, will you take your stock and run . . . or do you want to operate and grow with us?' And you know what my answer was to this question. By turning around now and asking for a cash deal, I vitiate the whole purpose of the merger—to become part of this great communications company and take part in its future growth."

"But Don, while I well understand your intentions, philosophy and hopes, I still must tell you the implications of what you are doing. Sure, you'll be part of the Cowles management and that is fine. You will be receiving $50,000 in dividends on the Cowles stock but that will mean only about $15,000 to $20,000 in net income to you instead of $40,000 or more on tax-exempts. But most important of all, there is no telling what will happen to the price of Cowles stock in the months or years ahead. Nor is there any guarantee that the 50 cents per share dividends will be continued. Or for that matter, whether any dividends will be continued . . ."

"Please Ed, don't talk that way. Cowles has a great ten-year growth record, both in sales and profits, and there is absolutely no reason to expect anything but increased sales and profits and continuation of the dividend payment. If anything, the dividend may well be increased."

"I understand how you feel, Don, and Ed Singer warned me . . . but I had to tell you. Don, please give this real deliberate, thoughtful consideration. You have spent twenty-two years building this business. You must now make sure that what you are doing will not jeopardize the proceeds, the investment of your hard work over these years. By taking cash and converting that cash to secure, Triple A tax-exempts, you are insuring the result of your work and achievement. You do not have this type of assurance when you take stock, no matter what kind of confidence you have in Cowles . . . I have said enough. Think about it. The decision is yours."

It is strange, but I did not give this hard-nosed, very practical, very sound advice any really serious thought.

My answer was immediate. I do not want cash. I want Cowles stock. I want a seat on the board, I want a position in this growing company. The stock could go to $20, $30 or even $50 a share. But most important of all, I yearned to "belong," to participate. I wanted to be a very important part of the Cowles organization. By asking for cash, I would give Whatmore and Cowles the feeling that I did not have confidence in the company, that I wanted to sell out instead of buying in, joining the company management and thus contributing to and sharing in the growth of the company—my company—in the years ahead.

Of course, I did not even know whether Cowles would consider changing the stock to a cash deal. . . . Or whether asking for a cash deal might cool or kill the entire deal. I wanted no part of it. I called Ed Singer and told him about my feelings.

"Don, I understand what you want and what you are trying to do," Ed said, "and I agree with you. I tried to explain this to Ed Vogel but he felt that it was his responsibility to tell you what he thought. He said that he couldn't live with himself if he didn't explain how he felt. But Don, I'm with you. You are doing the right thing, what you want . . . and may God bless you." Ed was a very pious man and rarely finished a conversation without a "God bless you."

The closing took place on November 30 in the Cowles board room. It was on a bright, crisp Wednesday morning. The atmosphere was relaxed and friendly. Taking part were Marvin Whatmore, who kept running in and out between signatures, Jack Harding, Frank Barry, his assistant who was to become MFI attorney, Ed Singer, Ed Vogel, Dave Regosin, Ezra Eisen, Bob Pulver (outside of me, the largest single MFI stockholder) and several bank representatives. Inasmuch as I had read and reread the various series and revisions of contracts, I merely signed the papers as they were placed before me by one of my attorneys— sometimes Dave, other times Ed Singer, and once in a while even Ed Vogel, the only one who did not smile at the closing.

At the end of the signing, which took over an hour, I received a batch of Cowles stock certificates totaling 135,135 shares. These were certificates for the various MFI officers and employees, me and my family and Bob Pulver. Bob Pulver was a personal friend—the only original investor aside from me in *Soft Drink Industry* when it was launched in 1946. He had long since gotten back his original investment of $10,000 through dividends and sale-back of stock of some of the shares to MFI. The Cowles stock he was now receiving was worth $150,000 at closing market price. Betty and I received a total of 101,000 shares with a closing market value of approximately $1,500,000. Of the total, we placed 20,000 shares in a ten-year revocable trust for my sons, Alan, Mel and Paul.

When I left the Cowles offices close to the noon hour, the attorneys remained to put the finishing touches on the various papers. I no longer owned the company I had founded, nourished and built and with which I had lived through at least two economic storms. Instead, I now owned an important piece— about three percent—of Cowles Communications, Inc., actually several pieces of paper in a strange company which others control. Could Ed Vogel have been right? Not really, I quickly decided. While my stock was now worth less than two million dollars, it was still a lot of money considering that I had started with so little. I had every reason to believe that long before my seven-year contract with Cowles would come to an end, our 101,000 shares would be worth much more than two million dollars. In the meantime, I was starting another lap—perhaps leap is a better word—in my career. It was a week before my fifty-ninth birthday and I felt no older than when I was forty-nine or even thirty-nine. And I felt a great sense of achievement.

FOUR:

The Herzes and the Cohens

I began to sense the beginning of a declining trend in Cowles Communications at my second board of directors meeting on February 15, 1967, just two-and-one-half months after my buying in to this great and growing communications empire. I had been elected to the board at its meeting on November 21—nine days before the actual closing.

I was still somewhat in awe of the assemblage at my second board meeting. But it was not quite the same as the first board meeting. But then nothing ever compares with a first experience in anything. The first visit to a new place, like our first trip to Europe, the first time we saw an opera at the Metropolitan Opera House. The first time on a train as a youngster. The first time on a plane. The first time driving a car. At my second meeting of the board I was still much taken with being part of the illustrious group of publishing giants. However, I had a strange feeling that maybe all that glitter was not for real. This feeling was unconscious. But the uneasiness stayed with me for a while—and kept returning at various intervals. It all started when Chairman Gardner Cowles asked Board Member Palmer K. Leberman, chairman of the board of Family Circle, Inc., to explain to the other board members the reasons for the decline in the fortunes of *Family Circle,* the company's second largest property, second only to the flagship, *Look.*

P.K. blamed a large anticipated loss for 1967 on losses expected to accrue from substantial advertising dollar refunds due to a sharp decline in circulation and a very large print overrun. He could not explain the unexpected decline in circulation or the inability of his staff to estimate effectively the number of copies to be sold during the last few months.

"We just don't know. It is the first experience of this kind that we have had since we have been publishing *Family Circle,*" Leberman said.

"What are we doing to correct the situation for the rest of the year?" Cowles asked.

"We're trying to find out the reason for the circulation drop and we are endeavoring to develop a better method of gauging the print run needed in the months ahead. Of course, we must be sure that we don't underprint just as much as that we do not overprint the number of copies needed."

I was quiet at the first meeting, saying very little except to answer questions. After all, I was a newcomer to this group. But somehow, I felt that I could not ignore what was happening to *Family Circle,* a magazine that had made as much as $2,000,000 and which was in danger of losing that much this very year. So, I raised my hand and this is what I said:

"I have heard some positive reports and recommendations made for the improvement of our various properties. Mr. Leberman, what positive steps are you planning to take on *Family Circle* in the months ahead, to correct what seems to be a very serious problem? And have you considered raising the price per copy of *Family Circle* from 15 to 20 or perhaps 25 cents?"

Instead of making an attempt to answer my questions, Leberman went on the defensive: "We certainly are taking positive steps. I have just explained, we are trying to find out the reason for the sharp decline in circulation and to find better ways of determining our monthly print run needs. As to raising the price from 15 cents, I am very much against it. This would be the wrong time to consider such an increase."

There was no point in pursuing this subject any further. Nor did any other member of the board ask any other question or make any statement. I had asked a question—perhaps naively—and I did not receive a direct, satisfactory answer. It bothered me, but I felt that I had made my point and that there was not much more that I could do.

Some weeks after the board meeting, I learned that two steps were taken by the executive committee. Executive Vice President Don Perkins was elected president of Family Circle, Inc., while P.K. Leberman was pushed upstairs to the office of chairman of the board of FC. Step Number Two was the announcement that the price of *Family Circle* was raised from 15 to 20 cents. *Family Circle*'s only direct competitor, *Woman's Day,* still trailing *Family Circle* both in advertising volume and circulation but beginning to catch up, followed suit, also raising the "newsstand" (or supermarket) price from 15 to 20 cents.

Don Perkins' tenure as president of *Family Circle* was short-lived because the hoped-for turnaround of FC did not take place. Whether this was the result of Don's inability to do the job, the lack of help and/or enthusiasm on the part of P.K. and his associates, the strong competition by *Woman's Day* or other reasons, was never explained to the board. If indeed it was known at all. At any rate, after a few months, Don was succeeded as president by Gil Maurer. Shortly after he was elected president, Gil was also named chief executive officer and it was P.K. himself who made the motion putting Gil in the top *Family Circle* post.

Gil's tenure at *Family Circle* was a bit longer than that of Don's, but within a year he was replaced as president by Fred Thompson, long-time top executive and family insider of *Reader's Digest*. Fred was married to a niece of the Wallaces (owners of *Reader's Digest*). His wife was said to be the only blood relative and heir to the Wallace fortune. During Gil's tenure, *Family Circle* losses were reduced substantially, but at the same time, *Woman's Day* went ahead of FC in circulation and accelerated its advertising gains, almost edging out *Family Circle* for leadership. When Fred took over the magazine, this one-time prime and very profitable supermarket woman's service magazine was in trouble.

By now, the much-heralded *Suffolk Sun* had been launched. Publisher of this first daily in the fast-growing Suffolk County of Long Island, with a population pushing one million, was Pat Cowles, Mike's only son— born to his second wife, Lois. (There was another Gardner Cowles "son," Charles,—the son of Gardner's present wife—who assumed the Cowles name, but was not legally adopted by Mike. He was editor/publisher of *Art Forum*, a magazine for artists and collectors. He thought the name Cowles would be a help to him and to the magazine.)

Great excitement and still greater promise surrounded the launching of the *Suffolk Sun* on November 21, 1966 in the new, sparkling plant in Deer Park. Many of the Cowles brass attended the launching ceremonies when the presses began to roll for the printing of the first issue at eleven that night. Betty and I dined out with friends that night, and when we returned to our apartment house at about 12:30, we met Marvin and Lois, who had just returned from Deer Park with a copy of the initial issue of the *Sun*.

"We had a hard time getting started, but the first issue looks great," Marvin said, as he showed me his copy.

"It does look fine," I said, taking a quick look at the front page. Separating "The" and "Sun" in the flag was a smiling sun—in yellow.

When I received a copy of the *Suffolk Sun* the next morning at my office, I was shocked. The printing was bad, almost washed out and hard to read. With the exception of one story, the news on the front page dealt with the national scene—and nothing pertaining to Suffolk County or any of its numerous towns and other localities. The lead story (with a Washington dateline) had the following headline: "Republicans Plot Budgetary Revolt." Other headlines: "Bishops OK War If Aim Just Peace," "The 'Black Death' Haunting Asia," and "Connor Denies Plan He'll Resign Post." Even the sports page covered national sports—nothing pertaining to sports of the towns of Suffolk County. This was not a local newspaper. Instead, it was an abortive attempt at a national newspaper on the style of the *Washington Post*.

Highly successful with small-town, growing-area daily newspapers in Florida and in Puerto Rico (the *San Juan Star*, the only English language paper in Puerto Rico), Cowles planned and launched the *Suffolk Sun* with great expectations. While there was no local daily in Suffolk County or any of its cities and/or towns, the *Suffolk Sun* did face formidable competition in *Newsday*, the highly successful and very profitable daily which covered the neighboring Nassau County of Long Island. When the *Suffolk Sun* appeared, *Newsday* had a circulation of over 400,000, 75,000 of which was distributed in Suffolk County. While the *Suffolk Sun* and Cowles may not have been aware of this serious competition, *Newsday* decided to be very much aware of the interloper and tried to kill it off before it got a foothold. It decided to do this by means of a three-pronged attack: by expanding its Suffolk County editorial coverage; by pushing for greater distribution in the adjoining county; and by making it difficult for the *Suffolk Sun* to get started, especially by disturbing its distribution and delivery program.

The Cowles organization did not seem overly concerned by the *Newsday* competition. It started off with a controlled (or free) distribution of 100,000 circulation, giving that figure as a guarantee to advertisers and moved to convert this number to paid distribution sales, with the long-range goal of attaining a paid circulation of 150,000 in several years.

Despite the fact that early issues of the *Sun* did not show the degree of excellence expected from Cowles with its experience in publishing good, solid newspapers, the reaction from advertisers and the community was excellent. And paid circulation began to come in at a nice pace—10,000, 25,000 and within six months, 50,-000. While the management of the newspaper made mistake after mistake, and as *Newsday* continued to bring all possible pressure against it, the *Suffolk Sun* in its first year nevertheless did make progress. Before the year was up, paid circulation hit 70,000 and the advertising linage amounted to in excess of 400,000 inches. But by this time, the first year's loss, including start-up costs of a million dollars, was in excess of seven million dollars. At the end of the *Suffolk Sun*'s first year, Cowles' working capital was reduced to less than $33,000,000—from over $35,000,000 (or a loss in working capital in one year of $2,229,000), the first such reduction in working capital in over ten years (the company's most important growth period). The company also posted a loss of $3,434,000 for the year against a profit of $3,786,000 for 1966. It was the end of my first year with Cowles and I began to be concerned about the company's future. Yet there was no evidence of much concern at the board meetings during 1967 or early in 1968.

And while I had a feeling of uneasiness, again more subconscious than conscious at this juncture, I was much too busy and much too involved with the growth program of my division to pay a great deal of attention to the overall picture of Cowles Communications, especially since it was impossible to get any reading of the development of any serious problem from the actions and attitude of President Marvin Whatmore with whom I had been working more closely than any other Cowles officer or executive.

In the spring of 1967, only a few months after MFI was merged into Cowles, I became involved in two major projects—plans to launch *Education News* and the acquisition of *Modern Medicine* and its affiliated publications. Because I had had my eye on *Modern Medicine* long before I merged with Cowles, I decided to make the move to acquire this company my first major project. After carefully exploring the situation at *Modern Medicine,* I determined that the best approach would be to call or write to Teresa Cohen, the widow of Jacob Cohen, the founder of this business in Minneapolis.

Of the over 350 medical publications, *Modern Medicine* was one of the "big four" in this exciting, very lucrative field. My own private research involved no major expense of any kind except my time, energy, enthusiasm and knowledge of the business magazine field. I knew where to obtain the necessary figures and other facts quickly and without showing my hand. One method I used to gather important information about the company and its people was to talk with other business magazine publishers, especially those who were acquainted with the *Modern Medicine* management, knew the company's history and were inclined to gossip. I made certain that the publishers I talked with about *Modern Medicine* were not themselves acquisition prospects or in a position to buy such a large and important company. And, of course, I gave no hint of my possible interest in buying the business. However, one publisher with whom I chatted about *Modern Medicine* said: "Don, why don't you try to buy this company? You may have a chance." I passed over his suggestion as if I had not heard it.

My investigation revealed that the management of *Modern Medicine* might well be interested in merging. The magazine, published every other week, had been the Number One non-association medical magazine in advertising volume in 1965, only two years previously. It had been second only to *JAMA*—the *Journal of the American Medical Association,* a weekly. It had been ahead of its principal competitor, *Medical Economics,* also a bi-weekly. But it had dropped from close to 5,000 to less than 3,000 pages of advertising in 1966, a very serious and most unusual decline. I reasoned that the management of *Modern Medicine* must obviously be scared in the face of such a huge page and dollar loss. It seemed obvious that they were doing something wrong after doing just about everything right over a long period of years.

I soon learned two reasons for *Modern Medicine*'s sharp decline in linage in 1966, which appeared to be worsening early in 1967. Reason Number One was the failure on the part of *Modern Medicine* management to change its format from a digest to a standard size.

Reason Number Two was the inability of management to make major decisions.

Until 1965, both *Modern Medicine* and *Medical Economics,* the two leading commercial magazines in the field, were digest size (5⅛ by 7⅞ inches). In 1965, after much study and soul searching, publisher William Chapman (whose father, Lansing, had started the magazine in 1923) decided to change the format of *Medical Economics* to standard size (8¼ by 10¾ inches). There was a practical business reason for this.

The change in size became necessary because the Food and Drug Administration had put through a ruling which required pharmaceutical advertising to physicians to include a so-called brief summary of the package insert in the advertisements that appeared in medical magazines. This meant that more space was now needed for the listings in the brief summary which, in some instances, was neither brief nor in summary form. A digest-size magazine page was no longer sufficient to carry the full story of the pharmaceutical products because of this new FDA mandate.

Had *Modern Medicine* and *Medical Economics* been the only two major publications covering the medical field, the pharmaceutical manufacturers would have had no choice but to continue to advertise in these two publications. But they did have a choice. They could use a larger number of pages in *JAMA,* the official organ, and this they did, in abundance. But also available to them now was another excellent journal, *Medical World News,* a weekly news and feature magazine, started in 1959 by Max Geffen, a legendary figure in printing and publishing. *Medical World News* enjoyed spectacular success almost from the start. Geffen teamed up with Dr. Morris Fishbein, long-time editor of *JAMA,* an imposing and controversial figure in medicine and medical publishing, Dr. Fishbein eventually was separated from his powerful position with the AMA because of his domineering attitude and un-orthodox approach. Max Geffen was a small, wiry man of sixty-five with an extraordinary personality. Using a fresh, sometimes daring editorial approach, he created the new weekly medical magazine in an attractive modern style, utilizing the newest and most effective graphics available. *Medical World News* moved toward leadership in less than three years of operation.

Bill Chapman of *Medical Economics* was aware of what was happening. He concluded that unless *Medical Economics* (and *Modern Medicine*) changed from di-gest to standard size, many pharmaceutical advertisers would move most of their campaigns to *JAMA* and *Medical World News*.

Medical Economics announced the change in its for-mat to standard size in 1965, and the change was made with its January 1966 issue while *Modern Medicine* con-tinued to publish in its original digest size. During the next two years *Medical Economics* did so well that it as-sumed leadership in the medical field in pages, and increased its advertising dollar volume and profit sub-stantially. It did so well that it soon acquired the Rein-hold Publishing Company and was on its way to be-coming one of the largest business magazine publishing companies.

At the same time, *Modern Medicine* began a de-cline which, by 1967, reached dangerous proportions. I had been aware of this situation and, through my private investigation, I was able to fill in details. Since the death of the company's dynamic, courageous found-er and chief executive, Jacob Cohen, the business had been operated by a committee of three: Mal and Jay Herz—brothers of Jacob Cohen's widow, Teresa—and Louis Cohen, brother of the late Jacob Cohen. Teresa continued to own a substantial part of the business—

more than twenty-five percent. She took over *Dental Survey* and two other dental magazines and ran these on her own while her three partners ran the major part of the business, including *Modern Medicine,* the company's flagship publication. She also took over the operation of *Postgraduate Medicine*, a successful monthly magazine for the general practitioner and internist. But she had sold this to McGraw-Hill before I made an approach to buy the company.

Inasmuch as Teresa's three partners could not agree on picking a chief executive officer—either from among the three, or from the outside—they decided to rotate the office of president. Moreover, no important decision could be made unless all three partners agreed. Each partner behaved as an antagonist of the other partners. Two of the partners had severely stubborn streaks. Thus, it was difficult if not impossible for them to make important decisions. Fortunately for the company, when Founder Jacob Cohen died, the business was in excellent shape. The company had been enjoying great affluence for some time, there was an abundance of capital and no debts. Moreover, the company enjoyed an excellent reputation with readers, advertisers and the business magazine publishing community. So much so that, while the old Associated Business Publications was inclined to be anti–Semitic, it elected Mal Herz, a highly respected member of the Minneapolis Jewish community, to its board of directors. And when the late Carroll Buzby, then president of the Pew (Sunoco) family-owned Chilton Company, had an opportunity to buy Topics Publishing Company (publishers of *Drug Trade News, Drug Topics* and other periodicals in the pharmaceutical field) he telephoned Mal Herz and invited Modern Medicine Publications to become a fifty percent full partner in the acquisition of that profitable operation. Mal and his partners accepted this generous offer since the total investment was less than half a million dollars.

The three partners continued to run the business in a conservative, "let things alone" manner. They faced no major decision until the question of changing the size of *Modern Medicine* came up. That decision-making meeting, I learned, was characterized by shouts and abusive language. Finally, two partners voted to change the format to standard size. The lone holdout was the partner who had been approached by Bill Chapman. He would not budge. *Modern Medicine* continued with its digest size and soon began its sharp decline in advertising linage.

Knowing this and a little more, I decided that it would be folly for me to approach any of the three operating partners. Mal Herz was then president. Had I followed the book and approached Mal Herz as president, I could run afoul of the other partners. Certainly, it would not be smart to approach Jay Herz or Louis Cohen, the former serving as vice president, sales manager and head of the company's foreign operations, and the latter as chairman of the board and editorial director.

I had heard that Cahners had attempted to buy the company but that after weeks of negotiations the deal was called off. I learned that Cahners' offer was in the neighborhood of eight-and-one-half million dollars, all in cash.

I decided that this was a propitious time to approach *Modern Medicine* and that the person to contact was Teresa Cohen, the founder's widow. I reasoned that none of the three partners could be antagonistic towards her, that she was more or less neutral. Most important of all, what happened to *Modern Medicine* and the affiliated publications was of the greatest importance and concern to her. The company was the brainchild of her beloved husband. Accordingly, only two months after the merger of MFI into Cowles, I sent Teresa the following letter:

magazines for industry, inc.

subsidiary of Cowles Communications, Inc.,
777 THIRD AVENUE   NEW YORK, N.Y. 10017   PLaza 9-5245 (212)
DON GUSSOW, President and Editor in Chief

February 7, 1967

Mrs. J. G. Cohen
Modern Medicine Publications
Southdale Park
Minneapolis, Minn. 55435

Dear Mrs. Cohen:

As part of our program of expansion now that we are a subsidiary of Cowles Communications, Inc., two of the fields that interest us are medicine and dentistry.

For this reason I should like to explore with you the possibility of acquisition of your company by us. We can offer you Cowles Communications, Inc. stock which, as you know, is listed on the New York Stock Exchange; a cash arrangement; a combination of the two, or whatever is most practical and desirable from both your point of view and ours.

Naturally, we would want to continue with your present expert, competent staff.

If you are interested in exploring such a possibility, please let me know. I should be happy to arrange a meeting with you in Minneapolis or, if you prefer, perhaps a meeting could be scheduled in our offices here in New York.

Of course, this entire matter will be kept in strictest confidence.

Sincerely,

Don Gussow

Don Gussow, President
MAGAZINES FOR INDUSTRY, INC.

DG:atp

Candy Industry and Confectioners Journal ● Candy Industry Catalog & Formula Book ● The Candy Marketer ● Dairy & Ice Cream Field ● Education News ● Food & Drug Packaging ● The Glass Industry ● The Glass Industry International Directory ● Packer/Processor ● Hard Goods And Soft Goods Packaging ● Inside Industry ● Soft Drink Industry ● Soft Drink Industy Annual Manual ● Soft Serve & Drive-In Field ● Books for Industry, Inc.

On February 14, I received her handwritten reply.

MODERN MEDICINE

65TH AT VALLEY VIEW ROAD, SOUTHDALE PARK, MINNEAPOLIS, MINN. 55435

Feb. 13, 1967

Dear Mr. Gussow,
Thank you for your letter of February 7th.
My associates in Modern Medicine are out of town & they will not all return until about the middle of March. When they return, I shall bring your letter to their attention and then one of us will write you.

Sincerely,
(Mrs J G) Teresa Cohen

I was delighted. Thrilled. I just could not wait for the second letter.

I did not receive a second letter but on March 8, Mal Herz telephoned me. He had just arrived from London where he had stopped over after a safari vacation in Africa. He said that he would be in New York that afternoon and the next day. He would be pleased to have a chat with me.

So, on March 9, Mal Herz and I had lunch at the Marco Polo Club at the same table Marvin Whatmore and I had lunched at about one year previously.

Mal dropped by first at my office and appeared much impressed. My "dream office" became a reality when we moved to 777 Third Avenue at the time that all-glass, 38-story skyscraper was completed in December, 1964. We have the entire twenty-fifth floor and part of the twenty-fourth.

My large office faces east and south. One of the two windows faces the East River and the UN and overlooks Turtle Bay. The wide south window reveals a good part of New York—from 48th Street to the Battery. My desk is a simple, functional Herman Miller table. Behind me is my old Herman Miller L-shaped desk on which I keep needed papers and copies of magazines. Behind that is a Danish rosewood paneled wall with bookshelves (holding books covering the fields our magazines serve, some of which we published) as well as specially constructed shelves that display the periodicals of Cowles Business and Professional Magazines. One wall is covered with paintings, three by my son, Alan: a large, colorful abstract called *The View from the Acropolis,* which Alan painted in Greece when he won the Prix de Rome of the American Academy of Art in 1954; a moody black and white sketch of the harbor of Monhegan Island in Maine; and a seascape called *Fish in Flight.* A watercolor by Reuben Tam, a mask-head from West Africa and an unusual lithograph (with a food packaging industry motif) by the famed lithographer, R. M. Davidson, are also on that wall.

The lunch with Mal Herz was pleasant and productive. I told Mal of my very satisfactory merger with Cowles: the autonomy of my operation, their great desire to place at my disposal millions of dollars in the form of stock and cash to build our division into one of the biggest and most important business magazine publishing companies, and the enthusiastic cooperation of excellent people—especially Marvin Whatmore and Gardner Cowles.

I explained that if *Modern Medicine* merged with us, its operation would not be disturbed. We would make available needed additional capital and research and promotional help that would enable *Modern Medicine* to build and grow, to solidify its already enviable position in the medical publishing field.

"It could mean having your cake and eating it too," I said. "You and your associates would have the security of a satisfactory capital gain—in stock or cash or both—and the opportunity to continue to run your own business, backed by the prestige and capital of the great and growing Cowles Communications."

I explained in detail why I had picked Cowles to merge our company with.

"Cowles is large but not too large. The company is in communications and nothing else. And it is in every phase of communications—consumer magazines, newspapers, TV, radio, book publications, educational software—the only company in every phase of communications except business magazines but with a very definite interest in business magazines. And now that MFI is part of it, Cowles is in business magazines with an appreciation of this important field and a great desire to grow in this area. Mal, your company fits perfectly into our growth pattern. Cowles will be very good for you."

Mal asked some specific questions which I was able to answer. He said he had heard some good things about me and MFI, and had always liked Cowles, particularly since Mike's brother, John, was well-known and respected in Minneapolis as the publisher of the *Minneapolis Star* and the *Tribune*, two excellent newspapers.

We decided that I would discuss *Modern Medicine* with Marvin Whatmore and Gardner Cowles and then send a specific proposal to Mal, after which we could arrange a meeting in Minneapolis.

I telephoned Marvin Whatmore and told him of my meeting with Mal. I suggested that we meet to discuss plans for the acquisition of this important business magazine company. He said that he would like to have Mike Cowles join us.

At eleven o'clock on Thursday, March 16, we met in Gardner Cowles' large, oblong, "lived-in" type office, which had a comfortable sofa and equally comfortable chairs. Gardner came from behind his large, plain, but attractive desk to greet us. A colorful abstract painting caught my immediate attention, and I asked the name of the painter.

"This is the work of my brother Russell."

Russell was the oldest of the three Cowles brothers—there were also three Cowles sisters. He was almost eighty, fifteen years older than Gardner, the youngest, and the only one who was not in the publishing business. John, the middle brother, was head of the Minneapolis Star and Tribune Company, which owned two excellent and highly profitable newspapers and a TV station, as well as *Harper's* magazine and a controlling interest in Harper and Row, the book publishers. John did not resemble Gardner, although, like his younger brother, he was tall. He looked more stern and had more of the appearance of a prosperous business executive. As a matter of fact, John was often referred to as "the businessman" of the three Cowles brothers. Gardner, who was a trustee of the Museum of Modern Art in New York and an art patron, was proud to have a brother who was a respected painter.

Several years later, I met Russell and his wife (his second, he having been married earlier and divorced) on Monhegan Island. I had heard that the Cowleses were on the Island—word gets around fast on this unusual lobsterman's island, ten miles from Port Clyde, Maine—and I had no difficulty finding him. I saw him at the wharf, and while he looked old and had difficulty getting around even with a cane, Betty recognized him immediately and pointed him out to me. He looked just like his youngest brother Gardner—an older, more genteel version of Gardner. We had him and his wife over for cocktails at our home and found him a very interesting person with a keen sense of humor. In his time he had been a bon vivant, and had lived the typical life of the artist. He had lived for five years in Italy, spoke Italian well; he also had an apartment in Paris at one time, and had also lived in Majorca and Venice—he traveled widely. He started as an abstract painter, moving to a representational style, and was known as a landscape painter.

Since 1954 he has been married to Nancy Cardozo, the writer and poet, a charming and cultured woman in her early fifties. She is a member of the famous Jewish family that included the late associate justice of the United States Supreme Court.

The Cowles brothers and sisters did not see each other frequently, but a mutual respect and family closeness prevailed among them. Although they lived in New York and other parts of the country, home was always Des Moines, Iowa. Given any good reason such as an anniversary of importance or some other family celebration, the entire family would track down to Des Moines on short notice and have a ball.

After a short discussion of Russell's picture in Gardner's officer, we got down to business.

I had brought to the conference copies of *Modern Medicine* and some of the other Modern Medicine properties. By now I was well-versed in the company and its publications. I reviewed and explained the position of the company and its periodicals in the business magazine field, particularly their importance in the medical and dental professions.

"While the company is presently having some trouble, in my opinion it is the most prestigious and potentially one of the two most profitable medical and dental publishing operations in the United States," I said.

"Which is the other?" Cowles asked.

"Chapman-Reinhold, which publishes *Medical Economics* and *RN*. *Medical Economics* is the largest and probably the most successful magazine in the medical field. Like *Modern Medicine*, it is a biweekly. It carries about 4,000 pages of advertising a year. Its billing is in excess of $10,000,000. *RN* is one of the two largest magazines for nurses."

I explained that *Modern Medicine* was Number Four among the approximately 350 medical magazines being published. "It is a poor fourth—behind *Medical World News*, a weekly, that is coming up fast. *JAMA*, the *Journal of the American Medical Association*, also a weekly, is Number One, while *Medical Economics* is a strong Number Two . . . But, while *Modern Medicine* is a weak Number Four, it still publishes over 2,500 pages of advertising a year, and I believe that it can be brought back to a strong, dominant position—a strong Number Three or possible Two."

"Don, why do you think *Modern Medicine* has slipped during the past two years?" Cowles asked.

"Because it is being operated by a committee, and because it failed to change its size when *Medical Economics* made the change from digest to standard size."

I explained the need for the change: "Because *Modern Medicine* continued to publish in its old digest size, pharmaceutical advertisers turned to greater use of the advertising pages of *JAMA*, *Medical Economics* and *Medical World News* and some of the lesser publications. Yet, *Modern Medicine* is a unique clinical publication in that it provides abstracts of the most important papers relating to all medical disciplines."

"What do you think we will have to pay for this business?" Marvin Whatmore asked me.

"I believe we can buy it for about $8,500,000 to $9,000,000 and I believe it will be a steal at such a price. It happens to be an excellent time to buy. The owners are more scared than they need be. Timing is just perfect."

"What's the next step, Don?" Marvin asked.

"You and I should visit Mal Herz in Minneapolis as soon as possible. I'll set a date."

"Go to it," Marvin said.

"Yes, I think we should move to buy this property," Gardner Cowles said as we ended the meeting.

On March 24, I sent the following letter to Mal Herz:

MAGAZINES FOR INDUSTRY, INC.

777 Third Avenue
New York, N.Y. 10017

PERSONAL & CONFIDENTIAL

March 24, 1967

Mr. M. E. Herz, Chairman
Modern Medicine Publications
65th at Valley View Road
Southdale Park
Minneapolis, Minnesota 55435

Dear Mal:

I enjoyed the opportunity of getting acquainted with you on March 9 during your short stay in New York.

I discussed our chat with Mike Cowles, Chairman, and Marvin Whatmore, President, of Cowles Communications, Inc. We are interested in pursuing our conversation and, with this thought in mind, I should like to follow up your suggestion to meet with you in Minneapolis early in April.

The most convenient date for Mr. Whatmore and me is Friday, April 14. We could drop by in the morning and continue discussions through lunch and wind up our meeting early in the afternoon. If this date is also convenient for you, please let me know and we will confirm it.

Kindest regards.

Sincerely,

Don

Don Gussow, President
MAGAZINES FOR INDUSTRY, INC.

On April 5, I received his reply:

MODERN MEDICINE

65TH AT VALLEY VIEW ROAD, SOUTHDALE PARK, MINNEAPOLIS,
MINN. 55435

April 4, 1967

Mr. Don Gussow
777 Third Avenue
New York City
New York 10017

Dear Don:

Sorry that there has been this delay in responding to
your recent letter, but I believe I told you I would be
attending a meeting the last week of March and I have
just returned.

We will be delighted to see you on the 14th. Let me
know the time of your arrival; and if you want hotel
reservations, let me know and I will be glad to take
care of it.

Looking forward to seeing you, and with my kindest
regards, I am

Sincerely,

MODERN MEDICINE
Mal

M. E. Herz
Publisher

MEH:njc

I followed this up with this memo to Marvin Whatmore:

April 5, 1967

Memo to: Marvin C. Whatmore
Re: Modern Medicine

Here is a copy of a letter from Mal Herz.

I have reservations for Friday morning, April 14, on Northwest's Flight No. 51 leaving Chicago at 8:50 and arriving in Minneapolis at 9:57 AM.

Inasmuch as Modern Medicine's offices are only about fifteen minutes away from the airport, we plan to meet in Mal's office at about 10:30.

I am planning to return to New York on Northwest Flight No. 230, leaving Minneapolis at 6:40 and arriving at Kennedy at 9:55 PM. Not knowing your plans for the return trip, I made a reservation for you, too, on the same plane.

Don Gussow

As our taxi stopped in front of the Modern Medicine offices, I could not believe my eyes. What was before us was one of the most beautiful buildings of its kind in an equally attractive setting. Of limestone contruction, the obviously new, white, classical building gave the feeling of a semicircular Roman forum. It was just as attractive inside as it was outside. Shortly after we announced ourselves to the receptionist in front of whose desk was a display of recent copies of the Modern Medicine publications, Mal Herz greeted us and led us to the elevator. We got off on the second floor at an immaculately clean, tiled hallway with doors to various offices. When we entered Mal's office, I was stunned by its spaciousness. It was a huge square office—about

30 by 30 feet. The windows looked out on a well-kept lawn, trees and a lake where swans floated. It was the middle of April and it was a warm, sunny spring day in Minneapolis. Mal's office was furnished in a manner not to my particular taste, with soft-cushioned sofas and chairs and a variety of end tables and huge lamps. Mal's desk was of curved, heavy-looking, light-colored wood. On the wall behind his desk was an abstract metal sculpture, again not to my liking.

When Mal opened the door to an adjoining office, a profusion of color—mostly bright purple—hit me immediately. Unlike the staid, conservative feeling of Mal's office, Louis Cohen's had a live, warm, exciting texture. It was loud but attractive. A profusion of photographs (of renowned physicians, we later learned) were on a wall. Several pieces of sculpture (heads of famous personalities in medical history) were on display. Louis' desk was small, attractive and classical—a modern miniature version of the rolltop desk minus the roll top. The furniture was luxuriously comfortable. It was a fitting office for *Modern Medicine*'s editorial director—the most creative member of the management triumvirate. While Mal Herz was a natural extrovert, a sophisticate and a bon vivant, Louis was warm and friendly—down-to-earth and less complicated than his partner. After a moment or two in Louis' office we returned to Mal's office for our initial business conference.

After discussing the medical publishing field in general and a brief review of the history of *Modern Medicine* and its affiliated publications, Mal took out a set of statements from a drawer in his desk and handed these to us.

"I thought you might want to take a look at our financials," he said.

This came as a surprise inasmuch as financial figures

are not usually made available until the parties' intentions of buying and selling a company have been discussed. Both Marvin and I then presumed that Mal and his associates had made at least a preliminary decision to sell their company to us, provided an acceptable price and satisfactory terms could be worked out.

A quick look at the figures revealed that 1965 had been a good year but that 1966 had seen a decline in sales and a sharper decline in profits.

"How do things look for 1967?" I asked.

"Not as good as we had hoped, but it's still too early to tell," Mal replied. In my language this meant that 1967 would not be a good year. It confirmed my belief that our visit was most timely.

At this point, Marvin began to ask some technical financial questions which Mal answered in considerable detail. It became obvious that both Mal and Marvin were figure-oriented executives. I knew this about Marvin, but it was interesting to learn that Mal had the same expertise. Marvin and Mal seemed to like each other from the start.

As Marvin and Mal continued their financial interchange, Louis said to me: "While these financial geniuses are reviewing and digesting the figures, why don't we adjourn to my office?"

Inasmuch as my interest in figures was not as keen as that of Marvin—and knowing that Marvin could handle this part of the job without my help at this juncture—I left with Louis as the figure men did their chores.

In Louis' office it soon became clear that Louis wanted to know in particular my frank reaction to the Cowles management "as people." How they behaved towards me. Whether I had operational autonomy. How closely any of the Cowles executives supervised my activity. . . .

"Marvin Whatmore appears to be a fine gentleman," Louis said. "Is he as nice as he seems to be?"

"Absolutely. He's really a fine person. He is a genius when it comes to figures, and he can calculate a set of figures at machine-like speed. But he is most considerate in his dealings with people. This is not the hard-nosed professional manager you expect to find at the head of a large public company."

"This sounds very encouraging. What kind of a man is Gardner Cowles?"

"Not unlike Marvin Whatmore, he, too, is a gentleman—perhaps even more kind and considerate than Marvin in his relations with his associates if that is possible—but he is quite different from Marvin. Marvin Whatmore is the kind of man you get to know on a first-name basis immediately, but this isn't the case with Gardner Cowles. He's inclined to be diffident. He seems to have a shell around him. Being basically shy, he must find it difficult to give much of himself as Marvin does with such ease."

"How do you find working with these men?"

"Great. But my contact is almost exclusively with Marvin and he is fine to work with. I remember our conversation after the closing of our merger. I asked Marvin: 'How do you want me to relate to you? How much do you want me to tell you of our operations on a day-to-day basis? What communications policy do you have?' This was his answer: 'I want to have the privilege of calling you once in a while and asking some questions. In turn, I want you to feel entirely free to call me any time you have something special to ask me. But, you run your own business just the way you have been doing it until now.' And this is the way it has been thus far. While we have been part of Cowles only since November 30, which is a very short time— actually less than five months—we have been working together almost since our first meeting in August, when we shook hands on our deal."

"How are the other Cowles executives, the others with whom you have come in contact?"

"Since I am a member of the Cowles board of directors, I have had the opportunity of meeting just about all the key Cowles executives. We have a big board—seventeen—only three of whom are outside directors: John Fischer, president of Teachers College of Columbia University, John Weinberg, a partner of Goldman, Sachs and Company, the investment banking house that has been Cowles' financial advisor for over thirty-five years, and John Perry, head of Perry Newspapers. I can tell you that I have not yet met one stinker. Of course, I cannot say that I like them all. Nor are there many like Marvin Whatmore, but as a group, I do find the Cowles executives exceptional. And they have been very friendly, very nice to me."

We continued our discussion through lunch in Louis Cohen's office. Then, Marvin Whatmore and I met Teresa Cohen in her office. She was a charming woman—alert, alive and very much younger in appearance than her age, which was just past seventy. After introducing us, Louis left, and Marvin and I chatted with Teresa for several minutes.

"Are you interested in buying *Dental Survey* and its affiliated publications too?" she asked.

"Of course," I replied.

After our short conversation, Marvin kissed Teresa and left for another meeting in town. I returned to Louis' office to continue our visit. I asked many questions about the entire business, which were answered fully by both Louis and Mal. Louis gave me a grand tour of the offices and I was impressed with most of the executives I met as well as with the manner in which they had departmentalized the operation. I was particularly taken with the library, which included hundreds of current medical journals from throughout the world, from which science writers abstracted material for use in *Modern Medicine*. Outstanding physicians in various medical disciplines were members of *Modern Medicine*'s editorial board, and they helped to guide the science writers.

I also met Burt Cohen, Louis Cohen's son, who was associate publisher of *Modern Medicine*. I spent over half an hour chatting with him and we continued our discussion as he drove me to the airport. The more I talked with him, the more I liked him. He was thirty-seven years of age, was a journalism school graduate and had worked for a business magazine publishing company in New York before joining the family company where he had been for more than eight years. I decided to keep my eye on him and to get to know him better.

My conversation with Louis and Mal emphasized "people." Not unlike Louis, Mal wanted to know how I related to and worked with Marvin Whatmore and the other key men at Cowles. I repeated and amplified what I had told Louis earlier—that my relationship with the Cowles people had been better than I had hoped for, that I was very comfortable with Marvin and the other key men with whom I had come in contact and that Marvin was a great guy to work with.

I met Marvin at the airport, and we spent most of our trip home discussing the *Modern Medicine* situation. Mal had given him two sets of financials, and we went over the figures.

"This is an excellent company which obviously did well over the years. They're having trouble this year, and, from my talk with Mal, it would seem that 1967 will be a very bad year for them," Marvin said.

"I have reached the same conclusion," I replied.

"However, the fact that they will have a bad year in 1967 happens to be good for us. We'll be able to strike an excellent deal—and I have full confidence that we can effect a healthy turnaround in 1968."

In looking over the figures, I saw that the company owned the building outright, mortgage-free, and had a very strong cash position—about $1,700,000—and that this figure also represented working capital or the net of current assets over current liabilities. They had no debt, either short-term or long-term.

After we discussed these items, Marvin asked me: "In view of this three million dollars-plus in net quick assets, do you still think we can buy the company for $8,500,000 to $9,000,000?"

"Yes, I still think we can—$8,500,000 for *Modern Medicine* and its affiliated corporations and about $500,000 (or possibly less) for the dental publications from Teresa Cohen. Obviously, they are going to ask more—perhaps $10,000,000 or as much as $12,000,-000, but considering the shape they find themselves in this year, I believe we can swing it for $9,000,000 or less."

"I think you're extremely optimistic, Don, but we're going to try."

In the weeks that followed, I studied the figures very carefully and presented Marvin Whatmore with a detailed analysis. I followed this up with several meetings with Marvin, and later on, with Marvin and Jack Harding, whom I learned to like and whose ability I began to respect. Jack gave the impression of a mild, easygoing person, but after seeing him in action, I concluded that one might be inclined to underrate him. He knew the law, he was a disarming negotiator and he knew how to get his point across.

I continued to be in touch with Louis and Mal. Louis and I seemed to click right from the start. Louis kept saying he was not a businessman, insisting that his great interest was the editorial part of the job, particularly his contacts and associations with "the doctors." I learned that he did have an unusually wide and close friendship with some of the country's foremost physicians.

As a result, I left the direct dollar-and-cents negotiations to Marvin and Jack, although they kept me informed and, in turn, I kept them in touch with every step that followed.

FIVE:

Joint Venture to Oblivion

While the negotiations continued for the acquisition of *Modern Medicine*, I became very much involved in the launching of *Education News*. As expected, the Louis Harris study pointed to a "great need" for a weekly or biweekly news-oriented publication for the educational administrator. Gardner Cowles took no part whatsoever in the *Modern Medicine* negotiations or discussions, or in anything else I was doing. He did take over the direction of the discussions and the launching of *Education News*, however. He called and chaired every meeting that dealt with *Education News* and he began to make every decision. Even the announcement (on April 17, 1967) of the launching of *Education News* was made under his direction. I did not like what was happening.

A crisis was reached at a meeting on January 23, 1967. In attendance at lunch were: Marvin Whatmore; Jack Harding; Gil Maurer, at that time president of the Cowles educational publishing division; and Dave Whitney, editor of the educational division, whom I began to

153

dislike and distrust more and more, although I found myself to be a minority of one.

Cowles opened the meeting by referring to the Harris study. Each of us had a copy of the eighty-page report.

"It would seem that we are on the right track," Mike said. "There seems to be a real need for a news type of publication for the educator. Now, should it be a weekly or a biweekly?"

"I prefer a weekly," I said. "With a weekly we would have a shorter, more newsy deadline and a weekly would give us newspaper delivery, provided, of course, we could obtain a second class permit which means over 65 percent paid circulation and this may be difficult, if not impossible . . ."

"So, what do you think we should do?"

"I believe *Education News* should start as a biweekly with a controlled circulation. This would mean our readers would not receive the periodical until a week or ten days after closing but it would still be the newsiest publication in the education field. All others are monthlies."

"No, it should be a weekly," Whitney said. "We have to accept the fact that *Education News* will compete with the weekly news magazines and with the *New York Times.*"

"That isn't so," I replied. "It's out of the question. If we plan to compete with the *New York Times* and *Time* and *Newsweek,* then let us forget the entire project. We can't hope to compete with the consumer news sources. Besides, *Education News* will be a trade paper—a business magazine—and not a consumer periodical."

"I'm not sure of that," Cowles said.

"I think that we'll have to make up our minds that *Education News* will be a business publication," I insisted. "Let us not make the same mistake Time, Inc., made when it tried to run its business magazines, notably *Architectural Forum*, like consumer books. That's why Time, Inc., failed with its business paper division, that's why they could not even sell the *Forum*—they gave it away."

"But *Education News* must not be a trade paper, like a cookie magazine. Education is a profession, not a trade," Whitney said.

"Education is a profession, but so is medicine, so is engineering, so is candy—or cookies, if you will, or glass—and professionals operate food and glass plants. A magazine for educators or physicians can be a business paper for these professions in the same way a dairy, glass or candy magazine is a business paper for these fields. *Education News* must and will deal with the business, the management aspects of the school field."

I realized later that I had received no help from Marvin Whatmore or Gil Maurer. Most of the argument involved Dave Whitney, Gardner Cowles and me. Gil and Marv took part in the discussion when it dealt with figures and other technical problems, such as the use of printing and paper.

After more heated debate between Whitney and myself, Cowles finally made the pronouncement: *"Education News* will be a biweekly. It makes more sense . . . Besides, the economics dictate it. But *Education News* can't be purely a business magazine. It will have to deal with the social problems now facing the educator."

"Of course, *Education News* will deal with social problems," I said. "How can we avoid them? But essentially, the periodical, as I visualize it, must provide news and information that the educator—the administrator—needs and can use in his daily work."

Since I had won my point on the matter of frequency, I felt that it would be smart not to push "the trade paper angle" at this time—but I planned to come back to it at a more propitious time.

Cowles then asked: "Where shall we locate *Education News?*"

"There can be but one place, at 777 Third Avenue, at the offices of Magazines For Industry," I said. "If MFI and I will be running *Education News,* than its location must be where MFI has its offices, where I have my office. I must be in daily contact with all members of the staff, as will Marvin Toben and several other executives and department heads of MFI . . ."

Before I could finish what I wanted to say, Dave Whitney broke in: "That is wrong, absolutely and unequivocally wrong. Since the Educational Book Publishing Company is located at 488 Madison Avenue, the *Education News* staff must be located here. How do you suppose our readers and the members of the editorial board—all noted educators—will feel if they hear that *Education News* is housed, not with the Cowles Educational Book Publishing Company, but with a trade paper division? Besides, as editor-in-chief of the educational division, I can be of help—on a day-to-day basis—to the editor and his staff . . ."

After more "debate" on the subject—a harangue between Dave Whitney and me, since Marvin, Gil and Jack just sat there and let us battle it out, Gardner Cowles finally made his pronouncement:

"The business office of *Educational News* will be at 777 Third Avenue—in the offices of MFI . . . while the editorial offices will be located at 488 Madison Avenue. I want to be personally in touch with the editorial staff of *Education News.* I want to see what the editor and his staff are doing, how they get the material . . . I want to help them." This is what Gardner Cowles had decided from the beginning—and apparently Dave Whitney knew it.

I was disappointed, let down. It was a mistake. I knew it. And I wanted to say: "Mike if this is what you want, then you know what you can do with it! Take the whole operation of *Education News* to 488 Madison Avenue. You operate it—or have Dave Whitney operate it—I want no part of it. Either I have complete charge, or I can't take the responsibility for the operation of it. There can be no other way."

Instead, I accepted the compromise, not willingly, certainly not enthusiastically, but I accepted it nevertheless. I said: "OK, if that's the way you want it, Mike . . . but it isn't my way of running a business, or what I consider the right way of starting a new magazine. I'll do the best I can. But it will be very difficult. Who will really be in charge of *Education News?*"

"It will be a joint venture between Magazines For Industry and the Cowles Educational Book Division," Gardner Cowles said. "You will share responsibility with Gil as president of the division, and Dave Whitney as editor. The publisher, sales manager and other members of the business department will be located at the MFI offices, as I said earlier, and the editorial staff will be here. I suggest that we create an operational editorial board, to consist of someone to be designated by you, Don—probably your editorial director, Marvin Toben—and Dave Whitney who will represent Gil, and Bill Attwood who will represent me. The board will meet regularly, say, once a month. It will report to Gil and you, and I will keep an eye on developments. I think it will work out fine."

I knew that I should not have accepted this compromise which I felt in my bones could not work. I knew that Gardner Cowles and Dave Whitney, aided and abetted by Dr. John Fischer, would not let me make *Education News* a business magazine for the educator, and I knew that my chance of success was marginal, at best. Yet I accepted the compromise. But, it was only a few months since our merger with Cowles, and I was still in awe of the Great and Legendary Creator and Editor-in-Chief of *Look* magazine. After all, this great editorial and publishing genius could do no wrong. Certainly he must know what he is doing. And isn't he committed to the educational field? I thought, I must give this thing a chance . . .

I left the office, knowing that I had made a serious mistake in accepting this ridiculous compromise, but not knowing just how sad and terribly costly a mistake it would prove to be.

And so, not very enthusiastically, I went ahead to develop a budget and staff for *Education News.* This was in the spring of 1967, and plans called for the publication of Volume One, Number One, in November. Which wasn't very much time—but more time, much more time, than I had had when I launched MFI's first magazine, *Candy Industry,* also a biweekly. I started in business on June 1, 1944, with six thousand dollars and a managing editor and a secretary. The first issue was dated August 19 and it was in the mail on August 15. It had a folio of thirty-six pages (11¼ by 14¼ inches) with forty 7 by 10 inch advertising units. I didn't need the entire six thousand dollars before the magazine was in the black. Not only did we make a profit with the first issue, but we ended the year in the black and before the year was up, we bought another magazine and, several months after that, we started a new periodical, our third biweekly.

In staffing *Education News,* we had to follow the directive of Gardner Cowles to hire an editorial staff of at least eight and to establish a Washington Bureau with at least two people. And of course, we had to use one of the news wire services, United Press International finally being our choice. This had to be a newspaper.

I did not fight the news service idea too much, but I could not see hiring an editorial staff of eight when I knew that four or five would be ample. But Cowles wanted twelve at first, then cut it down to ten—and when he finally said we could start with eight, I gave up the fight.

The criteria Cowles insisted on for an editor included: "A newspaperman of a big city daily with experience in education news coverage." I said that I preferred a trade paper editor, managing editor, publisher and sales manager. When I found the likely candidates, they were to be interviewed in turn by Gil Maurer, Dave Whitney, Marvin Whatmore and Gardner Cowles, in that order. Then a final selection would be made.

The editor I picked was Joseph Michalak who, at the time we interviewed him, was assistant to the president of the State University of New York. Before that, he had been assistant education editor of the *New York Herald Tribune* for about two years before its demise. And before that, he had been an education writer and reporter. He was a journalism graduate of Syracuse University. He had a strange, not-too-pleasant personality but Marvin Toben and I were impressed by his suitcase full of clippings of education newspaper stories. He certainly did a lot of reporting and writing on the subject of education. And his references checked out well. Of course, he was not a trade paper editor and I was concerned about his attitude toward trade papers. Every one of the four Cowles executives liked him and he was hired. As managing editor, we hired Bill Berry, who held a similar post with a weekly newspaper in New Jersey. He was acceptable to our editor—and to the foursome at 488 Madison Avenue.

For the jobs of publisher and sales manager, I wanted business magazine men, with at least one fully experienced in the education field. I used one of my favorite employment agencies as "headhunters" for this purpose. I provided a full and detailed job description and also indicated the kind of person I wanted for each spot. Of the dozen or so candidates that I interviewed, two came up to my expectations: Fred Bunting, who was sales manager of *School Management,* the leading school administration magazine at that time, and several affiliated publications—all in the education field, and Raymond Foster, who was publisher of *Pulp and Paper* and several other magazines of the well-known trade paper publishing company of Miller Freeman of San Francisco.

Ray was thirty-two and appeared to be a young, creative, brilliant up-and-coming business magazine publisher. Fred was thirty-seven. He had nine years of experience in the education magazine field, having started as promotion man, moving into space sales and eventually rising to the sales managership. He appeared steady and dependable. Since Ray had experience as both publisher and editor and the flair needed for the kind of sophisticated publication we planned to put out, I leaned toward him for the publisher spot, and toward Fred for the post of sales manager. However, I decided to get a reaction from Fred before making my final decision. I called in Fred and told him that he was one of the two that I had picked for the posts of publisher and sales manager. Then I described Ray Foster to him. Finally, I said: "Fred, because of his experience as publisher of several excellent business magazines, I am planning to make Ray publisher and you sales manager. What do you think?"

"I think it sounds fine. I would prefer to be sales manager anyway, since this is what I know best."

I felt relieved but also disappointed. Had Fred said that he wanted to be publisher, he would have gotten the nod—and I am sure that Ray would have accepted the title of sales manager or associate publisher in charge of sales. And Fred would have shown strength and confidence. I certainly had given him a choice of jobs and he picked the one with which he felt he would be more comfortable.

The foursome at 488 Madison Avenue agreed with my choice—for both the publisher and sales manager jobs. And even more than I, each of them was taken with Ray Foster's style and flair, although I noticed that Ray seemed nervous in the presence of Marvin Whatmore when I introduced him preceding a meeting in his office. But as the interview progressed, Ray came to life. Since everybody approved, Ray Foster was named publisher and Fred Bunting sales manager of *Education News*. Ray immediately got involved in promotion and in the job of securing an advertising agency. Fred got busy staffing and he was successful in bringing with him two of the best salesmen of the *School Management* operation—one for New York and another for Chicago. And a third was to follow—also from Fred's former company.

Joe Michalak was busy hiring editors and writers— all newspapermen and women with experience on dailies and with expertise in the education field. He did not hire a single trade paper editor or writer. And there was not much I could do except to protest, since he had the blessing of Newspaperman Gardner Cowles, aided and abetted by the other three at 488 Madison Avenue. While Cowles was willing to let me hire a publisher and sales manager with business magazine experience, he insisted on daily newspaper experience for all members of the editorial staff.

"Operating" *Education News* proved to be one of the most frustrating experiences in my long business magazine career. It was doomed from the start. I felt it in my bones in all my dealings and I knew it when the first issue appeared but I refused to believe it, hoping against hope that somehow a miracle would take place and that the magazine would begin to take off.

It had taken less than five thousand dollars to launch our first magazine, the biweekly *Candy Industry.* It involved an investment of about fifty thousand dollars (largely from the profits of *Candy Industry*) to put *Bottling Industry,* our second magazine and also a biweekly, into the black. And it took a quarter of a million dollars to steer *Food and Drug Packaging,* our third magazine, and again, a biweekly, on the road to success and profitability. But I could see a million dollars floating away on *Education News,* with very little of a constructive nature happening. Yet, I did not confront Gardner Cowles and say:

"Look here, Mike, either you let me run *Education News* the way I know it should be run—the way I successfully launched three other biweekly periodicals— or forget it. If you don't let me run it my way—at 777 Third Avenue—it will fail, and Cowles will throw away a million dollars or more. You might as well drop it now."

I rehearsed this little speech many times. I was tempted on many occasions to call Gardner Cowles, ask for a meeting and tell him what I thought. But I kept putting it off—tomorrow and tomorrow and tomorrow, and, having followed the habit of doing things promptly and facing even the most distasteful chores without hesitation, this was something new for me. And I did not like it.

I rationalized that I did not want a confrontation with Gardner Cowles. I was unwilling to take issue with Father. I didn't want to displease him even though I knew he was ruining our new and very much worthwhile project. And finally, I felt that a confrontation with Mike Cowles would be the end of my association with Cowles Communications and I was not quite prepared for that, at that time. Eventually, the confrontation did come—not quite in the way I had rehearsed it, but come it did—and it meant not only the quick end of *Education News* but also the beginning of the end for me as head of the Cowles Business and Professional Magazine Division and as a member of the board of directors of Cowles Communications.

For days on end, I kept asking Joe Michalak, the *Education News* editor, to draw up an editorial program for the first issue and for the publication as a whole. He kept promising me that he would do it, but as the days and weeks went by, he failed to deliver. I could have, and should have, fired him since this was insubordination but I knew that if I fired him I would hasten my confrontation with Gardner Cowles. At the same time, it could foul up the timetable for the first issue. So, instead, I drew up an editorial program myself. And after I did that, I roughed out a sixty-four-page "first issue." And I got a great kick out of doing it. My editorial plan called for the following:

BASIC CONTENT

1. *News*—Crisp, brief, well-written, lots of small items, smartly written headlines.

2. *Product Information*—Fairly large section, with bingo card.

3. *Special Feature(s)*—At least one in-depth feature.

4. *Format*—To be similar in size to *Food and Drug Packaging* and *Soft Drink Industry,* using 5-column page for news and 4 wider columns for features.

5. *News, Features, Departments:*

   (1)   Washington—news emanating from the Capitol.

   (2)   State Capitols.

   (3)   Educational innovations.

   (4)   Federal fund allotments.

   (5)   Federal and state legislation as it affects schools.

   (6)   New equipment and teaching aids.

   (7)   New school construction.

   (8)   Curriculum success stories.

   (9)   On-the-job training and teaching.

  (10)   Visual aids.

  (11)   Parent-teacher associations.

  (12)   Activities of parents in schools.

  (13)   Integration in schools, problems, activity.

  (14)   Underprivileged schools—news of research, improvements initiated, other activity.

  (15)   Specialized schools—for retarded, gifted, those with emotional problems.

  (16)   Teacher shortage—recruitment and training of teachers.

  (17)   Teachers' unions.

  (18)   Conventions, conferences, professional meetings, and trade exhibitions.

  (19)   New educational ideas.

  (20)   College preparation and outlook.

  (21)   Television—closed circuit educational facilities and activity.

  (22)   Use of computers.

  (23)   Buying habits and activity.

  (24)   School construction—innovations in architectural ideas.

  (25)   Equipment in schools.

  (26)   Food.

(27) Vending.
(28) Books.
(29) Expansion programs—applications and success stories.

I sent a copy of my suggested editorial plan to Joe Michalak, with additional copies going to the three other members of the editorial board of *Education News*—MFI's Editorial Director Marvin Toben, Dave Whitney and Bill Attwood. And I sent additional copies to Gardner Cowles and Marvin Whatmore. I also provided copies for Ray Foster, the *Education News* publisher, and Fred Bunting, the sales manager. I received favorable comment from Marvin Toben and Fred Bunting but heard nothing from the others.

I called in Joe Michalak and reviewed with him my editorial outline and also gave him a duplicate copy of my roughed-up dummy for the first issue. I instructed him to follow both—or at least use my material as a "guide." He promised he would do it. But he proceeded totally to ignore my plans and suggestions. It was only after repeated talks with him that he adopted a handful of the suggestions contained in the long editorial outline. Word came back from Marvin Toben that Dave Whitney had sneered at it and that Bill Attwood had made no comment whatever—either pro or con. Attwood, in turn, failed to offer any ideas of his own for the editorial approach and content to be used in the first issue or in subsequent issues.

Publisher Ray Foster kept running to 488 Madison Avenue, meeting various executives of *Look* and *Venture*. He had already made up his mind that *Education News* was too insignificant a project for his great talents. He would move to get the publisher spot on *Look* or at least on *Venture*. He expressed a special liking for the travel field.

He did take some time to run three "introductory luncheons" for prospective advertisers in *Education News* and their agencies. I attended the kick-off luncheon in the Persian Room of the Plaza Hotel in New York. About one hundred and twenty-five guests attended, mostly third- and fourth-echelon ad agency executives, including a good many free loaders. While they were invited and urged to come—mainly for window dressing—neither Gardner Cowles nor Marvin Whatmore showed. Representing Cowles were Don Perkins and Gil Maurer, in addition to Dave Whitney. MFI was represented by Marvin Toben, Burt Gussow and several others.

Publisher Ray Foster was toastmaster and he did so bad a job that I felt embarrassed by the whole thing. He smoked his big cigar as he made the presentation and the various introductions. The cards he used as visual aids for the presentation were much too small, so that even those in the front row could not read them. The only one he invited to help him in the presentation was Fred Bunting. Fred knew the education market and he could talk as a professional. But he was not a forceful speaker and because of the way the program was set up, he did not come through effectively. Ray merely introduced Gil, Don and me, placing greater emphasis on the introduction of the Cowles men than me. Why I permitted this sort of thing, why I did not insist on being on the program—at least for a brief talk on our plans—I will never know. I rationalized that "I must give Ray his head." I did and he flopped. I learned that the presentation luncheons in Chicago and Boston were no better—just not as well attended. At that point, I called off planned presentations in Los Angeles and San Francisco.

In the meantime, the deadline for the first issue was approaching—fast.

We had hoped to run a sixty-four-page issue, with at least thirty-four pages of advertising. Both Ray Foster and Fred Bunting, particularly Ray, seemed certain that we would have between thirty and forty pages of advertising in the first issue. But the ads did not come. We had actual orders for only five pages one month before the deadline, and just about all of these came from John Riley, one of our two Chicago space salesmen who turned out to be our top performer. Fred sold just one ad and Ray did not get a single order. As the days passed, we began to reduce our projections for the first issue—from thirty-four pages to thirty to twenty-five as "firm." When it finally appeared on October 12 (dated October 16, 1967), Volume One, Number One of *Education News* carried nineteen "pages" of paid advertising in a total folio of forty-four pages. Most of these "pages" were in the form of 7-by-10-inch units. There were only three full pages. *Look* and other Cowles "house ads" were used to fill out the issue.

It was a very disappointing first issue in many ways. I did not like the editorial content. I did not care for the layout, particularly the front page. Designed by *Look* Art Director Allen Hurlburt (who shortly thereafter became art director of Cowles Communications), the front page of the tabloid (which was supposed to have the appearance of the front page of a newspaper) looked more like the front cover of *Look* magazine. With the exception of several paragraphs of "Last-Minute News," half of the page was simply blank, while the flag began at the midsection, leaving very little space for news. The lead story dealt with U.S. Commissioner Howe's recommendation that the Federal government help finance the construction of schools in various cities of the nation. It was headlined: "Howe Backs U.S. Aid For School Buildings." The rest of the front page consisted of four other stories and one picture. The headlines were: "Catholic Rolls Dip Sharply In Big Cities," "Schools Face 30,000 Disabled By Rubella," "Race Plan Shows Some Negro Gain," and "Global Crisis Seen In School Shortage." The picture showed New York City teachers in a "walkout."

I called in Editor Joe Michalak and told him exactly what I thought of his first issue. He did not argue—not much, anyway, and promised that "things would shape up with the second issue." But that just proved to be lip service. He knew that he could promise me almost anything and then hide behind Dave Whitney's skirts. Or those of Gardner Cowles. After all, what did I have to do with the editorial content of the publication? At best, I was only in charge of the business aspect of the periodical. And that was open to question, too. Wasn't this a joint venture of MFI and the Cowles educational division?

I did no better in my talk with Publisher Ray Foster after the first issue. What I got from him was cigar smoke and promises. Promises that there would be more advertising in future issues. Though Ray made his office at 777 Third Avenue, he spent more time at 488 Madison Avenue. But then, he had decided from the beginning that he was working for the owners and publishers of *Look* magazine and not for MFI. And when he was away from his office, I could get little information of his whereabouts from his attractive secretary, whom he brought over from his previous job at Miller Freeman.

Sales Manager Fred Bunting was obviously discouraged, but he tried not to let on. He kept up a good front. He did explain that with government funds for educational software and hardware having been sharply cut, our first year would be a difficult one, but that we would get a good share of advertising in 1968, and that we would really shine in 1969, our full second year in business. "But insofar as the rest of 1967 is concerned," he said, "we will really have to scratch for every ad."

And he proved to be right. The second issue of *Education News,* published on October 30, carried only six "pages" of paid advertising, three of which were full pages. The total folio was twenty-eight pages. And things were no better in November or December. The lead story in the combined December issue carried the following headline: "Negro Teachers Plan Own National Union."

"But wait until 1968," Publisher Ray Foster said.

I could hardly wait. I asked for projections for 1968 and when I finally got them, before the end of December, they looked very encouraging. But when I asked how many pages we had in the house in the form of contracts and orders, the response was quite different.

"Actual contracts and orders on hand amount to only fifteen pages . . . but this year more than any previous year, contracts and orders are coming in late. We will know better by February how the 1968 advertising picture will look," Ray Foster said.

"How do you feel about it, Fred?" I asked Bunting at a meeting that I had with him and Ray.

"Ray is right, the ads are coming in slowly. There is much delay. And a great deal of hesitation . . . I can't be as optimistic as Ray . . . I think that 1968 will be a tough year—for us and all publications in the education field."

But he did not know or did not wish to tell me how bad a year 1968 would turn out to be—not so much for the entire education press as it would be for us.

While all magazines showed a decline in linage, including the leader, *School Management* (soon to be sold to Crowell Collier and Macmillan) and McGraw-Hill's *Nation's Schools,* which was quickly edging up on the leader, one magazine, a newcomer in the ranks, was doing exceptionally well as the Number Three book. This was the tabloid monthly product magazine, *School Product News*. As a matter of fact, it was pushing for leadership. It was published by Industrial Publications of Cleveland, and it was the most business-oriented of the educational publications.

One of the departments in my original outline that I had wanted featured in *Education News* was called, "News of New Products" but I had a real fight on my hands to get Editor Joe Michalak to include a few items in the first issue. As to featuring it, that seemed to be out of the question. The "New Products" page contained very few meaningful items. The biggest, with the largest picture, showed a man with an open-collared shirt, pointing to mops and brooms. The "story" was headlined "Built In Janitor's Station."

I finally got him to build it up to a page of copy but it soon became obvious that there was no enthusiasm on the part of the editorial staff for this department. Items used were of little import and they were presented in uninspired if not downright silly fashion. The editorial staff assumed a demeaning attitude towards anything that had a commercial appeal. We were not going to make *Education News* a trade paper, no matter what I thought. Or anyone else. Dr. John Fischer's admonition to Gardner Cowles was going to prevail, even if there were to be no advertising in *Education News* at all. After all, Gardner Cowles was committed to the profession of education and Gardner Cowles has millions. Who cares about advertising dollars? Who cares about making a profit from the education field? Gardner Cowles would continue to back *Education News* even without any advertising.

But that was not the way Gardner Cowles actually felt, even though he failed to convey his true feelings to the members of the editorial staff, to David Whitney, or to Bill Attwood or to Dr. Fischer.

One of the worst experiences that I had in connection with the publication of *Education News* took place shortly before press time of the first issue. It happened in the "bloodletting room" of *Look*.

The "bloodletting room" was on the eleventh floor, the editorial floor, of the Look building. It was a windowless room, about 24 by 14 feet. It had several tables, some chairs, but mostly standing room. For it was while people were standing or moving around that the work of the room was conducted. Members of the editorial staff (and at times, several others) examined made-up pages of *Look*—mostly feature pages—and then determined what pages, what features, were to go into a particular issue and what pages or features were to be discarded. On each of the four walls of the room, proposed *Look* pages, mounted on cardboard, were displayed on specially constructed display shelves. The editors of *Look,* including Editor-Chairman Gardner Cowles, went around the room, looked at the pages, and then said their pieces:

"This feature is lousy, it doesn't belong in *Look* . . . . This feature is too controversial . . . . This item is much too square . . . . This page is absolutely wrong—it belongs in a high school paper, not in sophisticated *Look* . . . . This layout is weird, absolutely weird, the reaction to a wild nightmare . . ."

And then the bloodletting started. Everyone in attendance had his say—pro or con. No holds were barred. Nothing and no one was sacred, as in group therapy. But after everything was said that was supposed to be said, the editor, Bill Arthur, made the decisions—which pages and features went into the particular issue under discussion and which were to be eliminated. Unless he felt very strongly about a page or a feature, Bill would

not include it in the next issue of *Look* if staff members
objected seriously.

I had not been privileged to attend a *Look* bloodletting but I was briefed by several staff members, including Gardner Cowles, on what took place. I was
told that feelings were not spared during the process
and that every staff member was encouraged to be completely frank and outspoken. Of course, constructive
criticism was preferred. Mere invective was not particularly appreciated. But no matter what happened or
what was said during a session, it remained in the
bloodletting room. After the session, men and women
who were involved in bitter argument would be seen
having a drink or friendly chat together.

I was taken on a tour of the famous room by Bill
Arthur, who explained in detail what went on behind
the closed doors every two weeks.

It was Gardner Cowles' idea that the *Education News*
staff hold a bloodletting session in the *Look* bloodletting
room before going to press on Volume One, Number
One. Since no one seemed to have any objection to
doing this, the time for the bloodletting of the pages for
the first issue of *Education News* was set and an announcement was made to the staff to be on hand and to
be prepared for comment and discussion.

I was not particularly excited about the upcoming
bloodletting. Nothing of this sort was done on any of
the MFI magazines, even when important changes in
format were being made. Nor was such a bloodletting
suggested on any of the *Modern Medicine* properties,
including the major change-over in *Modern Medicine*
itself, from a small, digest size to a new and very much
different standard size magazine. However, I was curi-
ous to see the editorial staff of *Education News,* with
whom I had little contact, in action—particularly under the circumstances of bloodletting. And I really did

expect some bloodletting. Nothing of the sort materialized.

In addition to the seven members of the editorial staff of *Education News,* the session was attended by Publisher Ray Foster, Sales Manager Fred Bunting, Art Director Allen Hurlburt, Gil Maurer, president, and Dave Whitney, editor of the Cowles education properties, Gardner Cowles, Marvin Toben and myself. Bill Attwood was ill and could not be on hand.

Editor Joe Michalak presided. Only a few dummied pages were put up for display, in a corner, interspersed with pages of the most recent issue of *Look.* The rest of the dummied pages were placed on the table in front of us, for those who wanted to examine them and make comment. Gardner Cowles walked around the room looking at some of the pages, then quickly shuffled some of the pages on the table. He made no comment. Just no comment at all. And since no one else made any comment, I thought that I would start off some discussion by asking the question: "How do you like the front page? Do you like the blank first half?" To my surprise, no one took up my lead to make any comment or attempt to answer the questions I posed. I then said: "Will you take a look at the New Products Page? . . . I am very disappointed in the page. . . . Aren't there better, more meaningful items than those that we are using?"

The reaction was a kind of annoyance on the part of the editorial staff. Finally, Assistant Editor Diane Divoky said: "We shouldn't have used this material at all." At which, Editor Joe Michalak smiled.

Several of us began shuffling the dummy pages on the table. But no one volunteered any comment or asked any questions. At that point, Gardner Cowles, who had not uttered a sound, said: "Sorry, but I have to leave for another meeting." That was all he said at the bloodletting session of the launching of *Education News*. But, then, he must have felt that he had said his piece in the "Message to Our Readers" on page 3 of the first issue, written for him by Bill Attwood. The last of the four paragraphs said:

"We happen to believe that American education is neither so good as its strongest advocates believe nor so bad as its more strident critics allege. But we also believe that a great deal needs to be done in the immediate future to make sure that it gets better and not worse. That is why we hope *Education News* will become both a forum and a source of ideas for those who are in a position to take constructive action."

A nice, harmless statement.

While Gardner Cowles had done some writing in the past, during the last ten years he had been doing no writing himself. Statements of this kind, speeches and quotations in news releases were prepared for him to read by Bill Attwood, the Cowles PR department and other staff members, or by the public relations vice president of the corporation. When I asked several men "close" to Gardner Cowles why this was so, why the editorial chairman did no writing of his own, I merely got blank stares. For some reason, he decided to write no more and that was it.

Since no one made any comment, the editorial staff looked bored and none of the others in the room were willing to say anything, I said to Editor Joe: "I guess the meeting is over." And we left.

"Is this what they call 'bloodletting'?" I asked Marvin Toben, as we walked back to our office.

"It may not have been bloodletting, but it was a very painful, frustrating meeting. . . . If you had an ulcer, you would have had some bloodletting all right," he answered.

By the end of December, with five issues under our

belt, averaging only six pages of advertising following Volume One, Number One, it became clear that 1968 would indeed be a very difficult year. We decided on a minimum folio of twenty-eight pages per issue and since most of our ad pages were really 7 by 10 units or about two-thirds of a page per unit, we were doing no better than 80/20, or eighty percent reading matter and only twenty percent advertising. A successful, profitable magazine—at least, in the business and professional fields—should have an editorial/advertising ratio of 60/40—sixty percent advertising and forty percent editorial, or close to it. This was the case with all of our other publications, with some doing as well as 65/35. We were losing a substantial sum of money each month, with no evidence of much improvement in 1968. This kind of situation called for drastic action and I began to think in that direction and then acted.

The first thing I did was to keep close tabs on the doings of Publisher Ray Foster and follow the activities of the rest of the business staff on a day-to-day basis. I did not like what I learned about Ray Foster's activities. He was spending too much time at 488 Madison and in areas other than managing *Education News*. And he was also developing some personal problems. Finally, his relations with Sales Manager Fred Bunting began to deteriorate. Shortly after the turn of the year, Ray asked to see me, and without much of a preamble, blurted out:

"Fred Bunting is leaving."

I was shocked. "Why? What has happened?"

"Oh, Fred got another offer which he felt was so good that he couldn't turn it down. . . . Don't worry Don, we can manage without him."

"What do you plan to do?"

"No problem at all. . . . We will name Art Eiger sales manager in his place and then hire a space salesman to do what Art is doing now—cover the Eastern market. We'll save money and probably get better results."

I did not like what I heard. I cut the meeting short and called in Fred Bunting. What I learned in the next hour or so proved both shocking and revealing. It took a little prodding to get the full story from Fred Bunting since Fred was a company man, did not want to criticize his superior and tried hard to avoid "personality" issues.

"Now that you have resigned, you can speak frankly, Fred. Ray Foster is no longer your boss. Besides, you owe it to yourself and to us to tell me why you chose to resign. What have you found wrong with the operation of *Education News?*"

"Maybe I should have talked to you earlier since I have found myself in an intolerable situation for some time," Fred replied. "But I just couldn't get myself to talk about the man who was my superior. I was probably wrong in not talking about it to you earlier."

A great deal of what Fred Bunting told me was known to me except for details. Fred told me of his inability to develop a working relationship with the editorial department, which continued to shun the business aspect of the magazine. Fred also told me how he had been unable to get through to Ray Foster to get moving on meaningful promotion and to help him with presentations and important sales calls.

Then came the blockbuster: "I hate to tell you this, but now that I have resigned I believe it is not unethical for me to do so. . . . Ray Foster has not been behaving the way a publisher should, especially a publisher of a new and struggling magazine. He is spending altogether too much time at the Look building and I don't know what he is doing there. He is not making calls with me or by himself. Outside of the Sheraton due bill, he has not sold a single advertising contract, and now he has gotten a Mexican divorce from his wife and is planning to marry his secretary and go on a two-week skiing honeymoon in Colorado, to be followed by more honeymooning in California."

"I thought he was going to Colorado and California on a business trip," I said.

"That's the way it appears on the surface—but what it really means is that *Education News* will help to finance his honeymoon."

I knew what I had to do immediately. And it was not very difficult. I induced Fred Bunting to rescind his resignation, which he was more than glad to do since he had a real commitment to *Education News,* and I named him publisher.

"You know, Fred, that I had you in mind for the publisher's spot at the very beginning. In an indirect but not very subtle way, I had offered you the publishership at the outset. You did not seem to take the cue."

"I really wanted to, although I had no experience as a magazine publisher. My expertise until I came here had been entirely in sales, sales managing and promotion. But I did feel competent enough to be publisher of a school-oriented magazine. When you seemed to be giving me the choice, I was tempted to say: 'I want to be publisher rather than sales director.' I didn't say it because I felt that the offer should have come from you—directly. Besides, I felt that you already had made a decision and you seemed to have some very positive feelings about Ray Foster, who did have experience as a publisher of several prestigious, successful business magazines. Now I have no question that I can handle the job of publisher well."

It was also Fred's recommendation that Art Eiger be moved up to sales manager.

"Art can double in brass. He can be sales manager

and still continue to cover his present territory in direct sales. We can save Ray Foster's entire salary," he said.

"And his pretty hefty expense account," I added.

Dismissing anyone is a very unpleasant chore. Over the years, I could count the number of occasions I had to fire an important executive but the Ray Foster case proved to be easy. I called in Ray immediately after my meeting with Fred Bunting and said: "I have bad news, Ray. We are dispensing with your services as publisher of *Education News*." And then, briefly, I outlined the reasons for taking this action.

He did not seem surprised. Or much disturbed. Which surprised me. He said: "I always wanted to go in business for myself. Now, I think I am going to do it—open a PR operation with one of my friends. Mr. Gussow, will you become our first client?"

I could not help but chuckle. What I really wanted to do was laugh out loud. Talk about audacity! Or chutzpah!

The *Education News* picture began to look a little brighter. Soon we would be receiving our first audit from the Business Publications Audit bureau, and while the publication did not even come close to approaching my standards for a business magazine, the need for a news periodical at the administrative level in the education field was so great that it began to develop rapport with its readers. Advertisers and their agencies began to look at *Education News* as a possible vehicle for their marketing stories.

Of course, the editorial content continued to deal largely with race problems in the school systems across the country, deemphasizing, leaving little space for business and administrative news and information. I decided that my next step must be to move the entire operation, including the editorial staff, to our offices and then to hire a new editor—one with an education background but one who was also business-magazine-oriented. Quietly, I began to make a search for such a person. I had several talks with Jack Harding and Marvin Whatmore and I soon found that both, especially Jack, were ready to back me up on my stand to move the editorial staff to the MFI offices. Before asking for a meeting with Gardner Cowles, I decided to prepare fully evidence to demonstrate the absolute need for my action. At the same time, I wanted to be able to show some tangible proof of increased advertising revenue, pointing to still greater improvement by 1969, the year in which we were to really make it with *Education News*.

My first step was to develop a strong, sophisticated sales presentation which Fred Bunting and his staff could utilize in their selling approaches during the spring and summer of 1968—for business for the second half of 1968 but, more importantly, for the calendar year of 1969, our target growth year. To help me do this job, I decided to retain William Maas, former vice president of sales and marketing for Cahners, recognized as one of the really top men in the business magazine sales and marketing field. Bill, at 41, left Cahners to start his own unique communications business for technologists. Since his first step was to obtain venture capital, he found that he had time to take on our assignment, about which he became very enthusiastic. And the fee he asked was small, about half the amount I was ready to pay. I discussed this with Marvin Whatmore and his immediate reaction was: "Don, it sounds good. Go to it."

And go to it I did. Within two weeks, Bill Maas, working closely with Fred Bunting, developed what I felt was a creative, masterful sales presentation and approach for *Education News*. The entire sales staff was brought in for a two-day conference on a round-the-clock basis in a motel in Westchester. Marvin Whatmore and I joined the group at the cocktail and dinner hour at the end of the first day's meetings. I liked what I saw and heard and so did Marvin. Not only was this a very good and timely presentation, but it helped to inspire Fred Bunting and his staff to a new pitch of enthusiasm. During the second day's meetings, Editor Joe Michalak was invited to view part of the presentation so that he, too, could share in the enthusiasm and, in turn, do what was needed with the editorial content of the magazine in the months ahead. Certainly, all of us felt that he should know of our new and intensified effort to bring in more advertising. At the very least, it would mean that he would have more editorial pages to devote to a greater variety of editorial coverage. As expected, he appeared to be only mildly enthusiastic, winding up by saying: "You fellows get more advertising and I will do my share in producing a bigger and better book."

I was so pleased with the job Bill Maas did for us on the *Education News* sales program, that I thought it might be a good idea to invite him to help me in the presentation to Gardner Cowles. He liked the idea, and in a few days he presented me with an outline of his planned study and presentation and an estimate of cost. His outline called for the development of a total plan— editorial, circulation and sales, from both the short- and long-range points of view. The cost was higher than his charges for his initial effort but, once again, it was less than I expected it would be. Marvin Whatmore was even more enthusiastic with Bill Maas' recommendations than I was and we told him to proceed. He said that he would have the job completed in eight to ten weeks. It was early in September that Bill completed the study and presentation. It was a constructive and sound program of action. But, in a way, it was also controversial. Bill pulled no punches in explaining why he thought *Education News* had not taken off as fast as it should have. He fully backed my contention that the magazine required a single management and physical location. However, he did not stop with his criticism and analysis. He also recommended a program of action, including a new budget which called for an even larger investment than was originally contemplated. However, he concluded that *Education News* could be made to be a viable, profitable and very important publication.

I liked his analysis and his recommended program, but I felt that we could accomplish just about everything outlined with a considerably reduced budget. After giving it full consideration and discussing it with Marvin Toben, I decided to show Marvin Whatmore and Gardner Cowles the study and program of action just as Bill Maas had presented it to me. I sent a covering memo asking for a meeting with Cowles and Whatmore so that both Bill and I would have an opportunity to discuss the program in detail and answer any questions that might come up. In my memo, I did not say that I felt that I could accomplish Bill Maas' recommendations in substance for less money, since I felt that I would explain this at the meeting. I was of the opinion that the right thing to do would be for Cowles and Whatmore to see the Maas report in toto without any comment. A meeting was set for the following week.

When Bill Maas and I arrived for the meeting at four o'clock on Thursday, September 26, in Whatmore's office, Gardner Cowles was sitting hunched over on the far end of the sofa in the conference area. He did not get up to greet us. As a matter of fact, he barely said hello. Cowles looked very tired, more tired than I had ever seen him. He looked like a man who had not slept the night before and had a round of meetings all day long. When we began our meetings, which Jack Harding

and Gil Maurer also attended, I realized almost immediately that we were not going to accomplish very much.
Cowles talked in a whisper and in a far-away, unin-
terested manner. Bill Maas and I had planned to make
this a spirited give-and-take discussion, but after listening to the listless chairman and watching the sad faces
of the rest—Jack, Gil and even Marvin, who is usually
ebullient at meetings of this kind, also appeared tired
and unhappy—the starch was quickly taken out of us.

Marvin began the proceedings: "We read your report. It's a good report, but what seems to be worrying
us is the substantial investment that we would have to
make from here on."

"Marvin, I believe that we can accomplish much of
what is recommended with a smaller budget . . . but I
wanted you and Mike to read the report just as it was
presented by Bill," I said, trying to save the day.

"Don, I'm very concerned about the future of *Education News*," Gardner Cowles said. "From advertiser
reaction thus far, I doubt whether we can make the
magazine profitable in 1968, or even in 1969 . . . and
the program recommended calls for a substantial additional investment. Can we really justify it at this time?
I don't know, I don't know."

He did not wait for my answer and he did not ask
Bill Maas to explain. Jack and Gil just sat there without
saying a word. And Marvin also sat without any further
comment, which was very unusual for him. Finally,
Cowles said: "Gentlemen, I'd like to give this a little
more thought . . . and then we will reconvene in a few
days."

On that ominous note the meeting ended.

"I never saw Gardner Cowles look so tired," I re-
marked to Bill Maas, as we left the office. "I'm afraid
that this could be the end for *Education News*. Ob-

viously, there was a lot worrying Cowles. I don't like
what I saw."

"Frankly, Don, I was shocked. They should not
have had the meeting this afternoon under the circumstances. It should have been postponed. This was a
tired, weary man loaded with problems—and the rest of
them know a lot more than we do about those problems.
Let's hope for the best, but I must agree, things don't
look good for *Education News* at this point."

Before the week was over, Marvin Whatmore telephoned, advising me that an executive committee meeting had been called for the following week to discuss
the future of *Education News*. "I'd like you and Marv
Toben to be here and be prepared to answer questions
with regard to budgetary needs, advertising volume on
hand for the final quarter, and projections for next
year."

"Should I bring Bill Maas?"

"I don't think so."

"Well, I would like to have Bill Buckley at the meeting."

"I'll ask him to attend."

Bill Buckley, formerly head of the book division of
Curtis Publishing Company, had been brought in as
chairman and chief executive officer of the Cowles education division, succeeding Dave Whitney, whose departure had been announced the week before in a terse
memo. Intercorporate gossip had it that the education
division, with the exception of the recently acquired
Cambridge Book Company, was in trouble. It appeared that a top-heavy inventory, accumulated over
the past two years, could not be moved at any price
and that operational figures had been overstated. Bill
Buckley was called in as pinch hitter and savior. I had
known Buckley and I had a lot of respect for him. He
was a fast-moving, smart-looking, tough little fellow of

about fifty. He minced no words, and he meant business. His was one of the very few divisions at Curtis that had consistently made a profit. I telephoned him to congratulate him on his new challenge.

"Talk about challenges," he said, "I sure have them here. I inherited a real mess—I had no idea it was that bad. The book inventory is a complete disaster. They've got books here—thousands upon thousands, that you just can't give away. Boring, square and off-beat, dated titles. . . . I'll have write-offs for years. I told Marvin that I need five years just to clean house and another five years to build a new, sound, profitable book company. What a mess! It's hard to believe that they would have let this go this far. It is beyond belief."

When Gil Maurer had been taken off as president of the education division and the *Venture* operation, in order to solve *Family Circle*'s special problems, Dave Whitney was made president, in addition to editor, while Arthur Diedrick was named general manager of *Venture* magazine. Both Dave and Art had been hired and trained by Gil. Gardner Cowles and Marvin Whatmore had great regard for Dave Whitney and Art Diedrick and their talents. I was not impressed with either from the beginning, and, as time went on and I began to know them, I developed a dislike for both. When I learned that I would have to work with Dave on budgets and all other matters on *Education News,* I find some common ground for a working relationship. made a luncheon date with him to see whether I could I tried hard to like him, but I didn't succeed.

It was at this luncheon meeting that Dave said: "Leon Lipkin will not talk with me. He just refuses to take my phone calls or communicate with me in any way. I don't know why." I could have told him why but decided that it would be a waste of time. Leon Lipkin was the founder and president of the small, and regional, but prestigious and profitable Cambridge Book Company, publishers of high school exam reviews and other software educational material, which Cowles bought in 1967. Leon, a highly competent entrepreneur and an independent operator, was disenchanted with the Cowles merger right from the beginning. While he was able to tolerate and/or deal with others at Cowles, he found that he could not work with Dave, and he made no bones about making his position known. He just refused to have anything to do with Dave. Of course, this meant the beginning of the end of Leon's association with Cowles and Cambridge, but Leon did not really care. He had sold his company for a combination of stock and cash and, not being an insider, he was able to dispose of the Cowles stock at his pleasure— which he proceeded to do. I met Leon only once, more or less by accident. It was on the day before he and his wife were sailing on the *Queen Elizabeth II* for an extended trip aboard. He wanted "to get away from it all" for a while, he told me. And as time went on, I knew what he meant.

The executive committee meeting "to discuss and resolve the future of *Education News*" was held in the board room on the morning of October 10, 1968. Sitting around the rosewood oval table was the entire membership of the executive committee. As usual, Gardner Cowles and Marvin Whatmore sat at the head of the table. Bill Buckley sat at the other end, and I alongside him. Jack Harding, Marvin Toben, Gil Maurer, Merrill Clough and Don Perkins also were at the table.

It was not long before we learned the real purpose of the meeting. Cowles said it simply: "Gentlemen, we have to decide whether we should continue publishing *Education News* or suspend it." It came as a mild surprise, not as a shock. I had feared that something like this would take place. If this was not the purpose of the meeting, then why convene the full executive committee? Nevertheless, I had hoped against hope that this would not come to pass at this meeting. It was a matter which Cowles and I, or Marv and I, should have discussed privately, preliminary to any decision as important as this.

"Don, tell us why you think that we should continue *Education News*," Marvin Whatmore followed up Cowles' initial statement.

"I can give you just as many reasons for suspending *Education News* as for continuing it," I said, "but if what you have in mind is to suspend it immediately, then I would say that that would be a serious mistake. We haven't had a full year's operation on the magazine, and while we are all disappointed—I more than anyone else—by the results and advertiser reactions to date, at this time we do not know what kind of year we will have in 1969. Advertising contracts for next year are first beginning to come in. We'll have a much better picture by December. And by January or February, we will have a pretty good idea what our 1969 advertising volume will look like—for the first half, and perhaps, even for the rest of the year. We have made a substantial investment thus far. Our budgetary needs through December and even through January or February will not be great. To kill *Education News* now would mean that our total investment thus far would go by the board."

"What is our total investment to date?" Jack Harding asked.

"I don't have the exact figures, but a good estimate would be in the neighborhood of $850,000," I said.

"What would you need from now through December and through January or February?" Marvin asked.

"We could manage with about $80,000 through December. If our advertising volume does not increase to any extent, we could publish through February with another $70,000. If the editorial staff were to be moved to our offices and the entire operation put under my complete charge, I have every reason to believe that I could reduce costs substantially and make *Education News* a profitable property by the end of 1969, certainly by 1970."

"Supposing you are right, Don, and *Education News* begins to take off in 1969, what is your potential for the magazine, I mean, what profits can you expect?" Jack asked.

"I believe that the short-term profit prospects—that is by 1970—are modest, say, about $100,000 to $200,000 a year before taxes. However, from a long-range point of view, I can see ad revenue of about $5,000,000 and pre-tax profits of about $1,000,000."

"That will mean a profit of only $500,000 a year after taxes," Jack said, "and that is not very much to look forward to—at best. I believe we can do better with our investment dollars from here on. While we are dealing with a much bigger investment in the *Suffolk Sun,* the anticipated returns are big. Our goals are much more ambitious there."

"You mean to say that a potential of net profit of $500,000 a year on an investment of less than $1,500,-000 is not good?" Marvin Toben asked. "For business papers, it is great."

"For a large public company such as Cowles, we must have much bigger goals," Jack said.

"Bill, how do you feel about suspending *Education News?*" Marvin Whatmore asked Bill Buckley. "I mean, will its suspension affect you in any way? Will it hurt the image of the educational book division?"

"If this is what you ask me, my answer is no, I

don't think dropping *Education News* will affect the book division, but that should not be the determining point in making up your minds about the magazine. I really have no business being here and less right to make the comment I am going to make but since I am here, I will say my piece. I am looking at, and listening to Don. He has not had full authority to run *Education News* and, at this stage in the game, he doesn't need *Education News*. Obviously, he believes in what he can do with the magazine under his wing. You already have a very sizeable investment in the property. You should give him the opportunity to show what he can do. You're not talking about very much money from here on."

"I have heard both sides of the question," Gardner Cowles said as he stood up, "I think we should seriously consider dropping *Education News* with the first October issue."

"You mean, we should not even try to sell it?" I asked, in amazement.

"We don't want to peddle *Education News*. It would not be dignified," Cowles said, then turning to Whatmore, he continued: "Marv, you know what we have to do. I have to leave now, for another meeting." And he walked out of the room.

When Cowles left, Marvin said: "Don, let me say publicly now what I told you in private. I think that it was a mistake to divide the operation of the magazine. The editorial as well as the business side of *Education News* should have been at 777 and under your direction. We will never know, but *Education News* may well have done better under such conditions. You have my apology—but I'm afraid it is too late to do anything about it now. You know that we must be careful with every dollar we invest from here on. I am afraid *Education News* must go."

"You mean to say that it is not worth $80,000 to see it through December—in the way I plan to work at it, Marvin?"

"We can't do it, Don. We need every dollar for the *Suffolk Sun*. And, as Jack said, we are playing for much greater stakes there."

"Then, the least we should do is to try to find a buyer. With the great interest on the part of so many publishers in the education market, I'm sure there must be at least one who will be interested in taking over *Education News*," I said.

"I am afraid we can't," Marvin said. "You heard Mike's feeling about peddling the property. Men, it's getting late. Let us take a vote on suspending the magazine." Jack Harding then read a resolution which said in essence that *Education News* would suspend publication with the first issue in October.

"All those in favor, say 'aye,'" Marvin said. The ayes were not loud, but they were fairly audible. "All those against, say 'nay'." There were no nays . . . and that was it.

"Marvin, you must give me a chance to try to sell the magazine—at least during the next twenty-four hours," I pleaded.

"Do you have any prospects?"

"No, of course not. But I think it will be worth contacting Harcourt, Brace or CBS . . ."

"All right, Don, I'll hold up the release on the suspension of *Education News* until tomorrow noon. It will take that long to prepare and dispatch it, anyway. So call Harcourt, Brace or anyone else tomorrow morning . . . and let me know by noon, please."

That wasn't very much time. But I decided I would try. I knew Jim Milholland at Harcourt, Brace. Jim was a fellow board member of the American Business Press and a friendly, understanding kind of a man. He was head of the company's business paper division and he was fairly close to William Jovanovich, Harcourt's president. Since Harcourt, Brace was very much involved in educational book publishing, and was expanding in the professional and business magazine area, they might be interested in taking over *Education News*.

Walking back to the office with Marvin Toben, I talked with him about the meeting.

"It is unbelievable," he said. "They were not willing to invest another $80,000 to $150,000 to save an investment of $850,000, with the possibility of developing a property that could bring in annual net profits of $500,000, yet they throw million after million into the *Suffolk Sun*, which is obviously the biggest drain on the corporation and is doomed to failure."

"Marvin, I talked my heart out to save *Education News*, as you heard, or at least to get a few months so that we might really know whether the paper would make it. You know what I think? It was all decided before we came to the meeting. Gardner Cowles had made up his mind to drop *Education News* and that was that. We just wasted our time and energy."

"I guess you're right. It makes sense. Didn't Cowles just walk out and tell Whatmore: 'You know what we have to do.' Marvin knew what to do all right—what his boss man wanted."

"Damn it," I exploded, "the least we can do is sell the magazine—if I only had several weeks! What in the world can I do in a few hours?"

It was just five when we returned to the office and I called Jim right away. He was not in, and I left word for him to call me in the morning. But by ten the following morning, he had not called and I called him again. I was told that he had my message but was in an early meeting and would call me later. He didn't call me until the following day. By then it was too late, and I never told him the reason for my call. I telephoned Marvin Whatmore at noon, as I had promised, and told him of my efforts to reach Jim.

"I'm sorry, Don, it's too late now. The release will be made available to the press this afternoon."

I was depressed, frustrated and angered. But not too surprised. Gardner Cowles was in character. He seemed to have the knack of dropping publishing properties prematurely. He seemed to be doing it time and time again. He gave up on *Quick* at a time when that little magazine was beginning to move. It could have been where *TV Guide* is today, one of the most successful of specialized consumer magazines. And *Quick* was there first with the same basic idea. By making a few changes in *Flair*'s format, such as the elimination of off-size doodads that were inserted in the magazine at ridiculously high cost, he could have made it with that original, beautiful and very readable magazine for a specialized audience. He dropped it after a few issues, losing a pile of money in the process. When the *Insider's Newsletter*, an unusual weekly newsletter of general interest, was beginning to generate an increasing number of valuable subscriptions and was looked upon by the publishing community as a winner, Gardner Cowles decided to drop it because "we couldn't get enough paid subscriptions to make this a profitable property" and "it just does not seem to have a big enough potential for us." The only publishing venture he stuck with was *Look*, his baby. It took all of fifteen years before *Look* began to make a profit.

My next job was to call in Fred Bunting and tell him of the upcoming demise of *Education News* so that he, in turn, could inform his staff. Fred was shocked. Shaken.

"What a terrible mistake," was his reaction. "We were just beginning to move with the book. I'm sure that if we had had the operation here, it would have taken off much faster. I don't know how I can tell Art and John and the rest. Our sales meeting carried them to new heights of enthusiasm. They have been out pitching. Really working their tails off. How can I tell them?"

It was painful, but tell them he did. And of course, Bill Attwood, as Gardner Cowles' personal representative, told Joe Michalak, who in turn, advised the staff. They were really shocked. "I thought Cowles had a strong commitment to *Education News* and the education field generally," was the editor's reaction.

The next day, when the news appeared in the *New York Times*, the *Wall Street Journal* and other newspapers and over the wire services, the telephone calls began to pour in—to me and to the Cowles' offices. Calls from other publishers and other would-be buyers.

"Why did you do this before trying to sell it?" was the question that was repeated again and again. What could we tell these people? That Gardner Cowles did not want to peddle *Education News* because it would not be the dignified thing to do?

One young, bright and highly respected consultant in the education field insisted on coming to see me. I saw him. "I could have gotten half a dozen good, serious prospects for *Education News*. I still want to try."

Among those who expressed interest in buying the magazine after the announcement of suspension was John Reilley, our midwestern sales manager. Quick action was necessary but, based on my experience of the past, I knew that quick action was not possible.

I telephoned Marvin Whatmore and told him of the calls that I received. "We did, too," he replied. "Maybe we acted precipitously. We have received so many calls, including some from the most prestigious publishers, a few offering joint venture possibilities, that Mike and I feel that we must explore them. I will throw those you received in the hopper . . . and we will be scheduling meetings. Keep your calendar flexible for the next few days. And we may need Bill Maas and Fred Bunting to help us with a presentation. Alert them."

The next two weeks were wild. Just about every day was devoted to a meeting with would be buyers of *Education News* or joint venture "partners." A team that included Bill Maas, Fred Bunting, Marvin Toben, Marvin Whatmore, Jack Harding and myself, started a series of presentations before representatives of some of the country's largest publishers and communications companies, such as CBS, Bill Benton's Encyclopaedia Britannica, Xerox, and a few lesser lights. Gardner Cowles was on hand for the presentation with the executives of CBS.

The presentation sounded great at the beginning. By the time the second week came around, it sounded canned. By that time, we were tired and weary. And with each day, the opportunity for a deal or joint venture faded. In the end, we couldn't even sell our list. Two weeks of exercise in futility. Yet, had we tried to sell or find a partner for *Education News* before announcing its demise, the chances of success would have been favorable. Even Gardner Cowles, Jack Harding and Marvin Whatmore seemed to agree on that.

SIX:

The Last of the "Buy-Ins"

The problems that I had to face in the launching, joint operation (or non-operation) and eventual premature demise of *Education News* did not prevent me from continuing to build the Cowles Business and Professional Magazines to new heights by way of acquisitions. Immediately following the successful, and, in many ways, spectacular purchase of the *Modern Medicine* group of publications on December 31, 1967—just one year after we merged our company with Cowles—I moved to buy several other publishing properties. Rather than using brokers, I decided on direct approaches. I had a fairly good idea of what was available and of who might be induced to sell. And, of course, I had definite goals on what fields and directions to follow and on what magazines and companies to buy.

Acquiring *Modern Medicine* and its sister publications in the medical and dental fields was considered a coup in publishing. Just about everybody and his uncle wanted to buy this prestigious company and, before us,

Cahners came close to a deal. When we were making plans to get into the educational area, I began to look at other fields on our list of priorities. These included plastics, food, paper, packaging and computerization. After carefully studying a magazine or group of magazines that I wanted to buy, I would telephone the president of the company and make a date for lunch. In most cases, I knew him. If I didn't, the chances were that he knew of me or MFI. And, of course, he knew of our association with Cowles, since this fact was widely published, circulated and talked about.

Among the smaller, but long- and well-established business magazine publishing companies that I had had my eye on, even before our merger with Cowles—as I had, *Modern Medicine*—was the Bettendorf Publications of Chicago, publishers of the magazine *Paperboard Packaging* and several other properties, all in the paperboard field. Since we were already publishing *Food and Drug Packaging*, this group of publications fitted well into our marketing picture. There was talk in the business magazine field that Harry Bettendorf, the president and principal stockholder, was interested in selling. Some said that he already had had some talks with one or two publishing companies who were would-be buyers. I was not able to confirm this. At any rate, I telephoned Bettendorf and told him that I expected to be in Chicago the following week and would like to have lunch with him. He said that he was aware of our merger with Cowles, and would be pleased to have lunch with me. He did not ask my purpose.

Instead of coming alone to meet me, Harry Bettendorf brought his first assistant and minority stockholder, Joel Ware. We met in my room at the Ambassador East, and then went to the Pump Room for lunch. It became obvious to me from the start that Bettendorf was ready to sell his company. He reacted positively to my approach and we returned to my room to continue our discussion.

I followed the same game plan with Bettendorf that I had used in acquiring *Modern Medicine*. I explained (in as much detail as seemed appropriate) the purpose of merging our company with Cowles and our program of expansion from that point on. "What we want to do," I said, "is to build one of the largest and most important business and professional magazine operations." I explained that I did not *sell* MFI but used MFI to buy into Cowles.

"We are not interested in buying your company, if what you want is to retire or walk away from it," I said. "We want you, like me, to buy into this growing, Big Board communications corporation. We want you to share in its growth. We want you to be part of our operation."

I sincerely believed in the "buy in" idea. It had great meaning for me as an "insider," board member and president and chief executive of the business magazine arm of Cowles. My plan was to bring a group of smart, experienced and industry-involved managers into our division, around whom we could build an operation that would approach in size and scope that of the magazine division of McGraw-Hill, of Cahners or of Chilton, the three biggest, at that time. My game plan had charisma and I proved that it could work.

Harry Bettendorf, who had an accounting and trade association background, acquired *Paperboard Packaging* in the late thirties. Through industry involvement, service and hiring good talent, he built the magazine into the Number One property in a field of two. However, eight years before our meeting, the magazine began to slip and, at this time it was Number Two. Eight years before, *Paperboard Packaging* had carried more than 1,200 pages of advertising a year. Now, ad volume was down to less than 700 pages. In turn, *Boxboard Containers*—now owned by the American subsidiary of MacLean-Hunter, the big Canadian publishing company—was the leader with about 1,200 pages of advertising. I had a fairly good idea why *Paperboard Packaging* had declined and *Boxboard Containers* had grown; I felt that we could turn the magazine around.

Additionally, we were buying more than just one magazine. Bettendorf also published a most unusual 12-page weekly newsletter called *Official Board Markets,* which carried advertising. The publication was recognized as "the bible" in its special field and was exceptionally profitable. Bettendorf also published two other newsletters in the same style, one of which, *European Board Markets,* was published in its small but growing London operation. And a study we made revealed that Harry Bettendorf was recognized as the most important publishing personality in the highly select paperboard industry. This was particularly true with the top management in the field, largely the older executives. What was needed was an infusion of new blood to deal with the younger, up-and-coming key men in the field. That would become one of our challenges following the acquisition.

Acquiring Bettendorf seemed fairly easy. Before our meeting came to an end, I made an offer, to which Harry Bettendorf and Joel Ware did not react unfavorably. They said that they would like to think it over. They also asked me to spell out my offer in detail in a letter.

When I returned to New York, I telephoned Marvin Whatmore and told him of my meeting with Bettendorf and asked for a meeting with him. When we met later in the week, I filled him in on details. I showed him several copies of the various Bettendorf periodicals and I left with him a copy of the latest audited annual report, brought up to date with unaudited figures, which I had asked Bettendorf to mail to me. This was a small operation, with sales of about $800,000 and a fairly good record of profit over the years. However, *Paperboard Packaging* was in the red, and the company as a whole was not making a profit at that time. I explained to Marvin Whatmore that I believed we could turn the business around within a year or two through cost reductions and extra sales effort. I also made it a point to show him how this operation was compatible with, and an important addition to, our packaging magazine.

"It will give us a greater opportunity for growth in the packaging field," I said.

"How much do we have to pay for this business?" Whatmore finally asked.

"It will be entirely a stock deal," I replied, "and I believe we can swing it for about 25,000 shares, but certainly no more than 30,000. Based on our stock's present price of $15 a share, our cost will be approximately $400,000, or a range from $375,000 to $450,-000. However, as you will see from the balance sheet, Bettendorf has about $150,000 in net quick assets—cash and marketable securities. Our deal would include the net quick assets, which means that we will buy the business for about a quarter of a million dollars."

"Do you think you can do this on that basis?"

"I believe we can. If we cannot, we won't make a deal. But I feel very confident that it will come our way. We will include a five-year contract for Harry Bettendorf and at least a two-year contract for Joel Ware. We need Harry since he is an important figure in the paperboard field. I am not sure we need Joel, but as part of the deal we may have to give him a two-year contract."

"You're on the right track and it looks like an acceptable deal," Marvin said. "Let me clear it with Mike and Jack and then get approval of the executive committee. I may call you in to answer some questions."

Following a brief meeting with Gardner Cowles and Marvin Whatmore in Cowles' office, during which the chairman asked only a few questions that I was able to answer without difficulty, the deal received approval in principle by the executive committee, and I was instructed to proceed. After several meetings, telephone calls and some correspondence with Harry Bettendorf, we finally had a deal. The price was set at 26,500 shares—equivalent to just under $400,000—and, of course, we captured the $150,000 in net quick assets, about $110,000 of which was cash and just over $40,-000 in marketable securities. Bettendorf would receive a five-year contract and Ware a two-year contract at acceptable salaries and incentives. Before the month was over, the closing took place in the board room. That was the first time Marvin Whatmore and Jack Harding had met Harry Bettendorf. Bettendorf expressed a desire to meet Gardner Cowles, and at the conclusion of the signing, Marvin and I escorted Bettendorf to Cowles' office. The chairman greeted Bettendorf and said: "Let me welcome you to our fold." Bettendorf appeared to be very much impressed and in turn, he tried to impress Cowles by saying: "I don't know whether you know it or not, but there is a town in Iowa called Bettendorf, named after one of our distant relatives."

"I was never in that town—but I've heard of it," Cowles said. And that was the end of the meeting.

With the acquisition of the Bettendorf group of paperboard industry periodicals, we were now publishing thirty-two business and professional magazines, newsletters, annuals and semiannuals, with a combined annual advertising volume of about $13,000,000, and a profit of $2,000,000 before taxes. Soon the advertising volume figure would rise to $15,000,000 and profits before taxes would exceed $2,500,000. We used very little cash, acquiring most of the properties with stock and notes. And the notes were being paid with profits and cash flow generated from our acquisitions. Phase One of our projected game plan of growth was now completed and we accomplished it in less than the three years of our target period. We were now among the ten biggest operations in the business magazine industry.

We were ready to begin our five-year Phase Two—to build our division into a unit with advertising volume of $50,000,000 and profits before taxes of about $8,-000,000. I knew exactly where I wanted to go, what to buy and what our priorities were. Early in 1969, I had several excellent companies lined up for acquisition, having done the preliminary work during 1967 and 1968. Two of these included companies with a combined annual volume of $10,000,000. One company was in the far West, the other in the Midwest. And we were also moving to expand our international division —in both the business and the professional fields. If everything had gone well, we probably would have reached our goal in less than five years, placing our division among the three to four biggest—in all probability right behind McGraw-Hill and Cahners. I also had visions of taking our division public, with control to be continued by Cowles Communications, of course. Such a move would give us additional leverage and would provide us with capital (and stock) that would not be dependent on the parent company as a source. I had watched other large multidivisional public corporations do this successfully and it appeared to be a good, sound program. I touched on the subject with Marvin Whatmore in an offhand, casual way, deciding to discuss it with him more seriously when I had fully explored the potentials and methodology. But this was not to be.

Following the premature demise of *Education News* and a loss of almost $1,000,000, the much bigger, more serious problems of Cowles Communications began to loom on the cloud-filled horizon. Serious storm warnings were there for all to see but those in power did not even bring these up for discussion at board meetings until it was too late.

But even as Executive Vice President Jack Harding was calling the executive committee's attention to "the great stakes" in the *Suffolk Sun*—potential profits in the millions as against earnings of "only" $500,000 for *Education News*—the daily newspaper was beginning to fall apart. At the very time Cowles killed *Education News* "to make available more investment dollars" in the *Sun* "where the action was," the morning daily had already lost about $10,000,000. The exact figure was never revealed—not even to the board of directors and in all probability not even to all of the executive committee. Cowles was not willing to invest another $80,000 to $150,000 to make *Education News* (for which we had a specific program) a viable, profitable property, but was ready and willing to pour additional millions into a daily newspaper that was sinking in a quagmire of endless, insoluble problems.

At the same time, Cowles as a corporate entity was facing a long series of other difficult problems. Early in 1969, Congressman Fred Rooney (the Democratic Representative from Pennsylvania) launched an investigation into *Look*'s subscription selling methods, which the Congressman (and others) felt had a foul odor.

Instead of taking prompt action to forestall further onerous complications, nothing tangible was undertaken until the "investigation" began to smell to high heaven and newspapers and other media across the country, including the *Wall Street Journal*, began writing about it.

As unbelievable as it may seem, *Look*, a most modern magazine, employing young, smart, "today" editors, housed in modern offices on Madison Avenue and doing many things that a magazine of the sixties should be doing, was following the most archaic circulation selling and fulfillment methods. Instead of computerizing its circulation in the early sixties, as Vice President Joel Harnett and several other younger executives had been urging for more than five years, Cowles continued to fulfill the over 8,000,000 circulation of *Look* by Speedomat and by hand, employing the services of 2,000 employees in its old-fashioned setup in Des Moines. At the same time, it was using subscription sales methods that had changed little from those developed at the turn of the century, including generally accepted but nevertheless high-handed procedures in bad taste, developed in the crew selling system (door to door salesmen, working a territory under a supervisor) of the twenties and thirties. Another method used was telephone selling, with a crew of salesmen making calls from a "boiler room" type of operations. Many of the calls were made in the evening.

While Time, Inc., and other magazine publishers followed basically the same subscription selling methods, Time, Inc., was years ahead of Cowles in that it had long computerized the circulation of *Life* and its other magazines. As a result, Time, Inc., successfully developed a direct selling program, particularly on books (largely reprints and/or developments of text published in *Life*). This proved to be highly profitable and provided the kind of cash flow that Cowles did not have but could have had. It was not until 1969 that Cowles, which then could ill afford it, finally launched a three- to five-year computerization program at an estimated cost ranging from $3,000,000 to $5,000,000. At the same time, and prematurely, Cowles inaugurated a new

direct marketing division under the direction of an
Episcopalian minister, to sell books, records and an
assortment of other items—including pantyhose—which
was aborted within a year, cost the corporation a bundle,
and proved to be the laughingstock of 488 Madison
Avenue and of magazine circles generally. Yet, it was a
"high spot" on the three-day program of the Cowles
1970 Seminar held in Orlando, Florida, March 8 to 10,
called "The Management of Change." In almost an
hour of dissertation that sounded more like a revival-
ist's sermon or a circus barker's pitch, Episcopalian
Minister Thomas J. Patterson, now Vice President—
Direct Marketing for the corporation, at the rostrum,
gave a most enthusiastic and inspired presentation dealing with the millions in profit potential in direct marketing of a long list of products. He devoted an important
segment of his talk to the problems and expense women
seem to have with pantyhose, today's and tomorrow's
product rage, and how the *Look* brand, of good quality
but low-priced pantyhose would soon become women's
salvation—and at the same time make a pile of dough
for Cowles Communications. Following his talk, the
evangelist-turned-salesman introduced his executive
staff of four key men and women for the new Cowles'
direct marketing operation: a manager of books and
records; a manager of the merchandise department (including pantyhose); a manager of direct mail promo-
tions; and a direct mail promotion manager. No one
asked, and he did not explain, what the different functions of the last two were to be. In an interview with
the *Wall Street Journal* in January, Patterson was
quoted as saying: "We aren't sure yet what dollar volume we might be able to build over the next five years
in this area (direct marketing) but I can tell you this—
it will probably become an important part of the company's business." In the same interview, Patterson ex-

plained how he had moved from a job as an advertising executive to become an Episcopalian minister in the early sixties and how, while serving a Long Island parish, he was sold on the idea of returning to secular life by a Cowles board member who happened to be a member of the congregation.

"Don't get me wrong," Patterson said. "I talked the whole thing over with my bishop and he agreed that it was the right thing for me to do. My faith has never been greater. You see, if you really love people and give them something they want and need, I believe they'll love you in return." From his spirited presentation at the Cowles Management for Change Seminar, there was no doubt in Patterson's mind that he expected to earn the affection of a lot of women who were going to buy millions of pairs of Look-brand pantyhose that would not tear as fast as the other brands of pantyhose which they were buying at higher prices. But this did not come to pass, because the direct marketing department was suspended before a single pair of Look-brand pantyhose was ever marketed.

This was the second Management Seminar of Cowles Communications. The first was held during a snow storm and in bitter cold in Des Moines, Iowa, the home of the Cowles family newspaper (but not that of Cowles Communications, Inc.), the *Register and Tribune*, and also the home of the *Look* circulation-fulfillment operation. It was here that *Look* had its beginnings. At each Seminar, Cowles management tried to make it quite warm and cozy for the participants, about one hundred corporate and divisional executives of the company. While it was much warmer in Orlando, Florida, than in Des Moines, Iowa, and it was pleasant to take a break in the pool (or with a drink at pool's edge), the general feeling was a lot warmer in the zero weather in Iowa than in the Florida sunshine. Despite the rhetoric, the second Seminar, in Florida, was held when the Cowles financial and operational situation had worsened considerably. The picture had looked much rosier early in 1969.

The main purpose of the first Cowles Management Seminar, held on February 3 and 4 in Des Moines, was to provide an exchange of information among the executives of the corporation's various and growing divisions. And to get acquainted. To make sure that the get-acquainted element worked right from the beginning, Seminar participants were doubled up, with single accommodations forbidden. And the doubling up was arranged strictly to help strangers get acquainted. You could not pick your roommate. And you could not make any changes. That was the rule, with no exceptions. And the whole thing came as a surprise. When I checked in, I found that my room was occupied, and I didn't know by whom. So I called the desk. I was told that I had a roommate, as did everybody else. And that was it.

My roommate turned out to be the new president of the educational book division, appointed a few weeks before the Seminar by Bill Buckley, the new chairman of the division. I do not recall his name but it doesn't matter, since he left as fast as he came—about a month or two after the Seminar. He was not replaced. There was no need for a president and a chairman. One would be enough.

Anyway, I did not enjoy having a roommate. Particularly this roommate. He snored right through the night and I couldn't sleep. The second night, I rushed to my room about an hour before the usual time. I went to bed quickly and tried to fall asleep but I couldn't. Just as I became drowsy, my roommate showed up, went to bed, fell asleep as soon as he hit the pillow and almost immediately began to snore, louder than during the first night. I couldn't fall asleep until early in the morning—when it was time to get up.

I did not have a roommate at the second Seminar. Some did. Maybe it was a matter of position or maybe Dick Collins, the very able corporation press chief who did the arranging, got my message from Des Moines. This was not an informal Seminar. It was well organized. It had a full day's program, each day. And we were kept on our toes. But I did sleep—every night I was there.

A principal purpose of the second Seminar, as enunciated by President Marvin Whatmore in a memo dated January 28, was "to answer questions about the various operations of the company." Questions about Congressman Rooney's charges? Whether the price paid for the *Ocala Star-Banner* was excessive? The future of the company?

"Advance knowledge will enable us to organize our presentations with greater precision and make it possible for panel chairmen to ask questions anonymously on your behalf," Whatmore explained in his memo. "Because most people are understandably reluctant to appear to be criticizing or second-guessing others, all questions will be treated in confidence, and the names of the questioners will not be revealed."

By now, the corporation had its full share of troubles. Not only did President Whatmore know it, all others at the Seminar knew it, too. And many did have questions and were not bashful about asking—anonymously. And some not so anonymously. While some questions were answered by both Whatmore and Cowles, several basic questions—especially those that were most embarrassing—remained unanswered.

Everybody in attendance knew that Cowles had suffered big losses in 1967 and 1968. And that 1969 was not much better. But how was 1970 going to size up?

That was the big question. In his talk on Sunday, March 8, Marvin Whatmore tried to answer:

"Our earnings from operations were improved significantly during 1969. We had a net loss for the year because of the costs of suspending the *Suffolk Sun* and because of the costs of phasing out some of our subscription-selling operations. The board of directors voted to pass the dividend rather than modify our favorable long-term debt arrangements."

And he told a little more—but not much. Mostly, he tried to show that things were not really as bad as they appeared. In fact, he tried to show that there was a great future ahead for the company and its people. Said he:

"Despite the losses from operations for nine-and-one-half months of the *Suffolk Sun* (in 1969), the company had an improvement before taxes of $3,553,000 or 89 cents a share. I think this is one helluva improvement. The turnaround which began for the company in 1968 is continuing."

As to the profit projection for 1970, Whatmore said: "I can't answer that question for two very good reasons: (1) Jack Harding would have a heart attack. The New York Stock Exchange takes a dim view of earnings projections unless the projection is made in the form of a news release and distributed to all investors via the wire services, and (2) there are just too many variables around right now, and a prediction made on March 8 might well have to be publicly revised by May 1." After listing some of the variables, he continued:

"So, although I can't give you anything that sounds like an official forecast or prediction for 1970, I will say the turnaround is continuing and I will be disappointed if 1970 isn't better than 1969."

Marvin Whatmore must have been disappointed, because 1970 was no better than 1969. Actually, it was much worse. While Cowles finished 1970 with a gain of $647,000 against a loss of $1,883,000 in 1969, the gain was the result of "extraordinary items," largely from the profit of the sale of profitable properties, almost all from the profit of the sale of the very profitable and growing *San Juan Star*, the only English-language daily newspaper in the capital of Puerto Rico. Total revenues for the year declined from $158,917,000 to $145,832,000 and there was a loss from continuing operations that amounted to $1,576,000 compared with a profit of $2,413,000.

Yet, in his talk at the Orlando Seminar, Whatmore said: "The company had a great forward thrust in 1969 and that thrust is continuing in 1970."

Gardner Cowles took a slightly different tack from that of Marvin Whatmore. He said: "I want to be as frank with all of you this evening as I know how to be. I want to describe in some detail the strengths and weaknesses of Cowles Communications, Inc., as I see them. I am very proud of our company, even though in recent years we have had a lousy earnings record."

He really did try, and a lot of us who heard him were impressed. And felt for him. He took the blame for the *Suffolk Sun* fiasco. Said he: "I was primarily responsible for the decision to launch the *Suffolk Sun*. It was a tremendous mistake. We lost a very large amount of money."

But mostly, he talked about *Look* and the future of that magazine. He said:

"I started *Look* some thirty-three years ago. I have been through good years and bad years with *Look*. I have put a lot of blood, sweat and tears into building *Look* and I am not about to see my lifework slide downhill. I am firmly convinced that we can surmount our present transitory problems and make *Look* even more important and more respected across this great country of ours than ever before."

But, as the months passed, the chairman was not very happy to see *Look* advertising volume continue to slide downhill.

He seemed enthusiastic about the prospects for *Venture*. Said he: "*Venture* is rapidly becoming America's Number One travel magazine. *Holiday* continues to slip. The travel field, in my opinion, is going to grow and grow. *Venture* may be profitable in 1970. I think it is also going to add prestige to our company."

Venture did not make a profit in 1970. As a matter of fact, it recorded a substantial loss. And early in 1971, Cowles announced the suspension of *Venture* with the July/August issue. *Holiday* continued to publish.

The presentations, speeches, and question-and-answer periods told us less about Cowles' problems than did private chats during the cocktail hour and at the pool. The three-day Seminar had its share of laughter and banter but there were not very many happy people in attendance. The company they were part of, or worked for, was in trouble and they knew it. That is why the Bettendorf acquisition was the last of the "buy ins" of Cowles Communications, Inc. The lid was shut tight on further growth by way of acquisition. The seeds of a reversal were beginning to take root. The disengagement of the corporation was starting.

SEVEN:

Why Not Try a "Buy-Back"?

So many times in our life spans we seem to wish away the days of our years. I just can't wait till tomorrow. . . . I wish it were next month. . . . If this cold winter would come to an end—and spring would only be here. . . . We're going through a terrible period —if only this were next year. . . . I just can't wait to see Johnny grow up and go to school. . . . Wouldn't it be nice if, with all the problems we have, we could fall asleep and sleep on for a few months or years and then wake up and find that the problems had just gone away?

But problems do not just disappear. I haven't been in the habit of running away from problems. I have learned from experience that it is best to meet them head-on. But if ever I came close to wishing away a number of days of my years, it was during the time that I decided to buy back our business—the entire business and professional magazine division, or at least Magazines For Industry—from Cowles.

On February 25, 1970, I approached Marvin Whatmore and told him that I had a "sporting offer" to make. The idea to buy back our business had come to me on several occasions and was triggered by the decline in the fortunes of Cowles Communications. With each board meeting, I became more discouraged about the prospects for the company. And as I began to get acquainted with Cowles executives and the various operations of the corporation, I came to the reluctant conclusion that I had been over-enthusiastic about this company and its future.

And, as I watched mistake after mistake being made —in the book division, *Family Circle,* the *Suffolk Sun* fiasco, the ineptness on *Venture* and, finally, the seemingly insurmountable problems that were developing on *Look,* I became a little scared. Then came the series of blasts by Congressman Fred Rooney on the "paid during service" (PDS) subscription-selling methods of Cowles and my fears were intensified. Of course, Cowles was not alone among consumer publishers as a target of the Congressman. The subscription-selling methods of Time, Inc., Hearst, Reader's Digest and others were questioned. But it seemed that his greatest thrust was at Cowles. *Look,* the magazine, and Gardner Cowles, the publisher and owner, were the Congressman's major targets.

Maybe if Jim Milloy had been well and still on the Cowles team, he might have been able to call off the Congressman from his attacks on Cowles and *Look.* Or maybe it was because of Jim, that Congressman Rooney behaved the way he did, that he acted as if he had it in for Cowles and *Look.* Jim Milloy had been a vice president of Cowles Communications for over twenty years, and while his function was to bring in advertising for *Look,* he made his headquarters in Washington, and was reputed to know anybody worth knowing in the nation's capital. No one inside or outside of Cowles could quite figure out what Jim Milloy was doing for Cowles and *Look* in Washington. But Jim was credited with a lot of *Look* advertising. When he started with *Look* shortly after the Second World War, advertising revenue of the magazine was about $1,000,000. Now, it was close to $80,000,000. Jim took the job on a nominal salary plus "a piece of the action"—in the form of an override—and before long, Jim became the highest earner of Cowles, being paid more than Chairman Gardner Cowles or President Marvin Whatmore. For years on end, his "take" was over $100,000 a year, and in one year, it was a whopping $190,000. But Jim was now in his seventies and had suffered several strokes, and was retired from CCI, though with a "nice" income. Obviously, he must have deserved it. It was probably only a coincidence, but Congressman Rooney's blasts at *Look* and Cowles came at the time when Jim Milloy began to fail and was soon out of the Cowles (and its Washington) picture.

Then the stock began to plummet, from a high of $21 to $15 to $10 to $7 a share. When I made the deal with Cowles, the price was $15⅞. When we signed the contract, it was $13¾ per share. And as an "insider," I could not sell stock except for a nominal amount (under SEC Rule #133, and with the prior approval of Cowles). By the end of 1969, I had sold 6,000 shares (at about $15 a share) of the 101,000 shares that I had received in the merger.

When the stock reached a low of $7 a share early in 1970, and the Cowles situation looked bleak, I decided to make an attempt to buy back our company—or the entire division which I had built since the merger in 1966. I also had another, more personal reason for wanting a confrontation with Marvin Whatmore. As president and manager of the Cowles Business and Professional Magazine Division, I was successful in making this one of the company's most profitable units. Only the broadcasting and newspaper divisions (exclusive of the *Suffolk Sun*, of course) were higher earners, but not by much. Yet my salary had remained the same as it was at the time of the merger, and the "other ways of compensating" that Marvin Whatmore had promised me in 1966 had not materialized. I was included in profit sharing beginning in January 1967, but since there was little profit from that time on, my share in the profits proved to be insignificant and eventually non-existent. Since I had moved to the Cowles profit sharing plan from the active, profit-producing MFI pension program, I was losing about $10,000 in pension fund money each year, in effect, reducing my annual income by this amount.

Additionally, in a subtle way, I was being isolated from the Modern Medicine (Minneapolis) operation, which I brought in, reorganized and made almost ten times more profitable in less than two years.

Then there was another factor. While until recently I had been able to buy business and professional magazine properties, because of the sharp decline in the price of Cowles stock and the heavy losses resulting from the operation of the *Suffolk Sun* (and other unprofitable properties), I was no longer able to buy magazines or companies. In turn, the substantial profits that I was successful in generating from my division were used to cover some of the heavy losses of the unprofitable Cowles properties.

I decided that I could no longer countenance this kind of nonsense. After much thought and a few sleepless nights, I came up with several options that I wanted to lay before Marvin Whatmore.

The meeting took place the morning of February 25, 1970. Marvin was his usual affable self despite the tremendous problems and pressures he was facing. The great charmer—easy to speak to, gracious and gentlemanly. While not a natural listener, he always gave the impression that he was extremely interested in what you were saying. It was most pleasant and comfortable to be in his presence.

After the usual amenities and a brief exchange on "the current business picture," in my division, and in the corporation as a whole, I went directly to the heart of the situation.

"Marv, it must be no secret to you that I have not been particularly happy, because of recent developments in my division, as well as in the Cowles operation as a whole. It is not only because our stock has slumped from $15 to $7 a share in a few months, and there is no telling where the price of the stock will go. Nor simply the elimination of dividends, which has cut my income by one hundred percent—from approximately $100,000 to $53,000, exactly where it was before our merger. While you promised that 'there would be other ways' in which I would be compensated, nothing has happened and you never really explained what you had meant. In the meantime, I am also losing about $10,000 a year in the pension fund or in deferred income—which really means that I am now getting $10,000 a year less than I received before we sold MFI to Cowles. This, on top of seeing the value of my lifetime of work dwindling sharply, is reason enough to feel distressed. But there is much more than that. During the last year or so, but especially during the last few months, I find myself being boxed in—isolated from the Modern Medicine operation—"

"Are you referring to the Pat Lyndon situation?" he asked.

"Yes—but that is only part of it, a small part of it. In the Pat Lyndon case, how do you explain the fact that I never received a copy of the massive report on his study of the international medical publishing situation?"

"Don, I really don't know. I thought that you had a copy."

"But if you thought that I had a copy, why wasn't I consulted when you began to discuss and then draw up a contract with Pat Lyndon—a rather important contract, involving a sizable investment? Am I or am I not the president of the Business and Professional Magazine Division? And if I am, then isn't the Pat Lyndon situation my supervisory responsibility?"

"Of course it is, Don, and I really don't know why you weren't involved. Jack Harding has had more to do with it than I have. He has had his finger in the international division. Don, I don't want to run Modern Medicine—no more than I want to operate MFI. It's your job. I'm sorry about the Pat Lyndon misunderstanding. What did Burt Cohen say?"

"Strange as it may seem, Burt says he, too, thought that I had received a copy of the report. But neither you nor Burt had ever asked my advice, although in fairness to Burt, it was from him that I learned about the contract planned for Pat. He called me to ask me what I thought about the contract. I was embarrassed to tell him that I had not seen a copy of the contract, nor the report. Eventually, he sent me a copy of the report and the draft of the contract. But is this the way to run a business?"

Marvin just looked at me—a little sadly—but said nothing. I continued: "You know, Marv, that I was never officially elected president of the division. Consistent with my contract, I just assumed the authority and the responsibility. But I've had to contend with many roadblocks. It took a year and a lot of pressure on my part before I was able to take the needed action to find and appoint a new publisher on *Dental Survey*.

I had to contend with the miasmas of Jay Herz, and the damaging situation brought about by the employment of his very sick son. I could go on listing problem after problem, obstacle after obstacle. But, despite all this, despite all of the unnecessary, harmful encumbrances, I was able to bring the Modern Medicine operation to its present spectacular position, with *Modern Medicine* now being the strong Number Two book in the field—in a highly competitive area with a great proliferation of new magazines each fighting for a share of the market. And when we took it over, it was slipping badly and fast. Profits this year will be about two million dollars before taxes as against $250,000 in 1967, the year before we acquired it."

Again, Marvin just sat there, looking sad and saying nothing. I continued: "Well, things can't go on this way much longer. If they do, you'll have a very unhappy manager on your hands, and the business is bound to suffer. At any rate, I can't continue under the present deteriorating circumstances. So, I have a sporting offer to make to you."

Marvin looked up, wondering what I would be saying next.

"I'm prepared to buy back the entire division—or at least MFI."

"It would take a lot of cash to buy Modern Medicine," were Whatmore's first words.

"I can raise the cash. In the case of MFI, I would like to trade you my stock in Cowles for this part of the business."

"I'm sorry, Don, we can't accept the stock. Under the terms of our loan agreement with IDS (Investors Diversified Services), we are not permitted to trade in our own stock. So, it would have to be a cash deal. Don, you're giving me plenty to think about. Let me give your proposition all of the thought it needs, and then I will take it up with the executive committee and let you know our decision. I'm terribly sorry, Don, that things have not worked out to your satisfaction—the way you hoped for. It is always enjoyable to meet and talk with you."

That was the end of the meeting. I was stunned. Whatmore did not seem surprised by my "sporting offer." And he made no move, said nothing to try to change my mind. He seemed to welcome the idea of a buy-back. When I left his office, I felt both relieved and saddened. Relieved that a buy-back—at least of MFI—was now a distinct possibility. And saddened that that man with whom I had worked so closely during the past three-and-a-half years, and for whom I had so much respect, did not make a single move to try to talk me out of leaving the company via a buy-back.

A week later, Whatmore called me, advising that he had given our discussion of the week before "a lot of thought" and then presented the matter to the executive committee. It was decided that they would not sell Modern Medicine—to me, or anyone else—but that they would consider selling me back MFI.

"Don, why don't we set a date—say, some time next week—and you come over for a meeting with me and Jack. Do you think you will be able to make a specific offer?"

"Yes," I said quickly. And a date was set for the following Tuesday, March 3, at 10 A.M. Before the meeting, I had to resolve two questions. What would be a price that I could live with and that Whatmore and Harding would accept, and where would I get the money? The question of price was not too difficult to resolve, at least in my mind. I could not possibly pay more than $1,500,000, and $1,250,000 would be fine. I would offer them $750,000 in cash, and $500,000 in notes to be paid off in five years. Where do I get

$750,000 in cash, or $1,000,000, if that should become the amount they insisted on as the minimum cash requirement? I decided to meet with Bill Lyon, regional vice president of the Irving Trust Company, who was in charge of five of the bank's branches, including the one with which we were doing business (at 245 Park Avenue), fairly new and one of the bank's largest and most affluent. I had known Bill for about five years, having met him when he was vice president and manager of the Park Avenue branch and we had moved our account there from the Rockefeller Center branch on West 51 Street. Magazines For Industry had been a depositor at Irving Trust for about twenty years and our record was good. We have carried nice balances— over $100,000 for the past five or more years—and the only loan we had made ($75,000) had been paid on time, and long ago. The bank had been making money on our account. Of course, money was becoming very tight in March of 1970, but I felt confident that Irving Trust would come to our help.

The meeting with Bill Lyon proved encouraging. Bill had called in one of his associates, an executive involved in corporate financing. In confidence, I explained what I had in mind, and what I was planning to do.

"Bill, I will need a million dollars in cash to swing the deal. What can Irving do for me?"

Bill Lyon is an unusual breed of cat for a bank executive. He is an optimist, enthusiastic, and neither looks nor talks like a bank VP of his stature. Before going into banking, he had been in the business world. And now in his early fifties, he was not quite certain whether he wanted to remain in banking or return to business management. He is affable, extroverted, interested in the arts, especially the theater, and he likes people and involvement with people.

His answer to my question was neither a direct yes

or no. Instead, he smiled broadly, and said: "So, at this time of the game, you want to buy back your business? You have a lot of courage. I'm all for it. And the way you describe the situation, you're doing the right thing. Don, we will do everything we can to help. Money is very tight, as you know, and getting tighter each day, but there are a number of ways of solving this problem . . . Eurodollars, private investors, the route of investment banking, equity financing, and several other approaches. We haven't seen your figures for some time, so why don't you let us take a look at some recent earning statements and your balance sheet, and by the time you have a definite deal with Cowles, we will try to set up the best financing program for you. So go to it, Don."

"Do you think that I ought to visit with Doug McNamara downtown in the meantime?" I asked.

"By all means. I'll tell him of our meeting. You call him and see if you can have lunch with him. Of course, you know that Mac has been under the weather during the past few months. He may need some surgery before long."

Unlike Bill Lyon, Douglas McNamara was more the typical banker—serious, conservative, forever thinking in terms of dollar investment and dollar returns. But like Bill, Mac was also a fine human being, considering the human factor in a loan transaction just as much as the profit-and-loss and the balance sheet.

I had known Mac since the early fifties and had been following his career at Irving Trust since that time. And he, in turn, had been keeping in touch with the growth of our company. When I first met Mac, he was vice president and manager of the Rockefeller Center branch where we had our account, when our offices were located at 18 East 49th Street and then at 660 Madison

Avenue. It was in 1960 that both Mac and I had to make an important decision—I as a borrower and Mac as a lender. We had launched *Food and Drug Packaging* in the fall of 1959, taking a giant but very risky step in moving from a small but profitable business magazine company, with annual volume of about $600,-000, to a breakthrough into "the big league."

The idea for *Food and Drug Packaging* came to me after our deal fell through to buy Breskin Publications (publishers of *Modern Packaging* and *Modern Plastics*) and after we failed to go public. By that time, I had gotten a taste of the packaging business and viewed it as a fine growth potential for a magazine. After a great deal of thought, and after talking the subject over at length with Burt Gussow, who was now ready to leave his job with Breskin and come with us to develop such a new magazine, I concluded it would be far better to create a specialized periodical than to compete with *Modern Packaging* and two other all-packaging national publications directly.

Burt thought we would do better if we started a plastics magazine, but I preferred the packaging field. When I discovered that the food and drug industries accounted for seventy to eighty percent of packaging materials and equipment purchasing and use, I decided that this was going to be our area of coverage. And since our experience was in the biweekly news magazine field, and there was no biweekly packaging publication, our new magazine was to be a biweekly, the size of our other two periodicals (slightly smaller than tabloid). And the name *Food and Drug Packaging* seemed to be a natural. Burt liked the idea and the approach, and on July 1, 1959, he left Breskin and started to work for us on the new project. He took with him Herb Friedman of the Breskin sales department, who became *Food and Drug Packaging*'s midwestern

manager. We staffed modestly and set the date for our
first issue as November 12, which gave us very little
time, but kept our start-up cost to a minimum.

Because we were overcrowded at 18 East 49 Street,
we moved into new, attractive and spacious offices in
the new Getty building at 660 Madison Avenue—at a
much higher rent than we were paying in the old building on 49 Street. And, for the first time, we used a
designer and architect to design our offices. This also
meant buying new furniture. While we kept our costs
down, they still represented a sizable, though necessary
and valuable, investment. Although I had a surplus of
about $250,000—built up over the fifteen years since
we launched our business on June 1, 1944—I was more
than a little scared. It was a tremendous step.

We did well with our first issue, but it soon became
apparent that we could not make it in 1960. Breaking
into the packaging field, even with a great salesman
like Burt, was not going to be a snap. It would take a
lot of work, time and plenty of money. Midway in
1960, our surplus had dwindled. All we had left now
was $75,000. And while both *Candy Industry* and
Bottling Industry were profitable, the profits from these
publications were not sufficient to support the new and
upcoming little "giant." If we were to continue with the
new magazine, the only answer was a bank loan. We
had no loans outstanding, and I had a dislike of getting
banks involved in our business. Even under the most
favorable conditions, I viewed such a step as restrictive.
Banks had to see profit-and-loss statements and balance
sheets, and banks that lend money to a business usually
insist upon required amounts of working capital and
place restrictions on certain expenditures. As an entrepreneur over the previous fifteen-year period, I had
tried to avoid "going to the bank." But there was not
much choice. I knew that the $75,000 we had left in

our surplus would go at a fast pace in the months ahead. I had to have at least another $75,000—or abandon the new baby at this juncture to save our two seasoned and profitable magazines. And so I arranged a meeting with Douglas McNamara. The date was set by Art Keller, a young assistant vice president who was in charge of our account and with whom I had been friendly over the past few years. I brought with me a copy of our audited annual statement for fiscal 1958, which ended May 31, which was fairly impressive. I explained to them that the 1959 statement would not be as good, although it would still show a profit, but that the 1960 figures would not be good since this report would reflect our investment in the new property. They knew about my negotiations with Breskin and, as a result, were able to share my enthusiasm for the potential of *Food and Drug Packaging*.

"How much money do you think you will need before you will break even with the new magazine?" Mac asked me.

"I will need another $75,000—on top of the $75,000 I have left from our surplus," I replied. "And this is the amount of the loan I would like, a loan to be paid off in three years. The prime rate of interest is 5 percent. You may charge me 5¼ but not much more."

Mac smiled and said: "OK, Don, we'll see what we can do. You will hear from us shortly."

Within two days, Art Keller telephoned and said that Mac had approved our loan for $75,000, for three years, but that the interest rate would be 5½ percent, and he hoped that I didn't think I was being overcharged. "Mac likes you, Don," he said, "and he thinks that you'll make it with the new magazine."

I liked Mac, too. We were contemporaries. He was a year and a half older than I was and, while our backgrounds were quite different, we had appreciation and respect for each other. I knew that Mac would be moving up at Irving Trust. And he did.

For the past five years, Mac had been senior vice president in charge of the loan department at 1 Wall Street, the bank's headquarters. Every loan of any consequence at any of Irving Trust's branches required his approval.

So, after talking with Marvin Whatmore, I telephoned Mac and we made a date for lunch for Wednesday, March 11.

I was warmly greeted by Mac when I arrived on the tenth floor of the 1 Wall Street building. We chatted for a while in his large conservatively appointed office. Then he showed me around and introduced me to his first assistant, after which we took the elevator to the top floor to the executive dining room for lunch. Only the most important clients and friends of the bank were invited to lunch in this well-appointed, very dignified dining club. The food and service proved to be superb.

While this was Doug McNamara all right, he was not quite the same spirited, enthusiastic, forward-looking banker I had known in the fifties and the sixties. He was still thin and pleasant. But it was obvious that he was not enjoying good health. But the more significant change that I noticed was his feeling of deep bearishness about our economy, the dollar and the banking business. As the chief loan officer of this highly respected, but very conservative bank, Mac must have gone through hell in "being forced" (as he put it) to disapprove so many big loans to so many important customers, in this critical period of tight money.

"Don, in my forty years of banking, I have never experienced this unbelievably tight, this terribly critical dollar situation," he said, looking weary and forlorn. "And it is world wide. Worse still, I can't see any improvement for years on end, and I am sorry to say that I have no reason to have any great confidence in our Administration in Washington."

I felt discouraged, but I proceeded to tell him the purpose of my visit. I relayed to him the problems that had been developing at Cowles.

"To buy back our business, Mac, I will need at least $1,000,000 in cash. From what you have told me, it is going to be a most difficult task to find that million, but there is no one who can help me better than you can, who knows as much as you do about obtaining funds in this difficult period. Of course, I must say Bill Lyons seemed encouraging."

"Bill called me and told me of your conversation. Of course, you know, Don, that as a Federal Reserve bank we are not permitted to lend money to buy a business, so we will have to get the money for you elsewhere. You have an established business and you have a good record over the past twenty-five years, so a way can and will be found to get you the money to buy back your company from Cowles. You may have to give up some equity, but that shouldn't bother you too much, since, under any circumstances, you will retain control. Maybe the pension funds of some of the companies with which I am acquainted would be interested. Let me give this thing some deep thought. Let me inquire around and, in the meantime, to bring me up-to-date, send me recent figures—going back five years, if possible—on Magazines For Industry, and I will see what I can do. You can be sure, Don, that I'll do everything possible to get you the money you need to buy back your business. You are doing what you have to do."

Mac said that he would call me in a week with some specific recommendations.

Precisely one week later, he called to advise me that the route to obtain needed financing for my buy-back, in his opinion, should be investment banking. Our deal was too small for a company the size of White, Weld, but a somewhat smaller company, he thought, might be interested. He said that he put to work a team of two young Wall Street investment-banking-oriented executives of Irving Trust, and he asked me to meet with them for immediate action.

I met with Jim Stewart and Henry Frommer that very afternoon. Directed by the bank's senior vice president in charge of the loan department to find suitable financing for me, these two capable bankers wasted no time. Jim Stewart (in his mid-thirties) was the older of the two, and he was a vice president. He was the very model of the up-and-coming young banker. He talked formally; he dressed conservatively; and he behaved courteously—all business, no small talk, and to the point. Henry Frommer was a different sort of man. He was in his twenties, and he was an assistant vice president, after two years with the bank. He was genuinely warm and friendly and he wanted to know more about the human element of the problem than about money per se. He was enthusiastic about the project, and was taken with both the challenge and the potentials involved. As the senior of the team, Jim wanted to take a crack at my problem first.

"We have several potential investors for you, Mr. Gussow," he said, "but the one that appeals to me most is a newcomer to the field of equity financing. The organization is headed by a young man who enlisted several other young investment managers to form a new company just a year ago. They are eager and sophisticated, and they have just completed an interesting buy-back program. I have just turned them down on a loan, and here I am, going to give them an opportunity for some new business. I turned them down on the loan because the figures and the proposition involved just did not fit into our banking picture under today's tight money situation. But I think this is a smart little investment company that may well be going places in the years ahead. The company is called Gibbons, Green, Laupheimer and Rice. How does this sound to you, Mr. Gussow?"

"It does make sense and if you think well of them, why not start right here?" As I was speaking, a flash went through my mind: Psychologically, this seems like a wrong approach. If Irving Trust turned down Gibbons on its loan request, then Gibbons, at least unconsciously, might end up giving Jim Stewart a dose of his own medicine. And then I had a second thought: Then again, Gibbons might try to make an impression on Irving Trust and go all out on this deal.

Jim Stewart then and there called Ed Gibbons and a date was set for later in the week in my office.

"Now, don't worry, Don," Henry Frommer said, "we have several good prospects for you. If the Gibbons negotiations do not work out, we'll be ready with the others—firms such as Oppenheimer. We'll get you the money all right. Doug McNamara speaks very highly of you and your business. We'll find a way."

On the appointed morning, Ed Gibbons came, bringing with him two young assistants, a mod-looking young man in his early twenties, and a very attractive young girl who talked and looked as if she had just graduated from Vassar—or perhaps Sarah Lawrence.

Ed Gibbons was thirty-five and looked and talked like a banker-turned-businessman, or vice versa. I was not quite sure. He explained that he and his associates had been connected with McDonnell and Company, the first major investment banking/brokerage company to develop financial problems and eventually liquidate its business, and later with Blyth and Company. A year ago, they started their own business to operate exclusively in the private investment capital field. They were not members of any exchanges. They preferred to operate privately on a very special, selective basis. He left with me a copy of the plan which represented their first and only successful buy-back program, mentioned by Jim Stewart, and asked me to provide them with basic financial statements, plus a review of our business and plans for the future.

"After we have had an opportunity to review the material, my assistants will meet with you to ask a series of questions, after which we will look at the entire picture and shortly after that, we will let you know whether we will be able to take on your deal—and under what conditions," Ed Gibbons said.

So began the work of obtaining the million dollars that I needed to buy back Magazines For Industry, Inc., as it was now constituted as a wholly-owned subsidiary of Cowles Communications, Inc. The date was March 19, 1970, and the days and weeks began to pass before me with a speed that seemed more like a dream than reality.

"We'll get you an answer in forty-eight hours" was soon stretched to two weeks. "We'll have definite word for you in a week" soon became five weeks. And all during that time, I was involved in more meetings, many telephone calls, a long series of letters and memos, and the endless preparation of financial statements and projections.

After eight weeks, one day, and five hours, Ed Gibbons called me (after several telephone calls from me) and said: "Could I see you Friday morning (it was then Wednesday afternoon)?" He did not seem very happy. We made a date.

On Friday morning, Ed came, with just one of his assistants this time, a pretty girl, Josie Sentner. They sat in the two chairs facing my desk. The girl placed a large manila envelope stuffed with papers on my desk in front of her. Ed began: "We like your field, Mr. Gussow. We learned a lot about business magazines from you and others whom we interviewed, and we think MFI has growth potential. We like your firm. I think you will do well with your buy-back—but I am afraid that we cannot be of help to you at this time. The money market has just about dried up during the past five weeks and what we were able to do then, we cannot do now. If your company had much higher profit, maybe . . . but even then, I am not quite sure. The money situation is really devastatingly tight now and is bound to get worse. We are new and small, as you know, and we have to be very careful. We may have to wait out this period altogether. We can earn ten percent without doing anything. I'm sorry, Mr. Gussow, we would have enjoyed working with you in this very interesting project." The girl said nothing. She just looked sad and pretty. They got up. She left the manila envelope stuffed with all the material I had sent her over the past five weeks, and they left.

"Let's keep in touch," Ed Gibbons said.

It was a sad morning—despite the fact that it was a beautiful day and my office was filled with sunshine.

What to do now? Give up? Or continue with the task of finding that elusive million in this outrageously tight money market?

I asked Nancy to get me Jim Stewart.

"Jim is away from his desk. This is Henry Frommer," I soon heard over my telephone. "I'm sorry about Gibbons. Ed had called Jim and told him of his decision. It's too bad. But don't worry, Don. Jim has asked me to handle your situation now and I am very enthusiastic about it. I have several very good leads. I'm going to explore them, and I will call you back early next week."

On Tuesday of the following week he called, sounding very excited: "I have good news for you, Don. I've found an investment banking company that is not only enthusiastic about your deal, but seems to be just right for you. It's a good company, one of the larger ones on the Street, as a matter of fact, and fortunately, they've done well during the last year, while so many investment bankers have had one of the roughest periods of their careers. The firm is Carl Marks and Company. Have you heard of them? . . . Bob Davidoff, vice president and head of their venture capital division, is awaiting my call to set a date with you."

I had heard of Carl Marks, of course, but it seemed strange that of all the Wall Street investment banking firms, Irving Trust would pick this unusual, more or less heretical outfit, certainly not one of the typically conservative, "establishment" investing banking operations.

"It sounds very good to me. Of course, I've heard of Carl Marks," I said, "I will be most pleased to meet with Bob Davidoff almost any time you can set a date."

"I must warn you, Don, that you will not be able to get exactly what you want—$1,000,000 for 40 percent of your company as you suggested—but I believe that you will get an offer of a fair deal, and Carl Marks is a fine company, well-financed, with about $35,000,000 in capital and more imaginative than most investment companies in setting up workable programs. Bob Davidoff is a good guy to work with. Most important of all, he seems to have an appreciation of your company and your buy-back concept."

The date with Bob Davidoff was made for May 29, 1970, which meant another in a long series of "lost weekends" for me. I had been in the habit of doing important things promptly—right now or tomorrow at the latest. The more I wanted quick action on the buy-back program, the more delays I seemed to encounter. Instead of "let's meet tomorrow," it was always "let's make it next week." Days turned into weeks, and weeks turned into months, and the number of "lost weekends" mounted—a waiting period for an important meeting on Monday or Tuesday or Wednesday always seemed to follow a preliminary discussion on a Wednesday, Thursday or Friday.

The meeting with Bob Davidoff in the Carl Marks conference room was pleasant and productive. I had met Henry Frommer at Irving Trust a few minutes earlier for a preliminary briefing and then we walked over to 20 Broad Street, just around the corner from the bank. And the building was very familiar to me since it housed White, Weld and Company, where I had been many times and, until recently, Goldman, Sachs and Company, where we made the deal with Cowles. The Carl Marks offices resembled the former Goldman, Sachs offices more than those of White, Weld—although not by much. The Carl Marks offices were the most crowded and most plebeian of the three. And Bob Davidoff was friendly and receptive. He was quite different from "Bus" Hovey and his associates of White, Weld and also different from John Weinberg and his group of men at Goldman, Sachs. Yet, all three were in the same business.

Joining us at the initial meeting was Harry Wise, Bob Davidoff's young, bright and sophisticated assistant. Bob was in his middle or late forties, tall, conservatively dressed but with longish sideburns. He had the ability to cut through red tape quickly and get to the nub of a situation without wasting a word or gesture. Harry was a member of the new breed of young Wall Street investment executives. Harvard Business School-trained, with a computer-oriented mind. But he was dressed a bit in the current mod style, and he had longish hair and sideburns. He was also interested in the arts, particularly in the theater, and said that he was a personal friend of Clive Barnes, the *New York Times* drama critic, and of course, he was acquainted with the *Times* writings and reviews of my son Mel who, while not *the* drama critic, was a drama critic and theater specialist for the *Times*.

After the briefest exchange of amenities, Bob Davidoff got right down to specifics: "Don, I have studied the financials of your company, which Henry let me have. Tell me, why do you think 40 percent of your company is worth $1,000,000, which in effect, places a total value for your whole company at $2,500,000?"

It was a good, logical and direct question, and I was not surprised that he had asked it. I was ready with an answer.

"Based on current earnings—and even the projection for the rest of this year—our company is not worth $2,500,000, certainly not under today's tight money situation, when you can buy good companies on the basis of ten times earnings or better," I replied, "but based on what I can do with this business and based on my performance with the entire Business and Professional Magazine Division of Cowles which I developed and operate, I think a million dollars for 40 percent of our business is a good deal. Given the proper atmosphere following the buy-back, and needed capital to expand, I believe that within three to five years I can build the new MFI into a ten-million-dollar operation, with operating profits before taxes of at least a million and a half." I then proceeded to elaborate on some of our plans for MFI, an outline of which he had before him.

Before the meeting of an hour or so was over, it was apparent that Bob Davidoff was as impressed with me as I was with him.

"How old are you Don?" he asked me.

"Sixty-two going on forty-nine" was my immediate

response and he chuckled, as did the others in the room.

"You sound more like forty-nine than sixty-two," Harry Wise commented.

"You have the spirit of a much younger person," Bob added.

"So, where do we go from here?" Henry Frommer asked.

"We like what we have seen and what we've heard," Bob replied. "Give us two weeks and we will give our answer."

"Does that mean that you are interested in pursuing it?" Henry asked.

"If our answer were no, we could have told you this right now, so, obviously, we are interested."

"Time is of the essence," Henry said. "Could you give us an answer in less than two weeks—next week, perhaps?"

"I will try, but it's doubtful. There is some work we must do. Let's say, we'll come back at you in ten days."

Ten days soon stretched to two weeks. Then followed a visit to my office and a luncheon meeting that included Marvin Toben at the Marco Polo Club, then another few days passed—and finally, almost three weeks after our initial meeting, Bob Davidoff said that he had his answer . . . could I meet him the next morning?

"Here's the deal as we see it—and which we are ready to undertake," Bob said, as we met again in the Carl Marks conference room on the morning of June 17. Harry Wise and Henry Frommer again make up the foursome.

"Don, you go to Cowles and tell them that you are ready to buy the company for $750,000—that, and no more—take it or leave it."

"But the price they are asking is $1,500,000 or possibly $1,250,000. They will think that I am out of my mind when I offer them $750,000," I said.

"I know this sounds like real chutzpah—but you have to have chutzpah—and besides you will be ready to offer them $750,000 in cash. Considering the liquidity problems Cowles has now, even $750,000 in cash could look good to them. Anyway, it will not hurt to try. All they can say is 'No'."

"And what if Cowles' answer is a resounding 'No'?" I asked.

"Let's try and find out," Bob said. "Now, here is our deal. Here is how you will have $750,000 in cash to offer to Cowles. We are prepared to make you a long-term loan of $400,000 at eight percent, amortized over a period of six years. We will also receive seven year warrants for which (if we should decide to exercise) we will receive 25 percent of your company at a total cost to us of $83,333 for the warrants. You will obtain $250,000 from a number of 'insiders'—executives of your company—and in return give them 25 percent interest. You will retain 50 percent of the company."

It was a tough deal and one which depended on a number of very questionable "ifs." If I could obtain $250,000 in cash from a group of insiders, if I could sell Marvin Whatmore and his associates on accepting an offer of $750,000 for MFI period, and a few more "ifs," including the practicability of making the annual interest and amortization payments on the $400,000 loan, and there was one more "if"—

"This makes it $650,000," Henry Frommer said. "Where will the other $100,000 come from?"

"That's where the bank comes in," Bob said, with a smile. "I will expect Irving Trust to provide $100,000 in revolving credit."

"Why don't you have lunch with me and meet some of the other fellows at the bank?" Henry asked Bob.

"Does this mean that the bank will pay for my lunch? I accept."

The weekend of June 20 and 21 was another in the long series of "lost weekends" for me. Of all the difficulties I had to overcome during the previous three or four months in my efforts to buy back our company from Cowles, none proved as challenging and threatening as the one that was thrown at me several days earlier.

At nine thirty on Wednesday morning, June 24, I had met with Marvin Whatmore and during the hour or so that followed, I told him a little of the grief I had gone through in my effort to develop the needed buy-back financing.

"There is no need for me to tell you that to obtain $500,000 today is as difficult as getting $5,000,000 under normal circumstances," I said. "You have been in the money market, you know. Anyway, I have a deal at last, and I'd like to tell you about it. It is not a great deal but it's the best that I have been able to obtain, and in some ways I feel embarrassed to offer it to you. However, I have found a way of sweetening the deal a little, and I also have an alternate proposal."

This preamble followed several previous chats with Marvin in which I hammered away at the fact that my leverage had been dissipated because of the sharp decline in the price of Cowles stock. I had to use that stock as collateral and it had slid from an average price of about $15 a share to $8 when I started talking to Whatmore at the turn of the year, to $3.50.

I said: "Whereas my 94,000 shares of Cowles stock were worth more than $1,500,000 about a year ago and $700,000 to $800,000 when we started talking 'buy-back' in March, the stock is now worth less than $350,000," I pointed out. "Anyway, I do have a deal and this is it: through the efforts of the Irving Trust

Company, the investment banking firm of Carl Marks and Company has agreed to give me a six-year loan (at eight percent) of $400,000, for which they will also receive seven year warrants to buy 25 percent of MFI for $83,333, the Marks loan to be made with my 94,000 shares of Cowles stock as collateral. Additionally, Irving Trust will provide a revolving credit of $100,000, thus providing outside financing of $500,-000. Carl Marks also suggested that we obtain $250,000 in investment from a number of 'insiders'—several MFI executives and possibly one or more of my personal friends. And this has now been arranged.

"When I first met with Carl Marks, I was asked what I considered a fair value for MFI and I replied that a fair price would be $1,250,000 and I also explained the basis for my evaluation and answered to the best of my ability.

"Bob Davidoff of Carl Marks told me, 'Don, maybe insofar as the future is concerned—possible future earnings, that is—MFI could be worth $1,250,000 or more, but based on today's earnings and past performance—and we must deal with today's and not tomorrow's earnings—MFI is not worth more than $750,000.'

"So, Marv, that is the best I can do—offer you $750,000 in cash, period, for MFI. However, I feel that that is too low a price regardless of current and past earnings and as a result, I would like to sweeten the deal by offering you ten percent of net profits each year for the next five years. This ten percent may not be very meaningful in the first or even the second year after the buy-back, but it could become very meaningful once we begin to build back MFI the way I built the Cowles Business and Professional Magazine Division. My goal is sales of more than $15,000,000, with pre-tax profits of $2,500,000. This is the worst of times to finance the buying of a business, but there is every reason to believe that our economy will make a complete turnaround in the next five years, possibly by 1972, and in the meantime we will tighten up our operation to maximize profits."

After asking a few technical questions, Marvin finally said: "Don, you have given me a lot to think about. I will call a meeting of the executive committee to discuss your proposition in detail. Jack Harding is in London, but he's expected to return on Friday. I will let you know our answer in three to four days." It turned out to be a long "four days."

In the meantime, I had called a meeting for Monday, July 6, of the same week at 5 P.M., of eight MFI executives—Jack Mulligan, Burt Gussow, Jerry Stevens, Marv Toben, Herb Friedman, Howard Grant, Jay Sandler and Saul Tarter—to tell them of my plans to buy back MFI and invite each of them to become an "insider" with an investment of $25,000 for 2½ percent of the total new stock outstanding following the buy-back.

I had called the meeting by means of a memo to each on June 26, the day before Betty and I left for San Francisco to attend the fiftieth anniversary convention and exposition of the Retail Confectioners International. I explained that the purpose of the meeting would be to discuss the future of MFI and their part in it. Naturally, the memo hit each of them like a bomb. Conjecture and speculation ensued, and since I was not there, they could not rush into my office (Burt had the habit of doing this more than the others) and ask questions. Obviously, it would be wrong for any of them to call me in San Francisco and ask, "What's up?" None did, not even Burt or Jerry, who might have found some excuse for calling. Nancy, my secretary, was away that week on vacation, and they were unable to try prying any answer from her. In any event, they would not have gotten very far.

Jetting home from San Francisco, I read a headline in the *Wall Street Journal* that stopped me cold. It read: "Cowles Selling San Juan Star to Capital Cities Broadcasting; Needs Cash to Improve Liquidity." It was strange for me to read this piece of momentous news 35,000 feet in the air—especially since I was a member of the board of directors of Cowles. But then, I had learned a long time ago that the controlled Cowles board merely serves as a legal rubber stamp to approve action taken by the executive committee which, in turn, is a rubber stamp for the decisions made by Chairman Gardner Cowles.

I showed the item to Betty, who was just as shocked.

"What does it mean? Will it help or hurt our deal to buy back MFI?" she asked.

"I don't see how it can help—and it might hurt. For one thing, getting $10,000,000 for the *San Juan Star* means that temporarily, at least, Cowles is solving its serious liquidity problem. Now I can understand why Marvin Whatmore felt he had good news when I saw him before we left for San Francisco. He said that he had a meeting with officials of IDS (Investors Diversified Services) in Minneapolis, the bankers who hold $15,000,000 in long-term (ten years) notes from Cowles, the first note ($1,500,000) of which is due on May 1, 1971. The contract with IDS requires that Cowles maintain a minimum working capital of $23,-000,000. I knew that as of June 1 we no longer had this minimum working capital. This meant that IDS could call the entire loan in default and could insist on Cowles paying up the entire amount immediately."

"This sounds very serious. Could they really do it?" Betty asked me.

"Legally, IDS could do it, but practically it will not,

because it knows that Cowles does not have the money and IDS is not likely to put Cowles in bankruptcy. However, IDS could insist on a higher interest rate—upping it from the present 4⅞ to 9 percent or higher. However, Marvin told me that at the Minneapolis meeting, IDS gave Cowles until the end of the year to bring the working capital back to the minimum requirement of $23,000,000. But I could not understand why Marvin seemed to be so relaxed about this 'concession.' Naturally, I felt that he would have to find a way to get several million dollars quickly—either by new financing or by selling off one or more properties. And since this is not a good time to obtain new financing or to sell a communications property, he was definitely in a bind. Now I know why he felt he had good news. He knew that he was close to a deal to sell the *San Juan Star*. That would provide more than the dollars needed to put the working capital over the required minimum."

"But how does it affect us?"

"Now that Cowles has $10,000,000, an additional $750,000 or even another million is of no great consequence. So, he might call off our deal. In another sense, the selling of the *San Juan Star,* a prime property, a good profit-maker with even greater growth, is a destructive if not a desperate step. And many within the company as well as outside it will now ask, 'What will Cowles sell next?' "

The implications of the news spoiled the rest of the trip for me. I usually feel relaxed on a trip like that. I find it restful, and after a drink, dinner and the movies, I usually take a nap and wake up rested. I could not nap, I could not concentrate on the drink, food or movie. I brooded on the possible dire implications of the sale of the *San Juan Star*—to Cowles, to the price of our stock, and finally to our pending buy-back of MFI and I tried to find possible solutions.

When I returned home, I found a batch of mail and other material from the office—just about everything that had reached my desk during the few days that I had been away. Included were two memos from Whatmore which attempted to explain the reason for the sale of the only English language daily of Puerto Rico —one memo to top executives, the other memo to all employees. Ironically, the second contained a better clue than the first to the reason for selling. The memo follows:

July 1, 1970

TO: Employees of Cowles Communications, Inc.

FROM: Marvin C. Whatmore

Earlier today, joint announcement was made of an agreement in principle for the sale of all of the stock of Star Publishing Corporation, publisher of *The San Juan Star,* by Cowles Communications to Capital Cities Broadcasting Corporation.

Capital Cities, which owns Fairchild Publications, Inc., *The Pontiac Press* (Pontiac, Mich.), eleven radio and five television stations in major markets, is known for the high quality of its operations. It is pledged to continue *The Star*'s dedication to public service—a dedication that won for it the highly prestigious Pulitzer Prize in 1961, just two years after its founding by Cowles Communications. The present top management and editorial policies of *The Star* will also be continued.

Despite our attachment to *The Star,* we accepted the offer of Capital Cities because it was simply too attractive to turn down. We believe this sale will benefit the entire Company by improving our corporate liquidity.

This was the July Fourth weekend and there wasn't much I could do except to anticipate reactions at the meetings I had set up with our own insiders and with the Carl Marks group. Another meeting with Whatmore was also in the offing, but no date had been set. It was not easy to divert my mind from the seriousness of the situation that I faced in the days ahead. But visits with Alan and his family, talking things out, reading, going for walks, seeing a movie helped a little to keep my mind off the main issue. My life's work and our financial security built over a twenty-five year period were threatened.

The book I found myself reading that weekend was *The Decline and Fall* by Otto Friedrich which dealt with the story of the *Saturday Evening Post,* with emphasis on its death throes. While I tried hard not to see any similarities between the problems faced by Curtis in its decline and those of Cowles, I could not help but conclude that the sale of the *San Juan Star*—an important, valuable, profitable asset—resembled the selling off of several important, valuable assets by Curtis. If Curtis had changed the direction of the *Saturday Evening Post* years previously or had sold or dropped that magazine instead of selling off valuable, profitable assets, the formerly great Curtis Publishing Company could have been revived and sustained. Despite the many costly complexities and painful emotional problems involved in taking such a step, the most practical, realistic move for Cowles at this time was to sell, drop or spin-off *Look* magazine. I had made the spin-off suggestion on a number of occasions at board meetings—to deaf ears. Cowles could have rebuilt the rest of the assets, most of which were sound and profitable. Instead, Cowles was beginning to follow the same route which led not only to the demise of the *Saturday Evening Post* but the ruination of the Curtis Publishing Company. While I hated to think of it in this fashion, I could not help feeling that the sale of the *San Juan Star* was the first direct step in the eventual ruination of Cowles Communications, Inc., which had so much going for it when I merged our company with it near the end of 1966. Outside of a costly proxy fight, there was not much I could do to stop this unnecessary destruction of a potentially great communications company. The only thing I could do was to continue with my plan to buy back MFI, rebuild it and then try to make up for the three years that I had lost during my association with Cowles. The weeks ahead were to be eventful.

EIGHT:

How to Get Venture Capital in a Tight Money Market

The first thing I did on Monday morning, July 6, was to call Marvin Whatmore to find out whether we had a deal. When could we get together? He said that he would call me.

Promptly at five o'clock, our eight insiders gathered in my office to learn about the future of MFI and their part in it. By this time—largely because of the news break on the sale of the *San Juan Star*—they thought they had a pretty good idea of what the meeting was about. However, except for Marvin Toben, my first assistant and confidant, none of the others actually knew. Some had guessed that I would announce that MFI had a new owner—some other publishing house such as Harcourt, Brace & Jovanovich, as one rumor had it. Others guessed that the meeting would deal with a possible buy-back—but how, and for how much?

My preamble was short. I reviewed the objectives of the sale of MFI to Cowles and touched on the situation as it existed at that time. Then I moved on to the current situation at Cowles as it affected our business.

"Because of a series of serious and costly mistakes made by Cowles during the past few years, we can no longer grow—neither MFI nor our division as a whole. Cowles has no money and you cannot use depressed stock ($3.50 a share today) to buy other magazines and/or publishing companies. More serious is the threat to our business we now face. Anything could happen from now on and I just cannot sit and wait for the possible destruction of our business, a business that I started twenty-five years ago and which we worked so hard to build . . . so, we are buying back our company. It has taken me five months to do it—first to get Cowles to sell it to me and then to obtain needed financing."

I paused for a minute, giving the eight prospective investors and key executives an opportunity to grasp the full meaning of what I was saying. Then I continued:

"Obtaining financing today—cold hard cash—is a most difficult task. I used just two sources: White, Weld, and Irving Trust. Through the help of Doug McNamara, senior VP, in charge of the loan department of Irving Trust, I have been able to obtain needed basic financing. Fortunately for us, I knew Doug McNamara when he was VP and manager of the Irving Trust branch on West 51 Street when MFI banked there. We became good friends and I continued my friendship with him as he moved up in the bank's hierarchy. Doug put two of his bright Wall Street-oriented young men on the job of securing financing for me. The younger of the two, Henry Frommer, took a special interest in our project and it was he who found and interested Carl Marks and Company in our proposition. Carl Marks will provide $400,000 as a loan, using my stock in Cowles as collateral. Irving Trust will make available to us a revolving credit of $100,000, or more, if necessary. Both the Carl Marks people and I felt that it would be a good idea to obtain about $250,000 from 'insiders'—mostly several key executives of our company. What I would like is an investment of about $25,000 from each of you. We have scheduled a meeting tomorrow morning at ten at the offices of Carl Marks. We will meet with Bob Davidoff, vice president, a partner, and head of its venture capital department, and one of his associates. Our financing program will be explained more fully and you will have a chance to ask questions."

"Will we have to commit ourselves tomorrow morning?" Burt asked.

"No. You will have several days to make a decision . . . and then sufficient time to obtain the needed funds to participate."

"Will our jobs depend on whether we participate or not?" Jay asked.

"No. . . . You did not get your job by investing in MFI and I see no reason why you should be required to become an investor now to keep your job. You will invest only if you want to do it, if you are convinced that investing is good business, that it is a good investment."

"Don, this is obviously a good deal for you. You are not putting in any money but we have to put up cash," Burt said.

"That's true. But I am the founder of this business and I have spent five months in the attempt to obtain financing. Moreover, I am using all of my Cowles stock as collateral, and I am giving up my contract with Cowles. Cowles is not selling MFI. It was my idea to buy it and the deal that I developed with Cowles is something no one could have made. The Cowles people feel they owe me plenty. All that is being taken into consideration."

"Don, are you saying that you can buy MFI for $750,000?" Jerry asked.

"No. This is the minimum cash that we need. Cowles made an evaluation of our business and the price they want is $1,500,000," I explained.

"Then, where will you get the additional $750,000?" Herb asked.

"It will be my job to work it out with Whatmore. I have some ideas and I do not expect to pay as much as $1,500,000. Anyway, we will discuss it in detail at the offices of Carl Marks tomorrow morning."

"Burt is right. You have a good deal for yourself, but I am not sure it is so great for us. Most of us have our money invested in stock and this is no time to sell stock," Jerry said.

"Well, you could borrow on your stock. While normally $25,000 is not a lot of money—especially for men like yourselves who have been substantial earners for many years—I realize that it is a difficult time to obtain this fairly small sum today. But if anyone really wants to invest—if he believes that the investment is a good one—I'm sure that he'll be able to obtain the needed funds."

While I was not surprised at the reaction from our "insiders," I was disappointed. I had hoped they would react more positively. Why didn't at least one of them say: "Don, this is great. We're so glad that you're buying back MFI. We are with you one hundred percent." While most of them seemed glad that I was moving to repurchase MFI, no one except Marv Toben expressed the enthusiasm or exuded the confidence that I expected. When I confided to Marv that I was planning to buy back MFI—that was late in February—he smiled broadly and said: "This is great, absolutely great. If you had not taken this step, I was ready to make such a suggestion. We can't do it soon enough." And, of course, when he heard the details of the plan, he offered to invest $25,000 or possibly more.

Burt and Jerry could become troublemakers once again, I felt, just as they were in 1960 when I made a heroic effort to go public. They pushed for every possible advantage, bringing their lawyers, causing unnecessary delay, so that by the time we were ready for an offering, the original underwriter walked out of the deal. By the time we found another underwriter, it was too late. The market for new issues turned sour and, in the weeks that followed, collapsed.

Because the experience of 1960 was still vivid in my memory, I did not cherish the idea of inviting Burt and Jerry to become partners once again—even at only two and one-half percent stock ownership for each. Yet the proposal by Carl Marks to invite several executives to participate as investors did make sense and I had hoped they might react positively. Apparently, they had not changed.

Things were a little better at the meeting the next morning in the offices of Carl Marks and Company— but not much. While Carl Marks is a successful, fully capitalized investment banking house, it is quite different from firms such as White, Weld and Goldman, Sachs. Founded forty-six years ago by the late Carl Marks, a German Jew with a bent for finance, it operated almost exclusively as a dealer in foreign securities. The company branched out in the domestic field, involving itself in block securities placements, serving as a stockbroker, handling a few underwritings, merger and acquisition activities and investment banking operations, including venture capital utilization and placement, with much emphasis on venture capital deals during the last few years.

I found it interesting and perhaps even significant that the prestigious Wasp bank, Irving Trust Company, handled the deal. A junior executive who happened to be Jewish selected an aggressive, down-to-earth no-

nonsense Jewish investment bank to help us buy back
MFI.

Carl Marks and Company, Inc., at 20 Broad Street,
had a four by four anteroom. Beyond a cashier's cage
was what looked like a stockbrokerage boiler room,
with scores of men sitting at old, worn, nondescript
desks, talking over telephones, mostly in loud voices.
Several TV sets and other paraphernalia of the stockbroker's craft provided quotations and other information. It was bedlam.

There was no receptionist in the anteroom. You had
to buzz before you could be "invited" inside.

Security was tight. I buzzed the buzzer, a girl asked
our business. Within a few minutes Harry Wise, a tall,
bright young assistant of the corporate finance department, appeared. He invited us to a "conference room."
To get there, we had to maneuver through narrow aisles,
zigzag past decrepit desks, old filing cabinets and paper-
stuffed wastebaskets. The "conference room" was small
and poorly air-conditioned. A small round table and
unmatched chairs awaited us. There were not enough
chairs for the ten of us and several folding chairs were
brought in. Bob Davidoff soon entered and I began the
introductions.

"Don't bother, Don," he said, "I will forget the
names the moment you mention them. We'll get acquainted as we go along."

Bob remained standing. He reviewed the deal, explaining everything in as much detail as possible. He
then asked if there were any questions.

There were a lot of questions from just about everyone except Marv, who knew as much as I did about the
deal. Some of the questions: What happens if I am fired
or I leave—what happens to my stock? Is the plan to
expand and eventually go public? Where will we get the
funds? Is Carl Marks handling the deal alone or will

there be other investors? Don is not putting in any cash
—he is putting up his Cowles stock as collateral—
How does this work? Will the company be able to han-
dle the annual interest and amortization of the loan?
How much time do we have to make our commitments?
To provide the money?

From the questions I could tell who was able to provide the needed amount of money to cover his pledged
investment and who was in a bind. The questions also
revealed who was likely to invest. It was obvious that
Jerry Stevens was in a bind to obtain any money because of his pronouncement: "Before I can invest
$25,000, I will have to consult with my lawyer, my
accountant and my financial advisor." Since he was
dead serious, it brought some laughter—the only levity
of the morning.

Several of the potential "insiders" expressed enthusiasm on the buy-back, with Burt leading the pack, which
was a dramatic change from the way he behaved the
night before. He said he felt very bullish about the prospects for MFI after a buy-back. And he expressed confidence as to the value of the investment. "Don proved
once before that an investment in MFI can be worth
many times its original cost," he said. "He can do it
again." He was selling. He was putting on an act before
the Carl Marks people and at the same time he was
making a play on my behalf and to me. I knew what
Burt was doing. And Marv did, too.

When we left the Carl Marks offices, I felt a little
encouraged about our "insiders." I was not sure that I
could obtain the entire amount needed—$250,000—
but I knew that I could at least count on $150,000.
That meant I would have to go to several friends such as
Bob Pulver, Dave Regosin and Ed Singer for the rest.
I thought Bob Davidoff and Harry Wise handled the
briefing very well.

As we were leaving, Burt intercepted me. "Don, I must see you . . . I have something that I must discuss with you." As we returned to the office together, he expounded: "I'm sorry that you didn't tell me about your buy-back plans earlier since I could have gotten you a much better deal than the one you are getting from Carl Marks. But I may still be able to do it. Won't you please let me try?"

This was typical of Burt. He had the contacts, he had the wherewithal, what it takes, to make a "better deal," no matter what the deal in question may have been. To get him off my back, I asked: "What investor do you have in mind?"

"Diebold. I was able to bring several deals to them. I don't know whether they have any money left, but if they do, they will go for this deal—and it will be total investment instead of a loan. Please . . ."

I could not help being impressed. I knew of Diebold and I knew of Diebold's relationship with Burt. He had told me about the one deal he had worked out with Diebold. It was a highly speculative, computer-oriented deal. And I knew of another in which Diebold made a substantial investment—Viatron Computer Systems Corporation—which was really like shooting craps. This "new idea" computer time-selling company had gone public several months previously and when I saw the prospectus I could not understand how anyone would buy stock in the company. The strange part of this story is that the stock was rationed to favorites and I probably could not have bought any even if I had tried. The stock opened at $15 a share and jumped almost immediately to $30—despite the fact that the prospectus revealed that the company had practically no money, no orders for equipment, equipment that was not yet even available, and no immediate prospects for any profits. What investors were buying was a highly speculative unproved computer idea known as System 21 and described in the prospectus as follows:

Viatron Computer Systems Corporation, organized November 24, 1967, is engaged primarily in the development of data processing devices which can be mass produced. The Company is developing certain components of a system, designated VIATRON System 21, which it intends to lease to its customers. None of the components of this system is yet in production, but prototypes or models of certain components have been demonstrated (see "VIATRON System 21" under "Business").

The Company incurred an operating loss of $1,254,351 from its organization to October 31, 1968. The Company expects to incur a substantially larger operating loss in its fiscal year ending October 31, 1969.

In addition to the risks inherent in any new enterprise, the Company considers that major uncertainties affecting its business include the following:

1. The major component of System 21 is the microprocessor (see "VIATRON System 21" under "Business"). The production model is designed to utilize metal oxide semiconductor (MOS) circuits. A prototype of the microprocessor using monolithic integrated circuits has been built and tested, but significant problems may be encountered in the development and production of a model utilizing MOS circuits. The Company's proposed low rental schedule will depend in large measure upon the successful utilization of MOS circuits for the logic of the microprocessor. To the best of the Company's knowledge, to date there has been no large scale production of MOS arrays for similar commercial applications.

2. The Company intends initially to have System 21 components manufactured by established independent suppliers, some of which may be located in foreign

countries. No contracts have been entered into for the manufacture of any components. There is no assurance that satisfactory delivery schedules or prices can be attained.

3. The Company has announced its products at low monthly rentals anticipating that its product, marketing and servicing costs will be lower than those generally experienced in the computer industry. There is no assurance that the Company will be able to achieve such lower costs.

4. The Company expects a major portion of its revenues to be derived from leasing its System 21. However, the Company has had no experience in large-scale leasing operations.

5. The Company intends that its rental agreements will be cancellable on thirty days notice, so that some or all of the rental agreements could be terminated within a short period of time.

6. Technological advances and the introduction of new products or services by others could adversely affect the Company's business. The Company anticipates that substantial competition may ultimately be encountered from other companies, many of which have technological, financial and other resources much greater than those of the Company (see "Competition" under "Business").

7. The Company expects that it will require substantial additional financing, and there is no certainty that the Company will be able to obtain such financing when needed (see "Use of Proceeds").

The prospectus went on to issue further warnings to prospective buyers of Viatron stock:

The technology involved in the design and manufacture of the Company's products is complex and subject to constant change. The Company must necessarily direct substantial efforts towards the development of additional, as well as the improvement of existing, components for System 21. There is no assurance that the Company's efforts will result in marketable components.

The Company holds no patents. While no claims have been asserted against the Company or with respect to its proposed products, there can be no assurance that patents will not be obtained by others or that patents owned or controlled by others will not be asserted against the Company or that licenses or other rights under such patents will be available if needed. Five present employees, formerly employed by Radio Corporation of America, have received letters from a law firm representing RCA reminding them of their duty not to use or disclose any confidential and proprietary information acquired during their employment by RCA.

There are a large number of companies rendering programming and other computer services, some of which are similar to those rendered by Viatron Programming, Inc.

The computer industry is highly competitive. There are many companies selling or leasing products or offering services similar to or the same as those offered by the Company. Many of the Company's competitors have established organizations, and most competitors have financial resources larger than those presently available to the Company.

The prospectus also revealed that, for the fiscal year ending October 31, 1968, the company had net revenues of $101,949, including $29,808 in interest income (interest on money received from "insiders" and other original investors, including Diebold), expenses of $1,356,290 and a net loss of $1,254,351 or a loss of $0.85 per share. Yet investors rushed to buy the stock at $15 per share and those who could not obtain any shares at the offering bought on the market in droves, pushing up the price to $30 per share and, before long, to $60 per share. Less than six months after the original offering, the stock was selling at $5 a share; System 21 was still not in existence; the president, chairman and others of the original groups of founders had been fired; and there was no telling what would happen to this company or the price of its stock.

In a news story headlined: "They Said It Couldn't Be Done, But Viatron Did It With Dispatch," the *Wall Street Journal,* early in 1971, said:

BEDFORD, Mass.—Base your new computer terminal on a technology that doesn't work just yet. Expand production space in the face of a sluggish economy. Price the terminal far too low, and then make your biggest shipment to a customer who won't pay.

These were only a few of the mistakes made by Viatron Computer Systems Corp. There were a few others—like losing track of some $6 million in debts that the company owed.

By expertly executing such blunders, however, Viatron has achieved what few other companies have managed to do. On sales of just $2.5 million in 1970, the company was able to lose over $30 million.

Stockholders are flabbergasted. Their shares, which were priced at $15 when first offered to the public in 1969 and which then soared to a high of $61, now sell for about $1.

Financial analysts are incredulous. "It's hard to understand just how Viatron did it," says an official of Shields & Co., the New York brokerage firm that underwrote Viatron's $35 million in stock and debenture offerings.

This week a federal judge issued an order that will almost certainly force the company into Chapter 10 of the bankruptcy act. Under Chapter 10, management loses control and a trustee is appointed by the court to manage what's left of the company. To stave off creditors' demands, Viatron management had since late February been operating the company under Chapter 11 of the bankruptcy act.

Viatron began its journey to spectacular failure in an ordinary enough way. Like many another company in the late 1960s, it was formed by a small group of businessmen, "computer" was put in its name and it was based on Route 128, the highway around Boston that's filled with electronic companies. Then its stock was easily sold to a technology-bedazzled public.

At least at this point, it would seem Diebold had a loser in Viatron. About a year earlier, however, when Burt convinced me to see the people at Diebold, the market was euphoric about the company. He made a date for us to meet with the president of the Diebold Venture Capital Fund on the afternoon of July 8, the day after our meeting in the offices of Carl Marks.

As we walked to the offices of Diebold at 430 Park Avenue, Burt began to hedge: "Of course, I don't think that Diebold will go for our deal—not because it isn't a good deal, it happens to be a great deal for them —but because of their shortage of cash. I believe that all they have left is $2,500,000 and I don't know how much they are required to have on hand to take care of current needs. Anyway, it can't hurt seeing these people. You have nothing to lose. And even if Diebold can't do it, George Pratt (the Diebold president) might offer some worthwhile suggestion. As you will see, I have fine rapport with him."

We soon found ourselves in the office of George Pratt, a friendly, informal man in his early or middle forties. He had a full head of black hair, long sideburns and a full black moustache. Burt kidded a bit about Pratt's new moustache.

"I've had mine since I was eighteen," I said. "I grew it originally because I wanted to look older when I looked for a job." I am not sure that this was the only reason. For one thing, my father had a moustache, and didn't I unconsciously want to be a man like my father? Betty once said: "Don, if you are going to have a moustache, it might as well be big and full." I took her suggestion—and now I am very much in style.

To join us at the meeting, George called in his young assistant, Dom Fitzpatrick. (One thing that I learned in my dealings with venture capital executives is that each of them has "a young assistant," sometimes very bright and at times female and very pretty.)

Burt, characteristically, took over the meeting. He outlined our plan of buying back MFI from CCI, and then he began to sell and sell hard. When he reached a point of oversell, I stepped in to bring him down to earth. I had figures with me and I presented these to George, explaining as I went along. I was interrupted by Burt several times, when he thought I was underselling.

From George's general manner, it seemed that he was interested in our proposition despite the fact that MFI was not a technologically oriented operation. Diebold had confined its investment to technological enterprises, including some wild, high flyers. Most of the companies in which they had invested seed money had not panned out too well and their interest now tended a little more to secure, seasoned investments. That is why the name of the company was changed from the Diebold Technological Fund to Diebold Venture Capital Fund.

Nevertheless, in his part of the presentation, Burt tried to show that there were technological involvement and profit opportunities even in MFI.

"We already have a deal for the development and use of input and output information for one of our magazines—*Food and Drug Packaging*—to cover the entire packaging function," Burt said, "and we will soon move in the direction of audiovisual communication for one or more of the industries we serve."

George seemed interested in our story and in our plans for the future—which included entering such fields as industrial ecology, paramedical and medical laboratory operations with magazines, newsletters and other forms of communications. We soon learned that George had a special interest in publications and in some of the fields in which we were currently involved such as packaging and paperboard.

Finally, he said: "Your deal sounds interesting. I can't make any promises, but it has real merit and it seems to be in the area of involvement of our new investment direction. Now, what do you fellows have in mind—specifically?"

"We'd like you to buy twenty-five percent of our business for $500,000," Burt said.

"Leave the material with us, and we'll come back at you soon."

"How soon?" Burt asked. "You know, Don has another deal pending, but I sold him on exploring potentials with you. We don't have too much time—"

"I'll have an answer for you on Monday." Since this was late Wednesday afternoon, this was real speed. It had taken Carl Marks and Company almost a month to give us their answer.

"Don, I think they're going to buy our dream. I really did not expect such interest," Burt said. Of course, for Burt, a Diebold deal would be particularly advantageous. Since Burt usually does nothing for nothing, he made it plain that, should Diebold buy twenty-five percent of MFI for $500,000 (a much better deal for us than Carl Marks') he wanted four percent of the MFI stock as his "finder's fee." It was a high price. Finders usually receive five percent of the amount "found." Five percent of $500,000 is $25,000.

On the basis we were offering MFI stock to insiders, $25,000 would buy two and one-half percent of stock, so four percent had a value of $40,000. However, I decided not to argue this point at that time, neither accepting nor rejecting Burt's request in the belief that we could work out his "percentage"—something I thought he should not have asked for at all.

By the time I returned to the office at about five o'clock, I began to feel encouraged about the MFI buy-back, but ambivalent about a Diebold deal versus the Carl Marks specific offer. Anyway, we had one definite financing plan and another possibility which could be even better. The big question now was: Will Whatmore accept my offer to buy MFI for $750,000 in cash and ten percent of net profit for the next five years?

While waiting for Whatmore's call, I began to receive commitments from insiders for specific amounts of investment. Marv Toben came in for $25,000 *plus,* Jack Mulligan for $25,000 *plus,* Jay Sandler for $25,000, and several others for lesser amounts. Burt and Jerry seemed in a real financial bind and I felt that while Burt would come in for $15,000, Jerry would conk out entirely. However, by Friday morning, it seemed that I would have little trouble in signing up employee insiders for about $150,000 but that $250,-000 would be difficult, if not impossible, without bringing in my friends.

It wasn't until 3:45 on Friday afternoon, July 10, that Marvin Whatmore called me. He said: "Don, the executive committee met to consider your proposition. We like the idea of ten percent of profit, on top of cash of $750,000, except that we would like to make it 'open end.' You will pay ten percent of net profit until $500,-000 is paid—or a total of $1,250,000."

His words were music to my ears. It was wonderful. We had it. I would have my company back.

Marvin went on: "So, if this is acceptable to you, why don't you have your lawyer—what's his name?—get in touch with Frank Barry and go to work on the contract? . . . But there is one more thing, Don, which I must tell you. One of our directors had a call from an attorney who said that he heard that MFI was for sale and that he would like to make an offer. As a public company, we have to listen to such an offer. So, I made a date to see this man. I have to, you understand, Don, particularly since you are an insider, a member of our board."

I was stunned. What could I do? I supposed Whatmore did have to see this attorney and listen to his offer—but he didn't have to accept it, unless it was far better than my offer.

"In the meantime, let's move fast and have your attorney and Frank draw up papers. OK?"

Just as soon as Whatmore hung up, I made a series of calls—to Davidoff, to my lawyer, Dave Regosin, several times to Whatmore, and a return call to Dave. The purpose of these calls was to act on Whatmore's suggestion "to move fast," to draw up some kind of paper in which details of my offer would be drawn, signed by me and sent to Whatmore. Somehow, Dave and Frank Barry could not agree on details or even the approach. Dave tried to reach Jack Harding but he had left for home, having returned from London the night before and still being under the jet lag. Frank and Dave finally agreed to postpone the drawing of the paper until Monday morning when they would have an opportunity to consult with Harding.

Marvin Toben and I discussed the new developments and decided to confer with Burt. This we did, and we decided that Burt should call Dom or George at Diebold for an "answer" inasmuch as we would soon have to make a choice between Carl Marks and Diebold as our principal financial sources, lender versus investor. Burt could not reach George, but Dom told him that he had been working with our figures. He promised to work over the weekend and call us Monday.

Another "lost weekend" for me. Tension. Speculation. Anticipation. I read a few more chapters of *Decline and Fall*. I saw many depressing similarities between the last years of the *Post* and Curtis and current events at *Look* and Cowles.

After only a few hours of sleep, I was up at five on Monday morning. I couldn't wait to begin making calls in my continuing effort to "move fast" on the buy-back.

I received a call from Dom, who advised me that Diebold was ready with an offer: they would buy twenty-five percent of MFI for $350,000 instead of $500,000. We decided to meet for lunch, with Burt and Marv Toben, to discuss details. And now I had to choose between Diebold and Carl Marks.

While the Diebold deal seemed preferable, I had several reservations. The stock Burt expected as a fee was unhealthy as a matter of principle. It could also prove shattering to Jack Mulligan who now wanted to invest $50,000 or more, so that he could become the largest stockholder in the new MFI. Jack had long had a gripe because he was "low man on the totem pole"—he had less stock in MFI than Burt, Jerry or Art.

Jack originally bought 100 shares for $500—way back. Eventually the 100 shares became 2,300 shares in the new, larger MFI. However, I had not offered to sell Jack additional shares and he in turn had not asked to buy any. When Burt, Jerry and Art joined us, their deals called for stock options, which they exercised as our business grew. Thus, each of the three had about twice the number of shares that Jack owned. Of course, they paid a much higher price for their stock than Jack did. But Jack somehow blamed me for his not having as many shares as the other VPs. Anyway, it was apparent that one reason for Jack's offer to invest $50,000 in the new MFI was his desire to be the largest single owner of stock outside of me. And I felt that he deserved this kind of consideration.

Thus it became difficult for me to choose between Diebold and Carl Marks. I did decide that no matter which investor and/or lender I chose, I must find a way to make sure that Jack would achieve his ownership objective. He would not be hurt again.

In the meantime, Dave and Frank could not get together to write a simple memorandum spelling out my offer to buy back MFI. Frank said he could not get a definite answer on "terms" from Whatmore. He told Dave there seemed to be "a difference of understanding about the balance sheet." This sounded ominous.

The balance sheet as Whatmore (in Harding's presence) spelled it out to me was the basis I used in negotiating for financing. It called for quick net assets of approximately $480,000, of which $100,000 was cash. Failure to get this kind of balance sheet at the closing would make it impossible for me to get financing. I telephoned Whatmore and asked that we meet to discuss the problem. Whatmore did not say very much, but I could tell from his tone that the meeting—set for that afternoon—would not be pleasant.

In the meantime, we were to meet with Dom Fitzpatrick who was to spell out Diebold's offer. At lunch, Dom confirmed that Diebold was ready to invest $350,-000 for a twenty-five percent interest in MFI. However, the offer had a "kicker"—if we did not make the projected profit in 1971, Diebold would get another six percent interest in our company.

"After all," he pointed out, "it is your projection.

Besides, we feel that 1971 is the key year for MFI. If you will do what you project in 1971, you will have little problem in making projected profits in the years to follow. But if you don't do it in 1971, then your company may not be as profitable as you would like to be in 1972 and the years after that. That is why that 'kicker' is important. We are not interested in the additional six percent. We want you to break your neck to make the projected profit."

We tried to argue this thesis. But he wouldn't budge. It was still a better deal than the one offered us by Carl Marks but not by much . . . and more and more, I began to lean towards Carl Marks. For one thing, I seemed to like Bob Davidoff and Harry Wise better than George Pratt and Dom Fitzpatrick. I also resented the fact that our Diebold dealings were with Dom and not with George, the top dog. Anyway, obtaining needed financing was no longer a problem. Either deal was acceptable.

The big question now was the balance sheet and the kind of buy-back deal Whatmore and Harding were now willing to accept. By now I was quite convinced that they had changed the rules of the game.

NINE:

The New Game Plan

Marvin Whatmore opened our crucial meeting that afternoon with a brand-new thought: "The quick assets belong to Cowles. You are correct about the figures in the balance sheet, Don. The quick assets are $480,000, but we can't give them to you."

I looked around the low conference table where Jack Harding and Gil Maurer sat grim-faced. No allies there. The threesome executed (in more senses than one) Gardner Cowles' decisions. They were in the inner-inner sanctum of the executive committee.

"But Marv," I replied in astonishment, "it was my feeling right from the beginning that this was the basis on which I was buying back MFI. Why did you give me the figures in the first place? Not once did you say that the quick net assets belong to you. There was no mention of it in any of our meetings."

"I'm sorry. In selling the *San Juan Star*, we got the quick net assets. That is the way it is always done."

"Always? When you bought MFI you *received* the quick net assets. When we bought *Modern Medicine*, we, the buyers, *received* the net quick assets. The same thing was true when we bought Bettendorf. The quick assets of $480,000 was the basis I have used in obtaining financing and it has taken me over five months to accomplish the impossible. Without the $480,000, we have no deal. All you are giving me then is good will and do you expect me to pay $1,250,000 for good will? Even if I were willing to accept such a deal, our money men would never countenance it."

"I am sorry, Don, but this is the best we can do. The $480,000 is ours."

"Maybe you can add that amount to the $500,000 you will be paying us on the basis of ten percent net of profits," Jack Harding said in a kind of whisper, sorry as he said it, that he was saying it.

"No, that won't do at all, Jack," Marvin interposed. "I am sorry Don. If you want the deal, the $480,000 belongs to us."

Gil Maurer was silent throughout the meeting.

"Five months of work, of agony—all wasted," I said.

The door to Whatmore's office opened, and his secretary whispered to him: "The others are in the conference room. The meeting is ready to start."

"I'm sorry, but I have another meeting to go to."

That was the end—the end of my work, the end of my dream to buy back my business. The sleepless nights. The tension. The uncertainty. The attempts to obtain financing. And now all this work was out the window. What now?

"The deal is off," I told Marv Toben. He shared my sorrow. I called Betty and told her the sad news, and she expressed great anger at Whatmore.

"That so-and-so," she said. "But then I never thought he was so great in the first place. You'll find a way darling. . . . We'll talk about it when you get home."

There must be a way—there must be an answer.

And I began to grope for it. What were my options now? One thing was certain: I could not accept the status quo. I could not remain in my present spot while I was being isolated from Modern Medicine. I must be completely in charge of the entire division, fully and unequivocally, or they must sell MFI back to me on some basis that I could handle.

I telephoned Harry Wise of Carl Marks and Company and told him what happened. He said: "Why don't you offer them part of the $480,000—say $100,000—and add that amount to the $500,000 to be paid out of ten percent net profit, open end. You can go to half of the $480,000, if necessary, but don't offer them that much right away. So you will be paying them ten percent of profit for 99 years—Who cares?"

This might be a way—this might be the answer, I thought. Anyway, I must call Whatmore and ask for a meeting with him, alone, to thresh out the whole thing. Say what I must say. Have a full confrontation, if necessary.

He was still at the meeting. I told his secretary: "Have him call me whenever he gets through with the meeting. I'll be in my office until six. If the meeting goes beyond that, please have him call me at home. It is important."

At six he hadn't called me. When I reached home, Betty greeted me by telling me that Whatmore had called. He was still in his office. I telephoned immediately.

"Marvin, we ended our meeting rather abruptly. I'd like very much to see you, alone, to thresh things out, and I believe that I have an answer to the quick asset problem."

He agreed immediately. "Righto. I'm not sure when I can make it but my secretary will call you in the morning and set a date."

For the rest of the evening my thoughts centered on at least one alternative solution to the balance sheet problem. Why not suggest a management contract for five years which would include a five-year option to buy MFI for $1,250,000? During the five-year management contract period, I could pay Cowles a fee of $100,000 per year. So now, I had a solution to the balance sheet problem (based on the suggestion given me by Harry Wise of Carl Marks) as well as an alternate plan. I was ready for the meeting with Whatmore.

I tried hard to focus on what I was doing—writing on Saturday and Sunday mornings, reading, watching a movie, visiting with our son Mel and his family—but my mind was on Cowles, MFI, the impending meeting with Whatmore and, most important of all, what would happen if no deal could be made. Prospects were bleak. I would do all I could to control the entire division but autonomy would be impossible. Cowles had his special hangup on *Modern Medicine.* I recalled that Don Perkins had warned me that I was being isolated from the Minneapolis operation and *Modern Medicine* in an effort to minimize my part in bringing in and setting up a highly profitable operation.

"A lot of people take credit for *Modern Medicine,*" Perkins had pointed out.

So, the next three years and four months—the extent of my contract—could be very rough for me. Cowles, in turn, would be going through a very difficult time, too. There was no telling what would happen to CCI. Cowles might just sacrifice all the valuable assets of this corporation in a futile attempt to save his very own baby, *Look,* and finally go under. This possibility was not remote, in my judgment.

I didn't really know Gardner Cowles and I didn't think anybody really knew this private person. He may well have had a compulsion to lose, to destroy, to go down with the sinking ship.

And Cowles Communications, Inc., in the eyes of the financial community, was sinking and sinking fast. Something drastic had to be done to bring it back and I had serious reservations whether Cowles could or would take drastic but necessary steps—such as dropping or suspending *Look*.

Thus, the present and future value of our 94,000 shares of Cowles stock depended on the whims of one man, a man nobody really knew and a man who may not even have known himself. A man who listened and made pronouncements. A man who ran a $175,000,000 public corporation as if it were his own private fief. Whereas the value of our stock had hit a high of $2,000,000 a year and a half previously (when it was $21 a share), it was now worth less than $400,000 (at $3¾ a share). It could go down to $1 a share and it could be worth zero. And more than eighty percent of what we had was in this stock. Not a very happy situation.

When I reached my office Monday morning at 9:15, a call had already come through from Whatmore's secretary, advising that he would see me at 11:30 the next morning. From that point on, nothing really mattered except that meeting. My mind was on it—completely. What I would say? How I would react to whatever he might say? I tried to figure out what he might do, what approach he might use. I decided to behave in a strong, positive manner—but to do it softly, kindly, disarmingly. I had to lead the meeting. I would have him do what must be done, but he must not know that I was doing the leading. It was going to be a tight-rope affair for me once again. I had learned to live with this sort of thing. Although I felt confident that I could handle it again the next day, I must confess that I did have doubts—doubts I must be careful to suppress.

As I was thinking these thoughts, Gil Maurer called and said: "Don, I think you were great at the meeting on Friday afternoon. You handled yourself superbly. I know what a blow it must have been to you to learn that the quick assets were not yours to have. You showed great restraint, and I want you to know that both Jack and Marvin appreciated it very much."

"Thanks, Gil, but it seems to me that the signals were changed. During all of these months, during my many meetings with Marvin, nothing was said about my not getting the net quick assets."

"Don, you're right. The signals were changed. I feel that I have to tell you this."

What Gil said I found extremely helpful. I now had added ammunition for a strong, positive approach in my meeting with Whatmore. From now on, nothing mattered until the meeting with Marvin.

At precisely 11:30 the next morning I was invited into Marvin Whatmore's office. Before I had offered to buy back the division or MFI Whatmore would come out of the office himself to greet me. Now, for the last few months, his secretary or her assistant would come out and signal me to come in. A little thing and probably not very significant, but it did represent a change in our relationship.

As I entered Marvin's office, we shook hands as usual but I found a weakness in his handshake that morning. There were dark circles around his small, bulging eyes. His brow and the rest of his face seemed more wrinkled than when I last saw him. He was beginning to show the wear and tear of the unprecedented pressures which had a firm, pincerlike grip on his vital organs and his psyche.

Here was a man whose whole life, whose almost entire interest revolved around business, the business of being president of Cowles Communications. The only avowed hobby he had was golf, which he did play on most weekends. But golf was not really his hobby. Work was his hobby. His vocation, his avocation, the marrow of his bones, his very lifeblood. Not only did he rush to work at eight each morning or earlier, walking briskly from his home on Sutton Place to Madison Avenue and 51st Street, after a cup of coffee and cigarette or two or three (or a little cigar, later on, when he tried to break his smoking habit—unsuccessfully—he had to have something in his hand, in his mouth). And he did not leave his office until late in the evening. Never before seven, and many times at eight or later.

His wife, Lois, went along with him. She rarely knew from day to day what time to expect Marvin home for dinner. And many times dinner was "out," usually with others, advertising agency people or advertisers. Lois must have been pretty when she was young. Probably a very attractive blonde. Now her hair was dyed, or she wore a wig, and you couldn't tell. She went along with Marvin in whatever he did or wanted to do, and regardless of a particular time schedule. She did not seem to have a life of her own. Her life was intertwined with that of Marvin—to a greater extent than the wife of any man of my acquaintance. Yet, she did not really seem to know what Marvin was doing, what his problems were, or what to say or do to help him.

Marvin kept her on a very strict budget, and while she complained about it from time to time—mostly to friends—she did nothing to change it. She did not seem to know or realize that her husband, her Marvin, was the president of a large publishing corporation, drawing a salary of $103,000 a year and earning dividends (when dividends were still being paid) amounting to another $60,000 a year.

She was a nice, kind, considerate, simple girl from Iowa and although she had been living in and around New York for over thirty years, in an apartment on Sutton Place during the week and in a most beautiful estate in Westchester during the weekend, she remained the Iowa country girl. At parties on the estate or in her apartment, it was Marvin who was the host, who greeted everybody and moved about from guest to guest, chatting, kidding, having a great time. Lois was there—but not really, not fully. She never became part of the Whatmore Publishing Big-Time, Big City, Big Estate Scene fully. More often than not, there was a sad cast to her still pretty face. She tried hard to be the wife of Cowles President Marvin Whatmore, whatever that was, but she didn't succeed because she did not really know how she was expected to behave as Mrs. Publishing Executive. Not having a false bone in her body, she could not wear a mask as so many wives of so many executives do. She did not even know what kind of a mask to wear. Betty and I often talked about Lois, whom we liked. We felt sorry for her.

Maybe Marvin knew how Lois felt and maybe he did not. He was just too busy, much too preoccupied doing his own thing, which was always behaving as The Most Charming Publishing Executive Of All Time. And charm Marvin had in abundance. Obviously, he also had his own private fears, frustrations and insecurities. But being with him, working with him, partying with him, one would never know it. He wore his mask, a most charming, smiling, pleasant mask, perfectly. Maybe that is why he had his ulcers. And maybe that is why, at times, he smoked more and drank more than was good for him.

Marvin, who was not a Harvard College or Harvard Business School graduate, was all Iowa. He graduated from Drake University (in Iowa) in 1932 and also

studied at the State University of Iowa. After a short
stint in a bank, accounting-trained Whatmore joined the
Des Moines Register and Tribune in 1935 in a clerical
position. Two years later, he was named office manager.

When Gardner started *Look,* he invited Marvin to
join him, and he soon became assistant treasurer, then
treasurer, a member of the board of directors as early
as 1943, at which time he was also made business manager of *Look.* His rise from then on was steady. In 1952,
he was elected vice president and promoted to the general managership, and in 1964 he was elected president
of the corporation, now a public company. Throughout
those years and the years to follow, he was Gardner
Cowles' man, doing the bidding of the chairman and
chief executive officer. Even when Marvin was finally
made chief executive officer in 1969, he continued to
defer to Gardner Cowles, who continued to call all the
shots.

Socially, the Whatmores and the Cowleses did not mix
—this, despite the fact that the Cowles' only son was
married to the eldest of the three Whatmore daughters
(they also had a son, Jim, who worked for Cowles).
For one thing, Mrs. Gardner Cowles was completely
the opposite of Lois Whatmore. She was an extrovert
and thoroughly socially oriented. She was very much
of the current scene still described as New York Society. Not the archaic New York Society, but today's
very mod New York Society. She chaired numerous
charitable functions and her picture appeared in the
New York Times society pages frequently. She knew
how to give, and gave, many cocktail and dinner parties
for such New York communications bigwigs as the Bill
Paleys, the Bennett Cerfs, the Andrew Heiskells (he,
the friendly competitor, chairman of the board of
Time, Inc.), the Arthur Hays Sulzbergers and the Ar-

thur Ochs Sulzbergers, and the many big names in the world of business and culture, including art and music. The Whatmores were not part of that scene, the Cowles' very urban, New York scene. The Whatmores preferred to be at their country estate—on all weekends and whenever possible.

Yet Marvin Whatmore's life was completely built around the fortunes (and whims) of Gardner Cowles. In his talk at the 1970 Cowles Executive Seminar in Orlando, Florida, he could say with real feeling: "Everything my family and I have is invested in Cowles Communications. We are not unique in that. Many of you have also invested all of your financial and emotional capital, your energies, your dreams and hopes in this company. I intend to make my investment pay off." He was speaking more for himself than anyone else in the room.

I thought of Marvin's words, presented with great emotion, almost at the verge of tears, at the Orlando meeting. At this stage of his career, he was facing what seemed almost insurmountable problems. Not only in his effort to make his investment in Cowles pay off but in keeping it going—at almost all costs—financial as well as emotional.

We were alone, but his door was open and his secretary could probably hear what we were saying, that is, if she really tried. Marvin started the conversation by telling me that he had had the scheduled meeting with the attorney who had told a member of the CCI board that he had heard that MFI was for sale and that he wanted to make an offer.

"Whom did this attorney represent?" I asked.

"He said he represented a 'group and himself,' that he had plenty of money and was ready to buy. He asked for figures and details. I told him that I could not give him any financial figures unless he made a firm offer or revealed whom he represented. I explained that I saw him because, as a president of a public company, I felt that I had an obligation to listen to any legitimate offer for any part of our business or division. I told him that if he wished to make a specific offer for MFI I would consider it. I doubt whether I will hear from him again. I believe he was on a fishing expedition."

I told Marvin that it was my belief—as well as the belief of my financial advisers and my family—that signals had been changed.

"I don't know what you mean by 'changed signals'," he replied. "You could have had a deal if you hadn't insisted that the net quick assets belonged to you—they don't."

"But this is the basis on which I approached investors, the banks . . . this is the way I understood the buy-back in the first place. In all our discussions—and we have had many meetings and telephone calls during the past few months—you never said that the net quick assets, the $480,000 or whatever the exact amount —belonged to Cowles. When I say the signals have been changed, I mean that for some reason you no longer want to sell MFI to me. Something has happened."

"The word in the Street is that Cowles is selling off the winners and staying with the losers," Marvin finally said. "This has been the reaction to the announcement of our impending sale of the *San Juan Star* . . . so, we have decided that at this time we are not going to sell anything—just nothing beyond the *San Juan Star*."

So, that was it! The signals had been changed. Gil Maurer was right. The net quick assets play was an alibi. They no longer wanted to sell MFI.

"This means, then, that the deal is off," I said. "It is not going to be easy to reorient myself and my staff.

Eight 'insiders' who are key men know that we were all set to buy back MFI. We are pretty close to the point of no return. It is going to be a helluva job to go back, to adjust to the idea and the reality that we will continue as a Cowles operation."

Marvin sat silently. He seemed to be at a loss for words. Or maybe he had a reason for not commenting.

I continued: "Marvin, if I am going to remain, if the deal is really off and there is no way to bring it back to life, then we must discuss my position, my responsibility, my future as president of the Cowles Business and Professional Magazine Division. It is obvious that I have been isolated from the *Modern Medicine* operation, the Minneapolis operation. I cannot tolerate being boxed in with MFI."

"Yes, Don," Whatmore said quietly and slowly, "it is true that you are being isolated from *Modern Medicine*—but Marvin Whatmore did not do it . . ."

"Exactly what do you mean?"

"I received instruction to isolate you. Word came through from Minneapolis that they would rather report to me than to the head of the business magazine division."

"Word from whom?" I tried to hide my anger. "From Burt Cohen? From Louis Cohen? From Mal Herz?"

"Burt Cohen has been totally loyal to you . . ."

"Then from whom? Not Louis Cohen. He's my friend. We are very close. But I cannot say the same thing for Mal Herz. Somehow, we never clicked." Herz's attitude of superiority annoyed me. MFI, he seemed to imply, was smaller than *Modern Medicine* and inferior to it. All that might not have mattered, but Mal Herz used the one expression that was guaranteed to make me see red. When he told me, "Don, I'm going to make you look good," I knew I was through with him.

One of my early friends, whose nickname was

Mersh, outwardly expressed interest in others but in reality was totally interested only in himself, and his favorite expression was, "I'm going to make you look good." When I realized what kind of blowhard he was, we parted company.

Years later, when I was editing *Confectionery–Ice Cream World,* the publisher brought in a kind of super-editorial-director-cum-space-salesman who was, in effect, another Mersh. He, too, was going to make me "look good." He got no help from me and my associates, and in six months the publisher had to pay him off and let him go.

Mal Herz was no Mersh. He was a man of substance and fine reputation. But his remark about making me look good made me suspicious of his intentions. I behaved courteously toward him but I did not seek his advice and I saw him infrequently. Burt Cohen was our manager in Minneapolis, and it was with him that I worked on a day-to-day basis.

At the same time, I developed a friendship with Louis Cohen. This was as much his doing as it was mine. He called me often and came to see me whenever he was in New York. I, too, would call him whenever I felt I needed his counsel. When I went to Minneapolis I spent as much time with him as I could. He asked many questions about our business and about Cowles and I answered those questions as frankly as I could without impugning my trust as a member of the board of directors of Cowles. Louis and his outspoken, friendly wife, Tess, were taken with Betty (which is easy to be) and we began to get together socially. They were over at our apartment several times, we had them out to dinner at our favorite restaurants in New York, La Cote Basque and Twenty-One. They seemed to speak our language.

Thus, I was a bit surprised when Marvin Whatmore

made the flat statement that "Burt Cohen has been totally loyal to you, Don." He seemed to imply that Mal Herz *and* Louis Cohen wanted "to report directly to Cowles management" instead of to me. While I decided to give Louis the benefit of the doubt, I naturally felt disappointed.

Marvin continued: "Not only does Minneapolis want to report directly to me but they have also hinted that they want a seat on the board. After all, they see the annual statement and they know that *Modern Medicine* makes a substantial contribution to the overall profit of the company. They know that their part of the business is the largest of the business and professional division —by far. They feel that they have a very important stake in CCI and they want to protect their interests. That does not mean that they do not have the highest respect or regard for you. They have said that. It is just that they feel their stake in CCI is bigger than yours."

"But how do you feel about it, Marv?" I asked.

"It isn't how I feel. It is what the conditions are. Perhaps if we were doing better at CCI . . . if MFI were a bigger, a more profitable operation, this thing would not have come up—but it has."

"As far as I am concerned, Marv, I can't continue to operate the division effectively under such circumstances. There can be no equivocation. As head of the Business and Professional Magazine Division, I must have full and complete authority. There can be no other way. You know, of course, that I have gone along with your wishes and have directed the Minneapolis division in a kind of 'keep your hands off' manner, treading gently, moving slowly, accomplishing what I could by indirection—by making them think that it was their idea to do a certain thing rather than mine. This has proved to be very difficult and, as a result, we have not maximized profits to the full potential, but since profits have been more than satisfactory, I have not moved to disturb anything. You know I took no important step without first consulting with you. It has proved to be most trying, and now the situation is becoming untenable. You must make a decision. Either I begin to have full and complete control of the entire division, or you move to sell me back MFI. Otherwise, I repeat, you are going to have a very unhappy manager on your hands. My contract, which still has three and one-half years to go, clearly spells out my function as president of the Cowles Business and Professional Magazine Division. There can be no other way. The choice is yours."

For a moment or two, Marvin sat silently, in deep thought, then he said: "I'll tell you what I'll do, Don. I'll call a luncheon meeting of the executive committee. Mike will be there and you can tell your story—fully— and we will try to clear the air."

"That's fine. I welcome it."

The date was set for Tuesday, July 21, the day after a special meeting of the board of directors called to approve the sale of the *San Juan Star* to Capital Cities Broadcasting Corporation for $9.75 million in cash.

This was the break I had been looking for. And I began to prepare myself for it as I never did for anything else before. For one thing, I decided that I would address myself to Gardner Cowles. To him and nobody else. I now knew beyond the shadow of a doubt that only one person made major decisions for the company. Gardner Cowles felt it was his company (despite the fact that CCI had 3,500 stockholders) and it was his function and responsibility to call all the shots, to make all major decisions. But he did it in a way that appeared to be democratic. He always made sure that major propositions were placed for board action after they were acted on by the executive committee. Everyone on the board or the executive committee always had an opportunity to discuss any proposition placed before them. Then Cowles would call for a vote.

But before placing any proposition before the board, Gardner Cowles made sure that every member knew exactly how he felt about it. Moreover, once the executive committee acted on a piece of business and placed it before the board, nothing was ever changed. Whatever the executive committee wanted, the board gave it. And whatever Gardner Cowles wanted, the executive committee approved, unanimously. In a nice, organized, "democratic" way, the executive committee did Cowles' bidding. And if Cowles erred, then Mr. Gardner Cowles would "take full responsibility" and that was that.

Knowing this, and knowing how Cowles behaved—impetuously and compulsively—I tried to set things up so that he would take the action I wanted him to take, impetuously and compulsively, at the proper time. I was now fighting for my life and I would thoroughly plan and rehearse every step from here on.

TEN:

A Legend in His Own Time
and the $15,000,000 Mistake

I was delighted that my meeting with Gardner Cowles (and incidentally, with the executive committee) was scheduled for the day *after* a special board meeting. I prepared a list of pointed questions that I would ask at the board meeting on Monday. My purpose was to demonstrate to Cowles and his key people that I could make trouble.

I planned not only the exact wording of my questions, but the way in which I would put them. I would not be adamant. I would not be unreasonable. But I would be mildly irritating. I would make it clear that I could be a problem.

The questions were:

1. Mike, why are we selling the *San Juan Star?*

2. Have we made any plans to determine how long the proceeds—the cash—of the sale would last?

3. What happens after the cash is gone?

Of course I knew the answers—particularly to the first question. So did everyone who would be present. We all knew that Cowles was trying to solve the problem of liquidity. But the question was guaranteed to irritate.

The second and third questions were a bit more difficult to answer. They were much more pointed. They would come as a shock. And they would show that I could be a pest, that I might be able to cause real trouble. Then they might go along with me on a reasonable plan of action.

The plan had to be reasonable. And it had to be good for Cowles—for Gardner Cowles personally, for the members of the executive committee and, lastly, for the company. Whether it was good for me was of no consequence from their point of view.

Basically, my plan of action gave Gardner Cowles only two options: one, to agree to give me full authority to run the Cowles Business and Professional Magazine Division; or, two, to sell MFI to me on reasonable terms—terms I had worked out and was ready to present specifically and simply. There could not be any equivocation. The choice was Cowles'.

While I preferred the buy-back, I decided that I could live with Option One, at least for a time. However, I was convinced that Cowles would move toward Option Two. While he did not understand the business magazine field, and did not really care to learn, he was very much taken with *Modern Medicine*. Besides, the Minneapolis operation (largely *Modern Medicine*) was a great profit earner. (Largely because of the tremendous profits from *Modern Medicine,* my division was now the second largest profit earner of all eight divisions of CCI, topped only by the broadcasting group.) Because he was enamored of Burt Cohen, and because of the pressure by "the Minneapolis division," Cowles apparently felt he could do without me. By selling MFI (now only marginally profitable) the company would get a nice chunk of cash, improving the liquidity that much more.

I spent most of the weekend rehearsing my plan of action. I awoke at four thirty on Monday morning. I felt as if I were rehearsing my first asking of the Four Questions on the seder night of the Passover, when I was four in the little Lithuanian hamlet of Pumpyan. By the time the sun rose, and the bedroom began to fill with light, I was in good shape, ready for the board meeting and the Three Questions.

The meeting started promptly at ten. All except John Perry were there. Everyone had the customary "black book" in front of him—a looseleaf binder with proposed resolutions to be adopted, sales and profits to date, by division, and revised budgetary figures for all operations and divisions for the rest of the year. Also projections for 1971—mostly blue sky, as usual. We were not permitted to take away the "black book" or any of its contents for a detailed, quiet study. The book and its contents had to be left intact in the board room. And since we went through each of the resolutions and each page of figures at a fast pace, it was almost impossible to "take back" any detailed figures—even if you had a very good memory. Of course, there was a large pad of lined note paper and plenty of sharpened pencils on the table. But there was a kind of unwritten law that said: "Note taking is not permitted." I found this out at my first meeting when I started making notes of figures and found that all eyes—piercing eyes—were on me.

At this meeting, I carefully and slowly moved a fresh writing pad in front of me. I turned pages and took notes furiously. All eyes were on me, but this time I did not care. There was no *written* law which said I could not take notes. And why provide us with large pads of lined paper and pencils if we were not allowed to take notes?

The meeting was opened by Chairman Gardner Cowles. The first order of business was the proposed approval of the sale of the *San Juan Star* for $9,750,000 in cash to the Capital Cities Broadcasting Corporation. After Cowles read the resolutions Marvin Whatmore explained that, in addition to the proceeds of the sale of the newspaper, CCI would also realize a minimum of $500,000 in cash from the sale of land that adjoined the *Star* property, thus giving the company more than $10,000,000 in cash. He also explained that the deal, scheduled to be closed in a few days, would be recorded as being effective on June 30. Thus profits from the transaction would offset the operational losses for the first six months, resulting in a net profit for the period of about $2,000,000 instead of a net loss of almost that amount.

Cowles then moved for a vote instead of asking if there were any questions.

I cut in: "Mike, before we vote on the resolution, I have several questions that I would like to ask—three, to be exact." All eyes were on me. Cowles seemed unhappy. Whatmore showed surprise. "My first question is: 'Why are we selling the *San Juan Star?*' "

Everyone looked befuddled. Cowles looked irritated. Whatmore's face turned a bit redder than usual.

It was a silly question. Of course I knew why we were selling the *San Juan Star*. Everyone in the room, with the possible exception of John Fischer, the president of Teachers College, knew the answer and the implications of the answer to this question.

The *San Juan Star*, one of the corporation's best and most profitable properties, was being sold because the company needed cash. Cowles Communications had two very serious problems—one of liquidity and the other of meeting debt restrictions. The second problem was even more pressing than the first. If the company failed, as of June 1, to meet the working capital requirement of its contract with its long-time debtor, the Investors Diversified Services of Minneapolis, then IDS could declare the entire loan of $15,000,000 in default. If IDS insisted on sticking to the letter of its loan agreement with CCI, it could put Cowles in bankruptcy or move to sell off sufficient assets to pay the $15,000,000. Obviously, the $10,000,000 net cash gain from the sale of the *San Juan Star* would not be sufficient to pay off this loan in full.

Cowles also had a revolving credit of $10,000,000 with the Manufacturers Hanover Trust Company. He had borrowed a large sum against that credit. Naturally, the bank was looking at Cowles' activities with a surgeon's eye. Bankers can be inhuman when they think they have to be, when the normal pay-back of a huge loan is being threatened. So, Charmer Marvin Whatmore, and Serious, Hard-working John Harding flew to Minneapolis in May before the loan reached the default stage and had a long, friendly but pointed conversation with the loan officers of IDS. The net result was an oral understanding that IDS would hold off the default procedure until December 31. IDS explained that it nevertheless felt free to begin default proceedings any time its officers concluded that it would be good business to do so. Anyway, when Jack and Marv had their first whiskeys on their return flight, they sighed with relief. They felt they were "safe" for several months. The decision to sell the *San Juan Star* had been made earlier and this was explained to the IDS people and that formed the basis of their willingness to go along with

CCI until the end of December. But time would be running out—and they had to move fast.

So, when I asked the question, "Why are we selling the *San Juan Star?*" I knew the answer and I knew it better than most of the board members in the room. Of course, the details of the problems were never talked about or even hinted at board meetings. We were there only to say "aye, aye, aye" to resolutions already approved by the executive committee. I had gotten the lowdown from Cowles men "in the know," from a word here and there, and much of it from "outside sources." It was amazing how much so-called outsiders knew about the operation of the company that the so-called insiders did not. By insiders, I mean the board members, most of whom are not really insiders at all. I was not one, and probably could never be.

I directed my question to Gardner Cowles. When he was able to catch his breath, he turned to Whatmore and said: "Marvin, you answer that question."

"We are selling the *San Juan Star* to improve our liquidity," Marvin said, slowly and almost in a whisper.

It was a superficial, incomplete answer, but I did not expect much more.

I continued: "My second question, Mike, is: 'Have we formulated any plans to determine how long this cash will last?' "

Again, Cowles turned to Whatmore for the answer. If Whatmore had been moderately annoyed by the first question, he was deeply disturbed by the second.

"No, we have made no plans with regard to the use of the cash. There really is no answer to this question—not at this time. We will use the money as we need it," Marvin said.

This was an evasive answer at best. Of course, I was not surprised to learn that no plans were made about the use of the funds. I knew the money was needed for at least two reasons: to satisfy the working capital requirement of IDS and to cover *Look*'s heavy losses that were increasing sharply each week as the advertising volume continued to decline.

"This brings me to my third question," I continued. "What happens after the cash is gone?"

This question was a real shocker. By this time, Whatmore was quite nervous. He no longer had to wait for a nod from Cowles to answer.

"Don, you are presuming that the money will be gone —that there won't be any left. You are making an assumption . . ."

"But isn't there the possibility that the cash we are receiving for the *San Juan Star*, one of our best properties, will be gone in the not-too-distant future, and if this could happen, shouldn't we know what we are going to do then?"

This was not the question of a friendly director and I knew it, and that was as far as I would go at this meeting. That was all the pressure I was going to apply at this time—but it was plenty.

"I really can't answer that question, Don," Whatmore said. "You may find the answer when we get down to the resolutions pertaining to our plans for *Look*."

The three questions caught the entire board off guard. Gardner Cowles looked sad and Marvin Whatmore had to make a real effort to compose himself.

Cowles again asked for a vote on the resolution to sell the *San Juan Star*. No other questions were asked. No other statements were made. Cowles got the ayes he wanted. I was silent. I had thought about voting nay, but decided against it. I felt that to do this could hurt me in my presentation the next day. I had applied just enough pressure. I had shown that I could make real trouble. And that was all I wanted to accomplish at this meeting.

The remaining resolutions were routine. One pertained to Shap Shapiro who since his retirement had taken on a series of jobs with various publishers. Because he received an executive pension and continued as a "consultant" to CCI, Shap had to ask for approval each time he wanted to take on an assignment. Thus, at every board meeting since his retirement, we were asked to approve several new jobs for Shap, including some far-out assignments. At this meeting, we approved his employment by a magazine called *Way Out*, published by a psychiatric hospital in upstate New York. That provided the only comic relief at the meeting.

Some hard facts we learned at the meeting were that *Look* was budgeted for a loss of more than $8,000,000 for 1970 and $4,800,000 for 1971. In 1969, the magazine had shown a "profit" of several hundred dollars. The $8,000,000 plus loss for *Look* and the smaller but substantial losses for *Venture*, the book division and other properties meant that in 1970 the corporation would show a loss—despite an $8,500,000 profit from the newspaper, broadcasting and business and professional magazine divisions.

Only the capital gain from the sale of the *San Juan Star* would make it possible for the company to show a profit for the year. But Wall Street and the investment public could see through this kind of "profit." Only operational earnings impressed the financial community, and there would be none for CCI in 1970.

Whatmore explained that a drastic cost-cutting program on the *Look* operation would save $2,500,000 in 1970 and possibly $6,000,000 in 1971. The losses budgeted for *Look* would have been much higher without the cost-cutting program, he said. The reductions meant eliminating about forty of *Look*'s editorial, promotional and sales people, including some high-priced talent.

Whatmore also brought out that the projected losses for *Look* were based on the publication of 1,200 pages of advertising each year. An increase could mean a reduction of the projected losses, he pointed out. But an increase was not expected for 1970 and was not likely for 1971. On the other hand, a decline in ad volume beyond 1,200 pages a year would mean bigger losses. That such a possibility existed was clear to most members of the board. A gain or loss would depend on at least two factors—an improvement or worsening in the economy of the nation, and on contract renewal action by labor and management in the automobile field. A lengthy auto strike would be disastrous for *Look* and other consumer media and would also worsen the economy of the nation. *Look* carried about seventy-five pages of auto advertising a year. A strike could mean a lot of advertising revenue lost, at about $50,000 a page.

I asked how many pages represented the break-even point for *Look* and Whatmore answered, "About 1,500 pages." And 1,200 were budgeted! The only hope was for *Look* to show some gains in pages each year, with the hope that some time in the future—say 1973 or 1974—it would once again begin to show a profit. It was not an encouraging picture.

It was no comfort that *Look* had been losing fewer pages than *Life* during the past few years or that the reported losses on *Life* (said to be $13,000,000 in 1969) were higher than those of *Look*. Time, Inc., was in a much healthier state than Cowles Communications, Inc. Time, Inc., continued to show profits in 1969 and 1970, although they were much lower than in the immediately preceding years. While Time, Inc., stock was selling in the low 30s (as against a high of $100 per share the year before), it was still paying a nice dividend, whereas Cowles had eliminated dividends.

The mass consumer magazines were under great pressures in 1969 and 1970. Some questioned whether they would survive beyond 1971. Even *Reader's Digest,* with the biggest circulation and the most successful of them all, was feeling the pinch of declining advertising revenue.

Gardner Cowles continued to be optimistic about the future of consumer magazines in general and *Look* in particular, at least outwardly so. What he thought privately or what nightmares he might have had no one knew.

After Marvin reviewed the figures on *Look*, Gardner Cowles made the following observation: "It took us fifteen years to make a profit on *Look*. In the twenty years that followed, right through last year, *Look* made a profit. And in some years the profits were high indeed. We have had problems with *Look* before, and each time we were able to solve these problems and come out of them stronger than ever. I am very confident that we will do it again. We are going to go through some rough times, but we are going to make it—and *Look* will once again come out of its problems stronger than ever."

While all of us hoped that his pronouncement would prove correct, there were quite a few who had doubts that *Look* would make it this time. Among the most vocal doubters was Barney Gallagher, who expressed his doubts in no uncertain terms in his famous (or infamous) and widely read *Gallagher Report*. In the issue dated July 28, 1970, he said:

COWLES COMMUNICATIONS— A RACE TO THE GRAVE

Chairman "Mike" Cowles can't postpone decision on ailing flagship *Look*—six months revenue down

$4,859,338, ad pages off 12.9%. Attempt to sell *San Juan Star* underscores desperation. Collapse of *Look* would cost company $41.3 million: $10.4 million in obligations to cancelled subscribers; $30.9 million in terminated paid-during-service accounts (banks loaned estimated $19 million on strength of PDS revenues).

Mike "hangs on." Continued dominance of 67-year-old founder major factor in current crisis. Typical "founding father" won't relinquish power. Permits sentiment to influence business decisions. E.g., "Mike's" son "Pat," publisher & president of *Suffolk Sun*, ran up operating loss of $3.2 million before tardy decision to fold newspaper last October. Look for major stockholder, Cowles director John Perry Jr., to demand action. John's 577,437 shares at 12¾ at time of sale of *Ocala* (Fla.) *Star-Banner* in July 1969. Now at 3¾. Perry's paper loss—$5.2 million.

Most targets of this type of "reporting" consider it good judgment not to respond, especially to the personal aspect of it. Until now, Cowles Communications as a corporation, and Gardner Cowles and Marvin Whatmore as individuals, had ignored a long series of "indictments" and unhealthy implications published in the *Gallagher Report*. Apparently, CCI and its two principal officers were no longer willing to tolerate them. Marvin Whatmore was goaded into writing this memo:

July 30, 1970

TO: Senior Management of Cowles
              Communications, Inc. and Affiliated
              Companies

FROM: Marvin C. Whatmore

As you all know, wild tales about the imminent demise of various companies including LOOK Magazine and, by implication, Cowles Communications are going around. The latest and most pernicious story appeared this week in *The Gallagher Report*.

Misstatements such as those made by Gallagher should not be dignified with a reply. However, since nonsense of this type can have an adverse effect upon our advertisers and upon the morale of our employees, I feel that I should set the record straight for you, your customers and your staff.

1. LOOK Magazine has been profitable for twenty-one consecutive years. It will not be profitable in 1970. We are confident the magazine can be returned to profitability. To expedite this, we have launched a major cost reduction program and a reorganization of our subscription selling subsidiaries. Our new computer system, designed to reduce costs while improving LOOK's marketing capability, is expected to come on-stream in the first quarter of 1971. We have also announced a new metropolitan area marketing program for LOOK under which its circulation will be reduced to 6,500,000 and over 80% of it concentrated in 60 top marketing complexes. This program has been well received by advertisers and advertising agencies. We have recently landed several major advertising schedules. If there is no major or prolonged automobile industry strike, LOOK will have a page increase in the fourth quarter.

The communications industry has been adversely affected by the current recession as have dozens of other major industries. It would make as much sense for an established business in other temporarily depressed industries—such as aircraft manufacturing, automobiles, artificial fibres, textiles, etc.—to cease operation on the basis of one bad year as for LOOK to do so. In short, it makes no sense whatsoever.

2. Cowles Communications has some very profitable operations and a considerable degree of improvement in those operations that are not profitable.

The Business and Professional Publications Division was ahead substantially in the first six months. The Broadcasting Division and the Florida Newspapers were up in revenues. XOGRAPH will be profitable for the first time in 1970 and chances for continued profitability in 1971 are good. Cambridge Book Company is developing new product out of profits. This growing operation will have a good 1970 and an even better 1971. FAMILY CIRCLE's circulation is so strong that we are raising the cover price from 20¢ to 25¢ with the September issue. FAMILY CIRCLE's ad picture shows signs of turning around.

The Cowles Book Company is reducing its losses; VENTURE's revenues should run slightly ahead of last year's figures.

3. The sale of *The San Juan Star* would increase our flexibility in the current tight money market. We are still in active negotiations for this sale and expect negotiations to be successfully concluded. Conclusions such as Gallagher's that the attempt to sell the *Star* "underscores desperation" of CCI are as inaccurate as are the reasons he gives for the termination of negotiations with Capital Cities and as farfetched as his attack on Gardner Cowles and his speculation about John Perry, Jr.

For Cowles Communications—like hundreds of other companies—1970 will not be a good year. I believe our corporate performance in the fourth quarter will be better, barring an even more severe downturn in the economy, and that our performance in 1971 will be improved. I am optimistic, with only some reservations because of a few jolts that may yet come (e.g. automotive strike).

A copy found its way to the Gallagher offices, but Gallagher and his staff ignored it.

While in many ways the Gallagher piece was vicious and devastating, it did contain an amount of truth. And the questions raised were in the minds of many others, including some Cowles board members and several large stockholders.

Despite Gardner Cowles' avowed optimism that "*Look* would make it this time, as it did in the past," there were many doubters, both inside and outside the company. And for good reason. For one thing, time was running out. The $10,000,000 in cash which Cowles Communications received for its very desirable property, the *San Juan Star*, would be sufficient to support *Look* losses (along with the corporation's other losses) for one year. This meant that *Look* must begin to make it in a substantial way in 1971. This did not mean that *Look* had to write 300 more pages of advertising than in 1970—the break-even requirement for the magazine. It did have to show an important linage gain—say, 100 to 150 pages more than the 1970 volume of approximately 1,200 pages (which represented a decline of more than 200 pages from 1969, and a decline of about 320 pages from 1968). In 1967, when *Look* earned about $4,000,000 before taxes, it published 1,650 pages of paid advertising.

If *Look* succeeded in writing about 1,300 to 1,350 pages in 1971, it would still mean a big loss for the Look operation, but it would be much, much less than the $8,000,000 loss budgeted for 1970. Most importantly, it would represent a positive indication that *Look* was beginning to make a turnaround, and if the economy continued to improve, increased linage could be expected in 1972 and in 1973. If all of these elements should fall into place, *Look* could make it by 1974 or 1975. But it would take money to support *Look* during this turnaround period. And that could require the selling off of other Cowles assets—obviously profit-producing assets.

On the other hand, if a lengthy automobile strike did

take place, and *Look* lost most of its seventy-five automobile advertising pages—on top of its already substantial page loss—and this situation was followed by only a minor linage increase, or no increase at all in 1971, *Look* would be in real trouble. At that point only the chairman's death wish for the corporation would result in continuing *Look* beyond mid-1971.

At the corporation's special board meeting on July 20, no one, least of all Gardner Cowles, could predict the direction *Look* would take.

Certainly, Gardner Cowles' optimism of the previous four years, in the face of the record, was not something anyone could bank on. And most assuredly, the financial community had no intention of doing it. Severe pressures were about to be exerted.

What was Gardner Cowles' record for the previous four years? It was a record of almost total failure, the most inexcusable, the most unconscionable being the *Suffolk Sun* debacle. If there were any phase of the communications business in which Cowles had thorough training and expertise it was, or should have been, the newspaper field.

He was born into a newspaper family on January 31, 1903, in Algona, Iowa. Immediately upon his graduation from Harvard, twenty-two-year-old Gardner joined the family operation, the *Des Moines Register and Tribune*, already the biggest and most important newspaper in the entire state of Iowa. Until early in 1936, when he founded *Look* magazine, he worked in many of the *Register and Tribune* editorial departments, from reporting to editing the Sunday picture page. He was creative. He had what was then called good newspaper sense. And he applied himself with an abundance of energy and great dedication. This, despite the fact that he was not particularly happy or at ease in his job. The reason for this was largely psychological. He was working for a strong, very able, dominating father. And preceding him at the *Des Moines Register and Tribune* was his highly competent and business-oriented older brother, John.

Gardner Cowles, Sr., got into the newspaper business by accident. As the president of a small bank in Algona, he lent a business friend a small sum to help him buy the *Des Moines Register and Leader*, the town's Number Three newspaper. In 1903, when the publisher couldn't meet his loan payments, the banker was about to foreclose.

Convinced, however, that the property could become profitable in time, in growing Des Moines, he bailed out the publisher in return for a partnership, and five years later he bought the paper for $300,000. The *Register and Leader* was $180,000 in debt and had a circulation of 16,000. Shortly thereafter, he bought the newly established *Tribune*. By the time young Mike graduated from Phillips Exeter Academy in 1921, the *Des Moines Register and Tribune* was flourishing.

From the very beginning, the elder Cowles put his newspaper subscriptions on a cash-in-advance basis. He also made it his business to deliver his paper to subscribers every day at the same time. In 1924, with readers of the two other Des Moines newspapers diminishing in numbers daily, he bought the *News* from Scripps-Howard. Three years later the last of the Des Moines papers, the *Capital*, called it a day. Thus, in 1927, two years after young Mike joined the family newspaper, the *Register and Tribune* was the only newspaper in Des Moines, publishing both a morning and afternoon edition and assuming a monopoly position. It also became Iowa's statewide newspaper.

Gardner Cowles, Sr., the son of a Methodist minister, believed in old-fashioned discipline. Self-educated, he had to support himself from the time he was fifteen.

Mike's mother was even stronger than her husband, although she never let on, and deferred to her husband on most issues. She also had a sharp sense of humor. Unlike her husband, she was a college graduate—the first woman graduate of Northwestern University in Chicago. She influenced Mike more than his father, of whom he was a little frightened, and with whom he never really had a good father-son conversation. While his father was interested solely in his business—first in banking, then in his newspaper—his mother had a much wider range of interests. She was involved in just about every intellectual pursuit.

Cowles, Sr., stern, ultraconservative, hardheaded, expected his three sons to enter the family business. Gardner and John, after graduation from Harvard, got in and stayed in. Russell, after Dartmouth, was forced into the business side, although his preference was editorial. Russell wanted to be a painter and when he found himself working in the classified department, sometimes until midnight, he rebelled. In later years, when Russell received the Prix de Rome of the American Academy of Art, his father conceded that "maybe Russell does have something in his art."

John liked the business side of the newspaper. But when it was time for Gardner to enter the family business and he expressed a desire to be in editorial, his father—apparently having learned from his experience with Russell—permitted Gardner to have his wish.

Young Mike was a good reporter and writer. At Harvard, he became editor of the *Crimson* in his junior year. Upon graduation in 1925, he stepped into the job of city editor of the *Register and Tribune*. (He remained active and fully identified with the paper throughout his career, even through the launching of *Look* magazine and the formation and operation of Cowles Communications.)

A year later, Mike became associate managing editor of the *Register and Tribune,* and within a few months he was promoted to managing editor, a post he held until 1931 when he became executive editor. The young managing editor instituted a technique of covering the state of Iowa and the entire Middle West by airplane for both news and pictures.

Young Mike launched George Gallup on his career of polling public opinion. Gallup was then an instructor in journalism at the University of Iowa. Following a conversation with the young teacher, Mike got the idea for a plan to measure reader interest. He asked Gallup to make this type of survey for the *Register and Tribune* and the Iowa instructor jumped at the opportunity. The initial results of the first series of Gallup studies revealed that newspaper readers were more inclined to look at pictures with brief and eye-catching captions than to read long columns of type. As a result, Mike developed a picture-story approach which helped to increase the newspaper's circulation. He replaced individual roto-gravure pictures with a headline and a series of related pictures with captions. It was Mike who decided that the Laurence Stallings' pictures of the First World War would make fine picture-copy coverage. And he proved to be right. In 1933, a roto picture service was established by the *Register and Tribune* and before long this service was successfully syndicated to a long list of newspapers in various sections of the country.

It was this innovation in picture-news coverage which led to the idea that meant the eventual launching of both *Look* and *Life.* The late Henry Luce has been credited with the creation of the unique concept in publishing *Life,* the first magazine that covered current news events in pictures. However, Marvin Whatmore has another version of the story.

According to Whatmore, it was after his success with

the roto picture service that young Gardner Cowles thought of launching a national magazine with picture-story coverage of major news stories. The elder Cowles showed only mild enthusiasm for his son's dummy copy and prospectus for the new venture.

Mike said: "I believe I can get started with about $80,000."

Banker-oriented Cowles the elder replied; "I think it will take more than $80,000 to make a go of a magazine of this kind. Anyway, you don't expect me to hand you over $80,000 for this wild idea of yours, Mike, do you?"

Young Gardner did, and said so. But his father's answer was a resounding no, and no matter how strong was the son's pleading, the elder Cowles remained adamant. However, the young Gardner was not going to be stopped. The more he thought of it, the more he liked the idea. But how could he raise $80,000, especially in the depression thirties? After days and nights of deep thought, he came upon a solution. Harvard's Gardner Cowles admired Yale's Henry Luce, who had proved so successful with *Time* magazine, the first weekly news magazine.

Whatmore gives the impression that it was Cowles and not Luce who was first with the idea of a picture magazine. At any rate, Cowles set a date with Luce for an early meeting in New York, at which the two editors agreed to form a jointly owned company (funded by Time, Inc.) to publish two picture magazines: one called *Look,* a biweekly to appeal to the mass market; and the other, *Life,* a weekly which would be a class magazine with a smaller circulation. The first issues would be launched at about the same time. However, when the first issue of *Life* appeared on the stands it was a complete sellout, and a few issues later, *Life* became a "mass" and not a "class" magazine.

Gardner Cowles became alarmed, if not downright sickened, over the unexpected events. A spirited argument with Luce ensued.

"What am I supposed to do now?" Cowles asked.

"I'm very sorry, Gardner," Henry Luce said haltingly. "This was not my idea. But when *Life* appeared on the stands, everybody just grabbed for it. It became a mass magazine. We did not make it that, it was beyond our control. And now my associates feel that we should let nature take its course. If the public wants *Life,* by God we are going to give them *Life*—in the millions."

Henry Luce then suggested to Gardner Cowles that they reverse the course of action—make *Look* the class picture magazine. Gardner would have none of this, and the end result was the transfer of *Look*'s ownership plus a substantial amount of cash from the partnership to Gardner Cowles. And it was with this capital that Cowles moved quickly to establish *Look*—as a mass picture magazine with a slightly different emphasis from that of *Life. Look* was to use larger pictures, it was to be printed on roto and it would pursue a more "sensational" approach. Cowles decided that as a biweekly or monthly, *Look* could not, and would not directly compete with *Life*'s weekly picture news coverage technique. The first issue of *Look* appeared on January 15, 1937. It was to be published monthly. Vernon Pope was its first editor.

Shortly after the introductions of *Life* and *Look,* an avalanche of picture magazines followed, some very lurid. As the years passed, only *Life* and *Look* survived. It took a long time, much perseverance and a great deal of ability and fortitude to keep *Look* going. After fifteen years, *Look,* by now a biweekly finally began to make a profit. Cowles proved he was not only a good newspaperman but had what it takes to be a successful magazine publisher as well. He had the guts to stick with a project in which he believed.

That is why it was shocking and unbelievable to see the same Gardner Cowles make just about every mistake in the book in the launching and operation of the *Suffolk Sun*. He had just about everything going for him: a professional knowledge of the newspaper business; $35,000,000 of working capital in his Cowles Communications and access to additional financing; the availability of needed research and expertise in interpreting and using it; and the experience and the ability to hire competent if not superior talent to run the newspaper.

Yet, from the very first move, he made mistake after mistake, which resulted in a loss of about $15,-000,000 and the collapse of his ambition to make Cowles Communications, Inc., the biggest, the most successful and the most prestigious enterprise in publishing—overtaking Time, Inc., McGraw-Hill and all the rest.

On August 15, 1966, Gardner Cowles and Marvin Whatmore addressed an association of security analysts and made a number of assertions about their hopes for the growing, exciting, "hot" Cowles Communications, Inc.

Cowles said he would "go out on a limb" in outlining the business goals of his company. He stressed the rapid diversification of the company, exemplified by a large number of properties acquired or started from scratch and, particularly by the impending publication of the *Suffolk Sun*. He pointed to heavy investments for the future in new properties such as *Venture* magazine, Xograph and products for the educational division—the so-called learning industry

—in addition to the *Suffolk Sun*. He pointed to a gain of 85 percent in earnings per share (from 8 cents in 1961 to $1.48 in 1965) since Cowles went public, and voiced an expectation of accelerated earnings in the immediate years ahead.

Although he conceded that Cowles' profit margin of 3.1 percent was low, he pointed out that this was an improvement, and predicted continued gains. He also noted that, although his company ranked 414th in dollars sales among the nation's 500 largest industrial companies, it ranked forty-eighth in profit as a percentage of invested capital. Annual dividends of 50 cents a share, amounting to about 30 percent of estimated 1966 earnings, could be moderately increased, he said, while leaving the company in a strong cash position for possible acquisitions.

Marvin Whatmore summarized the company's position and specific plans for its various properties. He pointed to an average age of fifty-two for senior management and forty-two for second-line management.

The magazine division, he said, is dominated by *Look* in both revenue and profits, attained through consistent growth in circulation and advertising. *Look* intended to intensify its efforts to increase advertising through a flexible system of regional editions, increased penetration of U.S. households, and editorial and subscription solicitation programs directed to better-education, higher-income families. *Look*'s annual advertising revenue goal by 1969, he said, was $100,-000,000.

Family Circle, which pioneered a system of magazine distribution through supermarkets, has "the greatest potential for growth of any consumer magazine in existence today," Whatmore told the security analysts. He pointed to a need to change the publication's image from that of a "store" book to a complete women's service magazine, and thus broaden the categories of advertising it carried. Food and other products sold in supermarkets provided 80 percent of *Family Circle*'s 1965 advertising revenue of $22,800,000. Soft goods, home products and other advertising categories, he predicted, would be tapped by *Family Circle* through physical upgrading—high-grade paper, printing and binding—of the magazine to achieve a quality image. After nine years of growth, *Family Circle* would show a decline in advertising revenue in 1966, about 12 percent, for reasons that Whatmore labeled "temporary."

Venture, The Traveler's World, in its third year of publication, would run 20 percent ahead. Seeking to reach households with average annual incomes in excess of $20,000, *Venture* faced the problem of increasing circulation without "diluting this selectivity"—a goal Whatmore hoped to achieve through mailings to card holders of American Express and credit customers of prestige stores such as Neiman-Marcus, Abercrombie and Fitch, and Bullock's. Cowles' goal was to turn the corner, from loss to profit, by the end of 1967. "If we do," averred Whatmore, "it will be somewhat of a record in magazine history. We look upon *Venture,* in our growing affluent society, as one of our productive 'seeds'."

Whatmore also summarized the positions of other Cowles magazines:

Insider's Newsletter, featuring news highlights, grew from 127,000 at the start of 1965 to 167,000. The British *Family Circle* (owned by Cowles and the Thompson interests in Britain on a fifty-fifty basis) is moving ahead from its position as the largest monthly women's magazine in the U.K., and the German *Family Circle* has an equally promising future.

The newspaper division, he went on, is part of a growth industry with a higher return on investment than

TV stations. Cowles' principles in starting or acquiring newspapers, he said, were: to locate in an area of population and industrial growth; to favor areas with universities since they tend to attract "highly desirable" industry; to become part and parcel of the community; to seek markets with definite needs for newspapers. The San Juan, Gainesville and Lakeland papers, he said, meet these criteria, and each is highly profitable. The upcoming *Suffolk Sun* "more than meets our criteria," he maintained. Whatmore pointed out that this paper "represents over a one-million-dollar pre-publication investment."

Whatmore also reviewed: Cowles' interests in TV and radio—three TV stations, two radio outlets, all "top-rated in fast-growing markets"; a publication sales division—selling subscriptions for more than 100 magazines through more than 500 franchised dealers; the education division—involving publication of an encyclopedia, acquisition of the College Publishing Corporation, expansion of its line of test-preparation books from 450 to 600; and Xograph 3-D printing—hailed as "the fourth major breakthrough in printing technology since the fifteenth century" by the *Saturday Review*.

The security analysts were impressed with the presentation and with Whatmore's prediction that "as a diversified . . . and still diversifying . . . communications company, our profit margins should continue to improve." Cowles' commanding ten-year record (from 1956 through 1965) showed a growth in sales from $40,300,000 to $137,200,000 and a growth in net earnings from $640,000 to $4,378,000. And the best was yet to come, especially the prospects for growth and profit with the new *Suffolk Sun*.

The presentation was expertly prepared and with added pictures, charts and graphs, it made a very nice package. A copy of this package was given to me so that I could see the kind of company of which I was becoming an important part. Copies of the package were also made available to the press on "a selective basis," and the press so favored reacted in kind. Cowles had a very good press in 1966. The stock responded well although not particularly aggressively. Which was healthy, of course.

I first learned some of the details of the plans for the *Suffolk Sun* in my first meeting of the board on November 17, almost two weeks before our MFI deal was consummated. A glowing picture was placed before us. Nobody asked questions. Everybody seemed pleased.

Although Whatmore had told the security analysts the pre-publication costs of the *Suffolk Sun* were a million dollars, no figures were presented at the board meeting. Nothing was said about the start-up costs, break-even estimates, anticipated expenses, or predicted revenues.

As a freshman member of the board, whose deal had not been completed, I asked no questions. At that stage I was in awe of the entire proceeding of my first meeting with the illustrious members of the board.

Several months later, I learned something concrete about the plans for the *Suffolk Sun*. At a meeting at which we reviewed plans for the launching of *Education News*, Whatmore explained that the Louis Harris public opinion polling organization had been commissioned to do the basic investigative research to determine the market potentials for the *Sun*. We were handed bright blue, hand-bound, eighty-page copies of the report of this study. This was done and the subject of the *Sun* was discussed because Gardner Cowles thought that it would be a good idea to have Louis Harris make a similar study of the market potential of the upcoming *Education News*. In addition to Cowles, Whatmore and me, the meeting was attended by Jack Harding, Gil Maurer and Dave Whitney.

The impressive *Sun* study had many tables and charts. The fact that Louis Harris knew little or nothing about running a daily paper and had never made a study of this kind before did not seem to matter to Cowles and his associates. They used the report as the basis for planning, directing and operating the *Suffolk Sun*. Harris was very much in the news as a pollster and measurer of public opinion.

Gardner Cowles explained that the Harris study revealed that Suffolk was the fastest growing county in the nation, that it had no daily newspaper of its own, that it needed one very acutely. The study also showed that such a daily should be a large-size morning paper, providing national as well as local news. The report also pointed to an immediate and enthusiastic response on the part of the community to such a daily—a newspaper that would appeal to all members of the family. Cowles then pointed to some of the charts and graphs which showed the age groups and their earning levels, how many commuted to New York City daily and how many worked in Suffolk County.

"What did this cost?" I asked.

"One hundred thousand dollars," Marvin Whatmore replied, adding: "But of course, we don't need to spend quite that much for the *Education News* study."

We were permitted to take the copy of the report "for a few days," to study it more carefully.

"But please return it next week," Marvin Whatmore said. "This is a confidential report and Louis Harris is very 'touchy' about anyone outside the top *Suffolk Sun* management seeing or using it in any way. Of course, we were not permitted to publicize the fact that Louis Harris made this study since he does not do any commercial work. He happens to be a friend of ours. He has done some public opinion studies for *Look* and he had made an exception in this case."

I was now one of the Cowles insiders. I was behind the scenes at the launching of the great new daily newspaper in the nation's fastest-growing community. It was not until a year later that I began to suspect some of the very costly mistakes that Cowles had been making on the *Sun.* When I had the full knowledge late in 1968, and began to feel the full impact of these unbelievable, terribly costly, downright crippling mistakes, I was shocked. But then it was too late to do very much about the problem.

The final blow came on Friday, October 17, 1969, when we were called to a special board meeting. While nothing had been said officially, I knew that the purpose of the meeting was to approve a motion to suspend publication of the *Suffolk Sun.* I did not know that Gardner Cowles III (or "Pat," as he was called), Mike's only son, who was the publisher of the *Sun,* was waiting to meet his father.

We met at 3:30 P.M. and by 4:20 it was all over. Chairman Gardner Cowles read the brief resolution calling for the suspension of the *Suffolk Sun,* effective after the publication of the next day's issue. He explained the reasons behind "the reluctant decision." While advertising linage was increasing—it carried 7,500,000 lines in 1968, an increase of 45 percent over 1967—circulation was not. Although 100,000 copies were being delivered to Suffolk County residents, as guaranteed to advertisers, the paid circulation was going below 70,000, having reached a maximum of 80,000 on November 21, 1967, its first anniversary. To deliver the over 30,000 free copies as well as to deliver the 70,000 paid subscriptions proved to be very costly. Cowles had called in a circulation expert from the *Minneapolis Star and Tribune,* the successful daily run by brother John and nephew John, Jr. The expert spent several weeks "on location" studying the problem, and then came back with a lengthy report. The report was not made available to the directors. However, the chairman reviewed the contents of the report briefly. He explained that daily newspapers traditionally make a profit on circulation and can never service readers at a loss. The minimum they can tolerate is a break-even situation. The *Suffolk Sun*'s circulation loss since it had been launched on November 21, 1966 had been $3,000,000 a year. The Minneapolis expert opined that more of the same could be expected and he recommended that the *Suffolk Sun* stop publication immediately. Cowles said that the heavy loss was due largely to the difficulty the paper encountered in obtaining newsboys who would get up as early as five in the morning so that the *Sun* could be delivered to subscribers before seven, as promised to both advertisers and subscribers.

"Young lads no longer find it a thrill to make a few cents or a few dollars delivering newspapers, as was the case in my time," Cowles said. "And even when we do sell a few boys to take on the task, they do not remain on the job very long. We have had one hundred percent turnover in newsboys on the *Sun* every month. A boy will work for several days, then his mother will call up and say: 'Johnny is ill today, he won't be able to deliver the paper.' And we never see Johnny again. This means that we have had to use delivery trucks to deliver individual papers and this has proved to be extremely costly. And so, reluctantly, very reluctantly, and sadly, I have had to reach the conclusion to suspend the paper after tomorrow's issue. There is a need for a paper like the *Sun* in Suffolk County and some day some publisher will find a way to publish one at a profit. The *Sun* is a good paper and is performing a service to the community, so I feel doubly sad—for us and the Suffolk County community. Maybe we were ahead of our time, but it was a mistake—a very serious mistake—for Cowles Communications to start the *Suffolk Sun . . .* and I take full responsibility for it."

It was not a very happy meeting. It was big of Cowles to say that he took full responsibility for the $15,000,000 mistake, based in large part on a failure to determine in advance whether newsboys would deliver the paper.

But who was absorbing this devastating loss? Not the chairman alone. All of the stockholders, including Cowles, of course. Shortly after the announcement of the demise of the *Sun* (and with Cowles Communications continuing to report losses), the price of the stock began to plummet. It went from $14⅞ the day before the suspension of the *Sun* to a new low of $4¼ about ten months later, on August 24, 1970. Some stockholders had paid as much as $21 a share on March 29, 1967, with the bulk of the buying at around $15 a share. When Cowles went public on October 25, 1961, the stock opened at $15½ per share and when the issue moved for trading on the New York Stock Exchange on May 10, 1966, the opening quotation was $17½ per share.

What Gardner Cowles did not ever explain to his board was the series of unbelievable mistakes in launching and operating the *Sun*. In the opinion of those "in the know" in the publishing community, these were the following:

MISTAKE NUMBER ONE: No meaningful projection was made of the capital needs to launch and bring the *Sun* to the "break-even point." Whatever cursory projections were made were highly underestimated.

Mistake Number Two: No goals were established relating to the time and cost of obtaining the necessary 125,000 minimum paid circulation to make the *Sun* viable.

Mistake Number Three: Gardner Cowles, whose stated business philosophy was "never to buy or start a newspaper except on a 'monopoly' basis," started the *Suffolk Sun* in a market that had already been crossed over by a highly successful, very powerful Nassau County (the adjoining county to Suffolk) daily. Just about everyone in the business knew that Harry Guggenheim's *Newsday* would not take the new Suffolk competition lying down. Immediately upon the *Suffolk Sun*'s entrance into the field, *Newsday* increased its circulation in Suffolk County sharply—soon reaching a total paid distribution of 125,000 in Suffolk. And, of course, *Newsday* upgraded its Suffolk County editorial coverage at the same time.

Mistake Number Four: Instead of concentrating the coverage of the *Suffolk Sun* in a central, carefully specified area with the greatest population density, emphasizing newsstand sales as well as home delivery, and then building on this kind of nucleus, the *Sun* decided on an all-county distribution—practically entirely on a home delivery basis. As a result, the distances between some individual subscribers were dozens of miles—and as much as fifty miles between groups of handfuls of subscribers.

Mistake Number Five: Shouldn't cursory investigation have shown that boys would not be available in the affluent sixties in lush Suffolk County to deliver the paper early every morning? This single sophomoric error piled up costs to the point of no return.

Mistake Number Six: With over forty years of solid, successful newspaper experience, did Gardner Cowles have to look to an expert from Minneapolis to tell him what was wrong with the *Suffolk Sun?* Did he need an outside opinion on why no daily newspaper could survive with a $3,000,000 annual loss from circulation? If he did, why didn't he call on expert help during the early months of operation, instead of waiting until $15,000,000 was dissipated?

Mistake Number Seven: As a good and experienced newspaperman, shouldn't Gardner Cowles have hired a local publisher, a local editor and a local staff who were familiar with, and had a feeling for, the Suffolk County communities? He brought in a staff from Florida—a young, relatively inexperienced group of newspapermen, who knew nothing of Suffolk County, its news sources, its needs and its problems and never seemed to learn.

Mistake Number Eight: Instead of making the *Suffolk Sun* the kind of local newspaper that was needed and wanted in Suffolk, a home town market, Cowles stressed national coverage. He competed with the *New York Times,* a newspaper that was readily available to all Suffolk County residents, many of whom did not buy it because they were more interested in local happenings than in national news. They read their local weeklies, several of which Cowles bought but failed to properly absorb into the *Sun.*

Mistake Number Nine: With newspaper technology and graphics advancing magnificently and explosively in the sixties, reaching new dimensions in automation, the *Suffolk Sun* built and equipped an old-fashioned, terribly dated plant with hand work throughout—from old-fashioned linotype machines to stone, hand make-up. This exposed the operation to the mercy of the powerful printing unions and the high cost of printing in the New York metropolitan area. If the unions (among the employees of the *Sun*) raised objections to automation, that should have been reason enough not to start a newspaper in Suffolk County.

MISTAKE NUMBER TEN: Gardner Cowles was playing with millions of dollars. It may or may not have been a mistake to name his only son, Pat, as publisher of the *Suffolk Sun*. But once that decision was made, shouldn't Gardner Cowles have given the publisher his head? Instead, Gardner Cowles tried to run the paper from headquarters at 488 Madison Avenue and treated his thirty-five-year-old son like a little boy. He directed Pat's every important step.

After the resolution to suspend the *Sun* was read, and the chairman made his brief explanation of the need for the action, he called for a vote: "Those who approve, please say 'Aye'." The ayes came quietly . . . "Those who oppose, say 'Nay'." There were no nays, although several of us, including me, made no sound at all. What was there to say? A decision had been reached—a decision that should have been made long ago and action taken at least two years earlier. The chairman had the votes in his vest pocket (he was wearing a vest, as was his custom). "There are no 'nays'—the motion is carried."

Executive Vice President, Secretary and Chief Lawyer Jack Harding rushed out of the board room to tell his secretary to advise the New York Stock Exchange of the action and to tell Dick Collins, the corporate chief PR man, to release the news to the press.

The meeting was adjourned and Gardner Cowles

walked over slowly to his office where his son, Pat, was waiting. "Pat, we just convened a special meeting of the board of directors and we approved a resolution to suspend the *Suffolk Sun* after tomorrow's issue . . . I am very sorry, Pat, deeply sorry. . . ."

Pat did not say a word, did not even look at his father. He just walked out quickly . . . and it was a long time before he was to see his father again. No one knew where young Cowles and his wife went. "To Switzerland," someone said.

Several months later, a news story appeared in the February 27, 1970 issue of the *Three Village Herald*, a weekly newspaper of Stony Brook, Setauket and Old Field in Suffolk County, announcing that Gardner Cowles III had bought the newspaper with his *own money*, that he and the paper would have no connection "whatsoever with Cowles Communications, Inc." and that it would be operated by Pat Cowles as an individual. He said that he had grown fond of Suffolk County and liked The Three Village community particularly. From this point on, the relationship between father Gardner and son Gardner III—Mike and Pat— never particularly chummy, became strained and remained that way for a long time.

A year later, Jim Whatmore, Marvin Whatmore's only son, left his job as assistant controller in production of Cowles Communications, Inc., to join Pat Cowles, Gardner Cowles' only son, in his growing weekly newspaper chain on Long Island, starting a partnership and/or relationship in some ways a counterpart to what happened to their fathers about thirty-five years earlier. It will be interesting to see what happens to the new Cowles and Whatmore enterprise in the years ahead.

ELEVEN:

Around the Rosewood Oval Table
—for the Last Time

The night before the special executive committee meeting I slept well. I was no longer concerned about any possible slipup. After the special board meeting on Monday, I had every reason to believe that things would go well for me at the Tuesday luncheon.

The scene was familiar. The spacious, lush reception room of the executive suite which had so electrified me when I entered it for the first time on August 5, 1966, had looked gloomier and gloomier each time I came into it during the past few months. It seemed as if there were no one in the executive offices behind the filigreed partitions. Even the charming, poised and spirited receptionist, Joan Bender, seemed gloomy.

"Hello, Mr. Gussow."

"Hello, Joan. I have a luncheon date with Mr. Whatmore, and—"

"I know." She went out to announce me to Marvin Whatmore's secretary. I sat down to wait.

Jack Harding was the first to come out, followed by Gil Maurer, and then Merrill Clough. We walked into the executive dining room.

How many times had I been in that comfortable and attractive dining room! How different the room appeared each time I was there, somehow blending with the mood of each meeting. This was the same room in which Gardner Cowles and the CCI bright lights had met with Henry Ford and other major industrialists— all big advertisers—and political figures such as Hubert Humphrey, the late Robert Kennedy, and Nelson Rockefeller.

The executive dining room that noon did not seem cheerful to me.

As Gil Maurer started serving the drinks, I said, "You make a fine bartender, I'd hire you any time you want to do some moonlighting."

"As a matter of fact, I am a good bartender," Gil said. "I worked my way through school as a bartender."

Gardner Cowles walked in, looking sombre. He smiled thinly and said: "Hello, Don." I replied: "Hi, Mike." Marvin Whatmore was the last to arrive, coming into the room briskly, smiling widely, as usual. The only member of the executive committee not in the room was Don Perkins. I wondered whether he was not there by design or whether he happened to be on vacation, ill or out of town. He was the only truly frank and outspoken member of the "insiders' team." I concluded that he was not wanted at this meeting lest he say something that could prove embarrassing or costly to Cowles or favorable to me.

"How's *Ecology* coming along, Don?" Marvin asked me. He was referring to a new magazine that we were planning to introduce later in the year.

"There really isn't much I can say at this time. It's much too early—"

"How many pages of advertising do you have, as of now?" Marvin pressed for an answer.

"We have sold the center spread . . . Another page or two. We don't have any of the paperwork yet."

"If you sign up ten pages you'll publish, is that right, Don?"

"Yes, Marv, that's correct. Our goal is sixteen pages, but ten is the minimum we need for the first issue. I have to quote Mike when he told Burt Cohen recently in connection with the plans for the new medical magazine: 'Don't get overenthusiastic even in the face of a favorable reaction. Wait and see what advertising pages actually come in.' We did get a fine initial reaction, but I have to wait until those orders begin to come in before I can say that *Industrial Ecology* will have a fighting chance to succeed."

The conversation turned to the general economy and its effect on advertising. I asked Cowles: "Mike, how do you view business prospects for the fall and the first quarter of 1971?"

"I think the recession is bottoming out. However, I can't see a great or speedy improvement, but in six to nine months, things will begin to get better," Gardner Cowles said. "It has been a very rough recession—almost like the depression of the thirties, much worse than a lot of economists or the men in government would admit."

I commented: "I lived through the depression of the thirties and I know what it means . . . what real tightening means."

He just looked at me. He did not say how the depression of the thirties had affected him. It was in 1938 that he had started *Look*.

Marvin finally said: "Don, I called this meeting on your behalf—to clear the air—so why don't you start discussing things now?"

I was well prepared but I tried to avoid "reading a speech." I glanced at the others and then addressed myself to Cowles: "Mike, do you remember when we first met here? Marvin, you, and I? I remember it clearly. It was August 5, 1966—a date I will always remember. It was the first time we met and it followed the luncheon meeting I had had with Marvin several weeks earlier. You remember, Marv, don't you? We had lunch at the Marco Polo Club on July 21. By the time the three of us met here, we had a basis for an agreement. When we were here then, Mike, one of the first questions you asked me was: 'Don, when you get our stock, will you take the money and run or will you operate?' I'm sure you remember my answer. I said: 'What you are buying in MFI, in my little business, is merely a nucleus on which to build a bigger, very important business magazine company. This is the real reason for my merging with Cowles, to make it possible for me to accelerate our growth, to utilize whatever resources you will make available to me—stock, cash, research, people—to expand and grow. Of course, I want to and will operate. I am not selling out, I am buying in. That is the way I look at my merger with Cowles.' "

He seemed to listen patiently, as did the others. I continued, still addressing myself to Cowles: "You will remember, Mike, that you asked me what fields I was interested in for growth, what were my priorities. I told you that I wanted to get into medicine, education and plastics. I had my heart set on buying *Modern Medicine* long before our merger with Cowles. I did not approach the Herzes and the Cohens because I felt that MFI was a much smaller operation and, as a result, it would be practically impossible to swing a deal of that magnitude, even if they had shown interest in my proposal. The first thing I did after our merger was to move to buy *Modern Medcine*. I had already done my homework and, as a result knew the *Modern Medicine* situation quite well. I followed up with some more of my own research. I didn't have to call on outside, high-priced research talent. I did not ask for, nor was I offered any research help from anyone at Cowles. On my own, I was able to determine that this prestigious, highly profitable business magazine company was having some serious trouble at that particular time and would thus be inclined to sell—to a desirable buyer and under certain favorable conditions.

"*Modern Medicine,* and the company that owned it and several other medical and dental publications, was in trouble because it was run by a committee of three following the death about a dozen years earlier of its founder and president, the very able and beloved Jacob Cohen. It is difficult, if not impossible, to run a business by committee, and the three men who formed the operating committee were unusual individuals—each one very different from the others, and each antagonistic to the others. What made the situation untenable was an agreement not to make any major decision unless all three partners agreed. As long as the company prospered and as long as the company did not face a critical decision, each partner went on his merry way, but once the three partners were faced with a crisis—as they were in 1965—they were at one another's throats and none would give way. The way out was to sell . . . and I soon learned that Cahners had been negotiating to buy the business, but that that deal had fallen through . . ."

Gardner Cowles listened attentively, and it occurred to me that he had not heard the details of the negotiations that led to the purchase of *Modern Medicine.* Obviously, Marvin and Jack, with whom I had worked on the deal, had not filled him in.

Before I could continue my story of the *Modern*

Medicine negotiations, Marvin broke in: "Why don't we sit down at the table and have our lunch?"

We took our drinks with us. I hadn't touched mine except for the first sip. Food was served. I was unable to eat. I drank half the coffee in a small cup; that was my lunch. I continued the *Modern Medicine* story as the others ate. I continued to address myself to Gardner Cowles.

"On February 7, 1967, just over two months after our merger, I wrote a letter to Teresa Cohen, widow of founder Jacob Cohen, explaining that Magazines For Industry, as the new business paper nucleus of Cowles, would be interested in buying her company. I received a reply several days later, written in longhand, advising me that her associates were all away from the office but that one of them would be in touch with me before long.

"Early in March, I received a telephone call from Mal Herz, who had stopped over in New York for a day following a short visit in London, after a two months' photographic safari in Africa. Mal and I met for lunch at the Marco Polo Club. What happened is now history. But I would like to fill you in on some details, Mike . . ."

I touched on the discussions and correspondence that I had had with Mal and others which finally led to the negotiations which resulted in the acquisition of *Modern Medicine* by Cowles.

"You will remember, Mike, the meeting Marvin and I had with you in your office in March of 1967, in which I outlined my plan to buy *Modern Medicine*. I showed you copies of several issues of the magazine together with copies of some of the company's other publications—*Geriatrics, Neurology, Lancet* and *Dental Survey*—and I reviewed the basic formula of the operation. It was not a lengthy meeting, although you asked several questions and I answered them in some detail. Marvin finally asked me what I thought we would have to pay for the property and I said that I thought we could do it for about $8,500,000 to $9,000,000. I pointed out that if we could buy it at such a price, we would be getting a real bargain. Incidentally, when I said that we could buy the Modern Medicine operation for $9,000,000 or less, I had no idea that the deal would include $1,700,000 in cash plus a beautiful building with a value then of close to $2,000,000. But that is exactly what happened. We paid $9,000,000 and got all this. Mike, if I did nothing else for Cowles, merely by bringing in the *Modern Medicine* deal, I earned every cent you paid for MFI and to me in salary, and a lot more besides. You owe me plenty, Mike."

At this point, Jack Harding came through with a shocker: "Don, I have listened to your recital of the acquisition of *Modern Medicine* and you seem to give the impression that you did the buying. I must correct you. You did not buy *Modern Medicine*. Marvin and I did. What you did was introduce us to the Herzes and the Cohens. Marv and I did the negotiating and the buying."

While I was horrified to hear Jack Harding, whom I considered to be a fair human being and my friend in many ways, speak the way he did, I was not too surprised. I remembered the words of Don Perkins several weeks before this meeting: "Don, surely you must know that a lot of the people at Cowles take credit for *Modern Medicine*—its acquisition and its success . . ." Maybe I should have known better, and in a measure, this was something that I had felt in my bones for a long time—but I hated to believe that was the way Jack Harding had felt about it.

"Wait a minute, Jack." I attempted to mask my

anger. "Of course, I got a lot of help from you and Marvin. Marv charmed them all in Minneapolis . . . kissing Teresa at every opportunity and referring to Mal as 'the brother I did not have and always wanted to have,' and as a lawyer in negotiations, you were superb, Jack. *But don't tell me that I did not buy Modern Medicine*—that you and Marv did. No such thing! You never heard of, nor knew anything about *Modern Medicine*. I did my own research and brought every piece of substantive information to you. It took a great deal of experience and knowledge in the field to make the right approach. You know I am not inclined to boast, but I must say right here and now that there are not too many business magazine publishers who know as much about this business as I do or have my wide acquaintance in the field. Not only was I able to determine the proper approach to use in the *Modern Medicine* deal, but it was I who determined the price to be paid, and you know very well that I was very much involved with you and Marv in the negotiations in Minneapolis, including the first and most important meeting with their attorneys. It was only after the agreement in principle had been reached with the Herzes and Cohens and the major details of the deal were worked out, that you and Marv took over—largely to iron out and write the contract."

"You must have forgotten, Don, that we almost lost the deal," Jack said. "It was Marvin and I who had to use all of our ingenuity to bring it back to life, and then see it through to fruition."

"I know all about this. The impasse you are talking about was the result of quibbling, which in turn brought about a hesitation on the part of the principals to sell . . . and a question on the part of at least one of them whether it might not be a serious mistake to sell to Cowles—or anyone else."

I had heard of the impasse. It was in early November. Betty and I were attending the soft drink convention in Houston and I decided to stop off in Minneapolis before returning to New York, to see what I could do to help save the deal. I learned it was Louis Cohen who became quite concerned about selling the business, largely because his wife Tess had considerable doubt about the judiciousness of taking such a step. Betty and I went to work on Louis and Tess. The temperature in Houston was in the eighties and it was in the low thirties in Minneapolis, and things were really cold in that city. We had dinner with the entire Minneapolis group—Mal and his wife, Jo, the Burt Cohens and, of course, Louis and Tess—but after dinner, when the rest left, we lingered with Louis and Tess. And then a lengthy discussion followed . . . a discussion that lasted into the morning. Betty and I really had to sell Louis and Tess, particularly Tess, and we sold like we never sold before. We told them what wonderful people the Cowleses were, how exceedingly well they were treating me, the autonomy that I had and the great future that was before us.

" 'If ever it was possible to have your cake and eat it too, a deal with Cowles will do it for you, Louis . . . as it has done for me,' " I said.

"While I was talking to Louis alone at this point, Betty and Tess were having a private chat of their own. Betty told me later that Tess's persistent question was: 'Tell me, Betty, in truth and all honesty: does Don have any regrets about his merger with Cowles? Are they really letting him alone?' Betty was able to answer in the affirmative, and convince her. It was quite a meeting that we had.

"I reported about this meeting briefly to Marv, when I returned to New York. I know that it was a crucial meeting and I'm sure that it played an important part in helping to bring the deal back on the track. I repeat, Jack, you and Marv were of tremendous help, but without me you would not have had *Modern Medicine*. I stayed with it through the critical part of the negotiations, revived it when it was dying, and what is most important of all, I brought the operation to its present great profitability."

"Actually, the whole thing—the buying of *Modern Medicine*—started at a cocktail party in Chicago," Jack Harding said, still trying to diminish my part in the buying of the Minneapolis operation.

"Jack, what are you talking about? . . . Let me give you the facts on the cocktail party," and after a brief glance at Jack, I continued to address myself to Gardner Cowles: "An important part of my research on *Modern Medicine*—especially with regard to determining the most effective approach—entailed several meetings with publishers who had personal acquaintance with the Herzes and the Cohens. One of the publishers with whom I met for lunch prior to my writing Teresa Cohen was Marshal Reinig (I told you about this meeting, Jack) who was president of Ojibway Publishing Company, a business paper operation in Duluth, Minnesota. I had known Marshal for some time and we had met for lunch several times. I knew that he was considering selling his company and one reason for my seeing him was to explore the possibility of buying Ojibway, but after some thought and study of his operation, I decided against pursuing it. Ojibway published about forty business magazines in a long list of fields, but the total advertising volume was in the neighborhood of $3,000,000. This meant that most of the Ojibway magazines were small, most of them much smaller than our magazines. And you know that one of the problems that I have had with MFI is that altogether too many of our publications were small. As a result, I had decided to buy magazines with large advertising volume and with still greater room for growth. I decided that I would not consider buying any magazine that did not have at least $500,000 in annual advertising revenue and a growth potential of at least $1,000,000. That is one reason I liked the medical field. Most of the magazines had advertising revenue considerably in excess of $500,000 and several, like *Modern Medicine,* could boast an annual ad revenue in the millions. Since only one of Ojibway's magazines was in the $500,000 ad volume class and many had sales of less than $100,000, I decided that this business was not for us. Besides, Ojibway also owned a printing plant and I didn't want to get into the printing business.

"There were, however, two magazines in the Ojibway stable in which I had some interest—*Drive-In Management* and *Foil, Film and Paper Converter.* These were the company's largest magazines and each of them fitted well with our special media mix. At this particular luncheon meeting with Marshal, I told him that I would not be interested in buying the company but that I would like to discuss the possible acquisition of both or one of these two magazines.

"Marshal replied: 'No, Don, I couldn't consider selling these two magazines. They represent the heart of our business.' Less than a year later, Marshal sold the entire Ojibway operation to Harcourt, Brace. Six months later, Marshal resigned from Harcourt and sold his stock—at about $100 a share. Only months later, the stock plummeted to less than $30 a share. Marshal left with a nice bundle of cash and Harcourt found that it had inherited a bundle of problems. The only thing Harcourt realized of any real value in the Ojibway deal was the unique computerized circulation fulfillment operation, for which it paid a very high price.

"Toward the end of the luncheon meeting, I was able

to engineer my conversation with Marshal to *Modern Medicine*. I did it in this fashion: After I explained our interest in buying magazines with hefty ad volume, I said: 'The field I like is medicine . . . Frankly, Marshal, we are looking around for some medical books.'

" 'You ought to buy *Modern Medicine*,' Marshal came right back. 'I understand that it can be bought. As a matter of fact, Cahners had been negotiating and I believe that the deal fell through.'

"I replied: 'We are very much interested in *Modern Medicine*. I have made a bit of a study of this operation, and I am ready to make an approach.'

" 'Good for you, Don,' Marshal said, 'but I am afraid you won't be able to get very far. It might well be a waste of time. However, I can help. I have a lawyer friend of mine in Minneapolis who could set up this deal for you. He knows his way around Minneapolis. He is acquainted with the Herzes and the Cohens, especially Teresa Cohen. Here, let me give you his name and telephone number. Why don't you give him a ring? It won't do any harm and it won't cost you a thing. Talk to him, and you'll see that he will be able to bring the deal to you.'

"I told Marshal that I didn't want to get involved with any lawyers, finders or what-have-you: 'I appreciate your suggestion, Marshal, but we have a policy at Cowles not to pay any finder's fees . . . Besides, I prefer to make the direct approach myself. This, to me, is a better way of buying a business.'

"Several days later, I received a telephone call from a Mr. Davis from Minneapolis. He was in New York. Marshal Reinig had talked to him about me. Could he drop by for a short visit? I tried to discourage the visit, but he persisted and he came over in about ten minutes. It was a very short meeting. It lasted no more than fifteen minutes. He said that he knew Mrs. Cohen personally and that he was certain he could arrange a deal for us to buy *Modern Medicine*. I did not like him, I did not care for his approach, but to put an end to the meeting, I asked him: 'What will this cost us, Mr. Davis?'

" 'About five percent of the sales price—or a minimum of $250,000.'

" 'Thank you very much, Mr. Davis, but I'm not interested. I appreciate your coming to see me, but we have a policy against paying finder's or broker's fees. We have no interest whatsoever in pursuing this matter with you any further. Thanks again.'

"Jack, I told you about this visit, about my talk with Mr. Davis. What happened was that Davis met Teresa at a cocktail party in Chicago several weeks after our visit and he asked her: 'I understand that you are selling your company to Cowles?' Teresa just looked at him and made no comment, and she told us of this meeting and asked us whether we had any dealings with Mr. Davis. You will remember, Jack, we discussed all this during our negotiations with her. She barely knew Mr. Davis and I assured her that beyond the fifteen-minute chat in my office, I had not seen Davis before or after. The *Modern Medicine* deal did not start at a cocktail party, Jack. . . . You know that."

I continued: "There is much more to the *Modern Medicine* story, Mike. After we finally acquired the business, there were some important decisions to make, decisions on the size of the magazine, decisions on who our manager in Minneapolis would be, and a long list of operational decisions. Who made these decisions? Who made sure that they were put in effect? Who followed up these decisions?

"Let's go back to a few months *before* the acquisition. It was in July, 1967. I was in Lou's office. Mal and Jay Herz were there with us. Marvin had been with us earlier but left for a meeting with IDS. With all three partners with me, I asked the question that had been in my mind for some time: 'Why didn't you change the format of *Modern Medicine* to standard size at the time your principal competitor, *Medical Economics*, did?'

"I anticipated the answer. From my own research I had learned that one of the three principals was adamant in opposition to the change in size of the magazine because 'the doctor wouldn't like it.' I knew that the subject had come up on a number of occasions, that the discussion had resulted in a bitter dispute but that the partner who was against the change proved to be immutable. As a matter of fact, I had confirmed this at a later date with Bill Chapman of Chapman-Reinhold (now part of Litton), publishers of *Medical Economics*, who was a fellow member (with me) on the board of directors of the ABP (the American Business Press), and with whom I had developed a friendly relationship. Bill told me of a meeting that he had with Mal Herz at a convention in the spring of 1965 in which he had asked Mal: 'What are you going to do about the change in the size of *Modern Medicine?*' Mal answered: 'Nothing, absolutely nothing . . . we are never going to change the size because the doctor, our reader, likes the present size of the magazine and doesn't want any change. . . .' Then Mal asked Bill: 'Are you going to change the size of *Medical Economics?*' to which Bill answered: 'In view of the fact that the pharmaceutical manufacturer advertiser now has to summarize his product in the advertisement and thus needs more space, I don't think either you or we have much of a choice.' Some weeks later, when a decision was made to change the size of *Medical Economics* from digest to standard size, Bill telephoned Mal and told him of the impending change, to become effective with the January 1966 issue. 'I didn't want him to learn about this from other sources, such as our salesmen or from the ad agencies, who would be receiving our announcement of the change,' Bill told me.

"While I had anticipated the answer, I wanted to hear it from 'the horse's mouth.' Mal answered me in this way: 'We didn't change the size of *Modern Medicine* because it made no sense to do it, since our reader, the doctor, did not want any change. He liked the small, digest size of the magazine because he could put it in his pocket and thus catch up on his reading whenever he had a free moment—' "

Jack broke in: "But, Don, surely you must have known by then that they made a study to determine whether it would be advisable to make such change, and that the study showed that it would be a mistake to make the change."

"I know all about this study. As a matter of fact, there were two studies, one a mail study, and another one that was done for them by Herb Mayes. The mail survey showed that the doctor did indeed prefer the small size. And I also knew that the conclusion reached by the great editor of consumer magazines (as in the case of the mail survey) proved to be wrong and costly —almost ruinously costly. As a matter of fact, it was Louis Cohen who told me about the Herb Mayes study. He told it to me in great detail, dramatizing it as only Louis can. That all came out after the meeting with the three partners.

"It was Mal who tried to answer my question about the size of *Modern Medicine,* and this is the way he put it: 'We had given this matter a lot of thought . . . and it was finally decided that it would be a mistake for us to change the size. However, we are studying the matter again now, and since the picture has changed during the past two years, we may go to standard size before long—perhaps next year.'

"At that point, Jay Herz chimed in, 'We should have changed the size of the book when *Medical Economics* made the change, and I said so.'

"After listening to the three partners 'explain' the failure to change the size of the magazine, I finally said: 'While I know that it will take several months before all contract details will be ironed out—and there is always the possibility that we may not have any deal at all—nevertheless, I feel I must express my opinion about the size of *Modern Medicine*. I believe it is most important that the format be changed to standard size, and it must be done with the January 1968 issue. The time to start is right now. I will be pleased to give you all the help I can.'

"Then Louis said, 'Mal, why don't we tell Don that we are already thinking in terms of design, that we are planning to commission a designer to do some preliminary work.'

" 'Yes, we are doing this. Isn't the art department working on the project?' Mal asked Louis.

" 'Yes . . . and we may be seeing something in a few weeks,' Louis replied.

" 'When you have anything to show,' I said, 'I will be glad to take a look, and then show it to Allen Hurlburt, the *Look* art director, who happens to be a great designer himself. At any rate, it is very important that you move as fast as possible in making the change, with the January issue. Hopefully, our deal will be completed before that time, but even if it isn't, you haven't anything to lose. This is something you must do. It's no longer a matter of choice.'

"When the meeting was over, Lou wanted me to linger in his office a while since it was two hours before plane time, and he promised that he would get me to the airport 'in plenty of time.' It was then that he gave me the details of the Herb Mayes study. He told me that when the partners couldn't agree on the matter of changing the size of *Modern Medicine*, he decided to take the initiative and make a study to find out whether it would be a good idea. At that time, Louis pointed out, Herbert Mayes was very much in the news.

"Louis then told me the story of the Mayes study: 'Herb Mayes was fired by *Good Housekeeping* after doing a great job there for about twenty-five years. He just walked out . . . and then sold himself to *McCall's*, where he soon became editor at $75,000 a year, a fabulous salary at that time. And within a very short time, he had completely redesigned and redirected *McCall's*, before long making it the hot magazine in the women's field at that time.

" 'Well, I was very much impressed with the Herb Mayes story, and while I had not met him, on my next trip to New York I telephoned him and told him what I had in mind. Surprise of surprises, after I explained the reason for my call, Herb agreed to meet with us in Minneapolis over a weekend—at our expense, of course —and discuss the possibility of making this study. Herb acknowledged at the time that he had never made such a study and knew nothing of the medical publishing field. After the weekend in Minneapolis, during which all of us were impressed with Herb Mayes and he with us, he agreed to make the study. I was so thrilled that this great editor was undertaking our little project that I didn't even ask what it would cost us. I felt it would be bad manners for me to talk about money.'

"Louis continued his story: 'After three months of meetings with the *Modern Medicine* staff and random interviews with physicians, the great editor of *McCall's* came back with a lengthy written report, attractively bound. It was his conclusion that it would be a serious mistake to change the size of the magazine, to alter its present uniqueness . . . that the doctor would not countenance a change. All this fully backed up Mal's contention. The price for this study: $25,000.' "

"But the decision to change the size wasn't really yours, Don," Jack Harding said. "They would have changed the size sooner or later. They did do some planning when we started negotiations."

"Maybe you're right and maybe you're not," I replied. "Let the facts speak for themselves . . . and the facts are that I continued to push for the change, and brought Allen Hurlburt into the picture almost immediately. If I hadn't pushed as aggressively as I did, they might have stalled for another year, and then it might have been too late. Only by pushing as I did was the needed, timely action taken. As a result, the January 1968 issue—the first under our direction—was in the new size and format. And it proved to be a huge success—esthetically, editorially and commercially.

"I'm telling you all this, Mike, and at some length," I addressed myself again to the silent Gardner Cowles, "because it appears that we have reached an impasse—a point of no return in my relationship with the company. As you know, I approached Marvin about five months ago with an offer to buy back the entire division, or at least MFI. I was surprised at Marv's reaction. I thought, and in a way, hoped, that he might say: 'Don, don't do this. I know the problems that you are facing just as you know the problems the company is going through . . . Stay with us . . . We need you . . . and we want you to do your share in helping us work out of our difficulties.' Instead, he seemed to welcome the idea—the idea of my buying back MFI and leaving CCI. Obviously, what I had suspected for some time was a fact. I was being isolated from the Minneapolis operation—boxed in. And since the major motivation of my merging with CCI was to build and run a bigger, more important business magazine company, I could not countenance this new development. I discussed this with Marvin and I told him that a decision must be reached: either I would run the entire division with full authority and autonomy, or the division—or at least MFI—should be sold back to me. He said that my proposals would be given serious thought. When, after several weeks of deliberation, he told me that CCI would sell me back MFI, but that you had no interest in selling *Modern Medicine* to me or anyone else, I spent five months of back-breaking work to obtain the needed financing. We were talking about cash, since CCI needed cash. The last few months have been the worst of times to obtain financing—cold, hard cash—as you well know, Mike. When I finally did obtain the needed financing and met with Marvin to move on the deal, the signals were changed."

Marvin Whatmore interrupted: "No, Don, the signals were not changed, circumstances changed. And besides, we had a misunderstanding on the quick assets in the balance sheet."

The way Marvin broke in and the manner in which he said what he did, made it clear to me that he did not want me to repeat the conversation we had had the week before. Particularly, he did not want me to quote him when he had said, "Don, we are not selling anything anymore. After our sale of the *San Juan Star,* the word in the street is that 'Cowles is selling off the winners and keeping the losers.' "

"Well, changed signals or not," I said, "the deal to sell me back MFI seems to have been called off. Mike, what must be resolved now is whether I am going to run the Minneapolis operation—completely, with full authority and the way it should be run—or whether you will sell me back MFI . . ."

Again, Marvin interjected: "Don, it isn't as simple as that. As I have told you, Minneapolis has asked to report to me directly instead of to the head of the business magazine division. They feel that the tail should not be wagging the dog."

I cut in: "Marvin, who at Minneapolis made this request?"

"I prefer not to name names . . ."

"It certainly wasn't Burt?" I pressed the matter.

Jack Harding chimed in: "No, it wasn't Burt . . ."

"No, it wasn't Burt," Marvin repeated, "Burt has been loyal to you in every way."

"Then who at Minneapolis?" I asked again.

"It was Mal and Lou," Jack said.

"I don't believe it was Lou. We have become friends. I'm not surprised that it was Mal, but not Lou."

Harding repeated: "Lou, as well as Mal."

"Let me say," Marvin began, "there is no disrespect or any lack of regard for you on the part of Mal or Lou —or anyone else in Minneapolis. They like you and respect you, Don, and they have nothing but praise for your ability. But they feel that they represent the second or third largest profit center in the corporation and, as a result, want to report directly to the chief executive officer. They also want a seat on the board, as I told you . . . and as a matter of fact, at least one of them, Mal, questioned whether MFI should be part of Cowles at all."

Lightning struck. There was the crux of the situation. I now realized that I could not possibly run the Minneapolis division with the authority and autonomy I needed and wanted, but that I could and must buy back MFI. I knew what I had to do, what I had to say.

"Mike, in view of what Marvin and Jack have just said, we've got to bring things to a head. The situation as it now exists is intolerable and I cannot countenance it. You know that I have a contract as President and General Manager of the Cowles Business and Professional Magazine Division. That contract runs for another three and one-half years. From what was said here today and from what was done during the past year—and especially over the past few months when you moved to isolate me from the Minneapolis operation—you have already taken some overt steps to abrogate my contract. *And when you abrogate my employment contract, you also vitiate the MFI purchase agreement.*"

Whatmore turned to Harding: "Have we broken the contract, Jack?"

"No, Marvin, we haven't," Jack replied.

"Marvin, I did not say that you broke the contract. I said that you took some overt steps to break the contract. Unless you end my isolation from Minneapolis—unless I am able to run *Modern Medicine* and the entire division with full and complete authority, as is spelled out in my contract—you will be abrogating my employment contract and, in turn, the MFI purchase agreement, and I will not tolerate any of it."

"But, Don, you really have been running *Modern Medicine*," Marvin said at this point, "We haven't interfered with you."

"This has been true—up to a point. I assumed authority right from the beginning, the way it was spelled out in my contract. I tried to run the Minneapolis operation the way it should be run. But even from the outset, roadblocks were put in my way. I had to use kid gloves in dealing with various people in Minneapolis. I could not take urgently needed steps or move as quickly as was necessary in some areas without the constant fear of 'stepping on toes.'

"Let me give you a few examples, Mike. You may or may not be familiar with these. As I explained earlier, when I had made the decision to make Burt Cohen our manager in Minneapolis, Marvin asked me to 'move slowly' in making the change. I knew that we could not afford to continue with the status quo—that we had to change from a committee-of-three operation, to a single decision-making manager, reporting to me. This was essential from the start, it was my first priority, and I made no bones about it in my talks with Marvin.

"When I told the three partners what I wanted to do, they said: 'Yes, Burt is a fine choice. As a matter of fact, we have been looking at him as our hope for the future, but Burt isn't ready for the job. Maybe in a year or two.' I knew the problem that I faced and would face, but I decided that Burt would be our manager beginning January 1, 1968, the day we took over—and not a day later. Marvin finally agreed but pleaded with me not to discuss it any further with the three partners.

"At any rate," I continued, "on December 31, when the contract to buy *Modern Medicine* was finally signed, I met with Marvin and told him that 'beginning tomorrow, Burt is our manager in Minneapolis.' He suggested that I wait a while, explaining that Mal asked him to hold off taking this action for at least a year. I would have none of this and explained to Marvin why we could not wait even for a week. Waiting could mean losing very valuable time in putting into effect a direct-line, profit-maximizing program. Marvin finally acquiesced. Burt became our manager as of January 1, 1968, and what has happened since then is history. Burt, under my tutelage and my direction, has performed exceptionally well, despite early resistance and roadblocks."

"Burt is a very fine boy," Jack said.

"Yes," I said, "he is a fine man. I have trained him. He has great potential. He is not fully trained yet, there is still work to be done.

"Then there was this situation on *Dental Survey*. I had heard that the publisher on that magazine had a serious drinking problem, and I mentioned this in our first meeting with Teresa Cohen, who was running *Dental Survey*. She said that it was not true, that the publisher was merely a social drinker, that he had a wide acquaintance in the field and he should remain on the job. Of course, once we took over the operation, I realized immediately that we would be losing ground if we did not make a change in *Dental Survey*, but because Marvin Whatmore had promised Teresa that 'we would go easy,' I had to wait an entire year before I made the needed changes . . . and it proved very costly —a valuable year wasted.

"I could cite a long series of other examples where roadblocks were put in my way in Minneapolis. Take the appointment of Pat Lyndon as head of the international division. Here I was not even consulted at all—"

"This is true," Marvin said, "and I still don't know why you were not consulted. It was just an oversight."

"This was not the only oversight. There have been many more. Mike, it just cannot go on this way. Either I run the Minneapolis operation, or sell me back MFI. Mike, I brought you a gold mine in *Modern Medicine* and it's all yours . . . dig it . . . but remember that you owe me plenty. Maybe Mal Herz is right: MFI is not for you. You ought to give me back MFI as a gift!"

There was a bit of spontaneous laughter. It was funny, all right, but my outrageous demand had just enough validity to temper their mirth.

Jack Harding then said: "This is not the best offer you've made this morning." Some restrained chuckles followed.

Whatmore than turned to Gil Maurer: "Gil, you've been in touch with Minneapolis during the past few months. What is your feeling about the *Modern Medicine* situation?"

"I really haven't been that much in touch," Gil said, "but from my cursory observations, I feel that they don't really mind working with Don. They certainly don't mind consulting with him. But they do believe that the tail should not wag the dog."

"So, here is more evidence, Mike," I said, "that things cannot go on as they are now. This nonsense about 'they don't mind consulting' with Don, that 'the tail should not wag the dog.' "

I kept pounding at my main theme: "I am manager of an important, profitable division, and it was I who bought it and made it profitable despite the many roadblocks. I must have full control in running it, and I can tell you that there is still much to be done to maximize profits, to solve some problems that still need solving. Otherwise, sell me back MFI. Isolating me from Minneapolis makes my position untenable. This change in my function and my status, if permitted to continue, means an abrogation of my contract—both my employment contract and the MFI purchase agreement. I cannot and will not tolerate it. The best answer for you, Mike, is to sell me back MFI. It is not only good for me, it is good for CCI. MFI is much too small for Cowles unless it is used as a nucleus for growth, but now that you seem to want to continue to isolate me and MFI from the Modern Medicine operation, it makes no sense for you to have MFI . . ."

"Don, what would you do with MFI under your own ownership that you cannot do today?" Marvin asked.

"Plenty. In the first place, I wouldn't have to pay the huge CCI management fee; that reduces our profit considerably. Then, I would streamline our operation, including the accounting department which has been in a mess since our merger. I would call in our investors

—executive employees of MFI—and tell them that our future—theirs and mine—depends on the success of MFI, I can assure you, Marvin, that they will go to work as they have never worked before. There is no secret that demoralization has set in at MFI, particularly during the past year, for a long list of reasons—all emanating from Cowles—and I don't have to cite chapter and verse.

"But most important of all, once again, we will be able to build MFI. We have been standing still for almost two years. Yes, we could begin building MFI in the manner that I built the Business and Professional Division for Cowles at the outset of our merger."

"But if we are to sell you back MFI, the net quick assets must remain with us, Don," Marvin said.

"Marvin, my entire basis for obtaining financing has been the balance sheet as you gave it to me at the beginning, with the net quick assets going to us. But I don't want to argue about it now. We have had plenty of discussion on the subject. Let's say that there has been a misunderstanding, but if you really want to sell me back MFI, we can work it out."

"Do you have another plan, Don?" Marvin asked.

"Yes, I do have another plan, a modification of the old plan but with an important, workable addition. Here is what I propose to do. I propose that we take the balance sheet, whatever it will be at the time of the closing, or at whatever cutoff date we agree on, say, July 31, and then take one-half of the excess of current assets over current liabilities of Magazines For Industry, Inc., as reflected on the consolidated balance sheet of MFI, to be certified by Ernst and Ernst, Cowles' accountants. This will be on top of the $500,000 which we have already agreed to pay you out of future profits."

Marvin quickly consulted with Harding and Clough,

reviewing figures in a half-whisper, and then Jack Harding said: "I'm afraid that we might face a stockholders' suit—Don is an insider."

"I don't think you need worry about a stockholders' suit," I said, "I am not getting a bargain. MFI is worth much more to me than to any other buyer. Besides, you have had a respected, professional appraising company make an evaluation, and this appraiser said that you could sell MFI for $1,250,000. Under the plan you could be receiving more than that for MFI and that is no great big bargain for me."

"How will this look on the balance sheet, Jack?" Marvin Whatmore asked.

"It will show as a loss," Harding answered.

"Why don't you combine the loss from the sale of MFI to me with the profits from the sale of the *San Juan Star?*" I suggested. "Then the total combined transaction would be a plus, a very sizable plus."

At that point, the Chairman made his pronouncement. Until that moment, Gardner Cowles had been sitting in silence, listening but not saying a word, looking unhappy most of the time but always listening. Now he said: "Don, I am going to recall the executive committee right now. Men, I must give Don an answer in a day or two."

Silence fell upon the room. A few seconds seemed like minutes. Marvin Whatmore finally said: "I guess that's it."

I had my cue. I got up quickly, saying quietly, "Thank you . . . goodbye." I opened the door.

"In the meantime, I hope you do well with *Industrial Ecology,*" Whatmore said. I left quickly.

TWELVE:

Goodbye CCI—Hello
New York Times

On my twelve-minute walk to my office, I tried to visualize the scene at the executive committee meeting after my departure. It did not seem too difficult.

"Marvin, do you think we will miss Don very much, I mean, in the operation of the *Modern Medicine* group?" Gardner Cowles began.

"Don has done a good job. He has set things up well. Now *Modern Medicine* can run by itself—under Burt's management. Burt's a good boy, you know."

"What about *Dental Survey* and *Nursing Homes*, Marvin? Don't we have problems there? Do you think that Burt will be able to handle them without Don?"

"I think he will, and we'll give him guidance. Gil will be taking over, Mike, to fill in where Don will be leaving off. So, I don't see any great problem here. Besides, the morale should improve. You know that both Mal and Lou made a big fuss about the 'tail wagging the dog'. Of course, they like Don and they worked well with him, but they know that most of the profits from the division come from *Modern Medicine,* their magazine, and they take full credit for it."

"So, you don't think that Don's leaving will give us much of a problem?"

"I don't think so, Mike," Marvin said.

"How do the rest of you feel?"

"I think the way Marvin views the picture is just about right," Jack Harding said. "Don has done well, but I think he has served his purpose. Minneapolis can now operate on its own—with our supervision. Besides, unless we give Don full authority and autonomy, he could begin to give us trouble, Mike. You heard the questions he asked at the board meeting the other day. So, I go along with Marvin."

"Gil, do you think you'll be able to handle the Minneapolis situation?" Cowles asked.

"I don't foresee any problems. As a matter of fact, I have been at it for several weeks now, and I must say that Don has cooperated, although he must have known full well what I was doing. I feel confident, Mike, that I can handle things. Burt is good to work with. Don is right in saying that Burt still needs supervision and training, but I can help him."

"What about the price, Marvin?"

"For one thing, we will get $750,000 in cash, and this is important. Every dollar we can generate now is very helpful."

"But do you think we can get more out of Don?"

"There is some chance, but facing reality, I must say that it's doubtful, Mike, at least for some time. Don will have a tough time making money with MFI as it is now. He'll have to make many changes and he'll have to move fast. He needs at least one big magazine and I don't see him getting it for some time. Maybe in three to five years we will get some money. The best we can figure is $750,000 cash at the closing, and not very much more."

"How will the sale look on the balance sheet? Does it have to show as a loss?"

"Not necessarily," Gil said. "If Ernst and Ernst will let us figure MFI's contingent liability as an asset, we may come out ahead."

"Does that make any sense to you, Jack?"

"It does. Gil and I discussed it and we went over the figures. I think that Gil might be right."

"What do you think, Merrill?"

"I really can't say. Jack and Gil didn't consult me. I suppose they will go over the figures with me in due time."

"What about a possible stockholder's suit, Jack?"

"There is always a chance of that, Mike, but I doubt that we will have one with regard to the sale of MFI. We do have an appraisal from American Appraisal, and their appraised price is $1,250,000 to $1,500,000, so I think that we are in good shape here. No matter to whom we sell the property, it will be difficult to get more than $750,000 in cash in today's tight money market . . . and no court will assume to tell us how, under what terms, we should sell a subsidiary. Any lawyer for a group of stockholders would know this."

"Besides," Gil put in, "we are going to have at least a half-dozen other bids, and the way things are working out, I don't think we will need any higher bid and no more than $750,000 cash."

"Yes, Gil is right," Jack said. "He and I are working with several publishers on these bids. We might get more if we sell the MFI properties piecemeal, Mike, but that could take months. In the meantime, we will have Don to contend with, and he could well bring a stockholder's suit himself. Don is a fine, quiet gentleman, but he is getting a bit desperate. There is no telling what someone in his place might do—this is his life work, Mike."

Then came Gardner Cowles' pronouncement: "Gentlemen, you have made the decision. Let's sell MFI back to Don. Jack, you work things out as to details and whatever legal problems you may foresee. Are there any objections?"

There were none.

What I did not know on July 21 and what the other members of the executive committee did not know either, was that Chairman Gardner Cowles and President Marvin Whatmore had already begun preliminary discussions with Arthur Ochs Sulzberger, president and publisher, and Ivan Veit, executive vice president, of *The New York Times,* for the acquisition by the *Times* of most of Cowles' profitable properties, including the *Modern Medicine* operation of Minneapolis.

For a long time, I had known that Gardner Cowles had been very much in awe of the Sulzbergers and *The New York Times.* With most newspapermen, *The New York Times* was the zenith. And to Iowa Newspaperman Cowles, the *Times* was the Top of the Mountain. Gardner Cowles knew and admired "Punch" Sulzberger as he knew and admired his father, the late Arthur Hays Sulzberger. If he were to lose his prestigious image as chairman of the empire that bore his name, he could find no better substitute image than an important, major association with the *Times*—as a holder of a substantial number of shares and as a member of the board of directors of The New York Times Company.

At first, Gardner Cowles alone started private conversations with Punch. Then as the *Times* president brought in his executive vice president in charge of "development programs," Ivan Veit, Gardner invited Marvin Whatmore to share his carefully guarded secret. It was not until a deal seemed possible that Jack Harding entered the picture. And it was not until an agreement in principle was reached that the other members of the Cowles executive committee were called to a meeting and the full story told.

The official joint release was made available to the press on October 28, three months after my meeting with the executive committee.

It was an excellent buy for the *Times,* which some time earlier had decided to go the way of the *Los Angeles Times-Mirror*—to become a diversified communications operation. While there had been talk of going in this direction during the latter years of Arthur Hays Sulzberger, it was not until Punch became president and publisher, and later, in full command of The New York Times Company, that he began to move in the direction of substantial, diversified expansion. Not only did he have the backing of his mother, Iphigene, but also other members of the Sulzberger family. And his key men, now a new group (and his own). Not new at the *Times,* but *Times* men whom Punch liked, and with whom he felt he could work in building a significant, diversified communications empire.

The Cowles properties represented a valuable purchase for the *Times.* They provided much room for growth.

But good as the deal was for the *Times,* it was probably even better for Gardner Cowles. Not only did it save his financial neck, around which a noose had undergone massive tightening during the previous months, but it also bolstered his sagging prestige in the publishing and financial communities. As he approached his sixty-eighth birthday, he had a last chance for some sort of comeback. And the *Times* deal proved to be a magnificent way of doing it.

At the last Cowles board meeting that I attended (on

May 15, 1970), I asked Chairman Cowles whether negotiations had been in progress for the sale or merger of Cowles Communications into another, possibly larger public company, consistent with rumors that had been floating around at that time. The chairman replied, slowly and hesitatingly: "There have been some discussions."

I suspect that the "discussions" referred to could well have included some earlier talks with the Sulzbergers of the *Times*. These things take a lot of time, much preliminary talk and much more time in actual negotiations.

Said President and Publisher Arthur Ochs Sulzberger in announcing the agreement in principle: "The [Cowles] acquisition will be an important step toward the diversification which the *Times* has been seeking. We believe that all of the properties have a large potential for further growth and profitability. Also, we are pleased that Gardner Cowles has agreed to join the board of directors of the *Times*. He has a wealth of experience in newspaper and magazine publishing and in the broadcasting field. His judgment and counsel will add strength to the New York Times Company."

Interesting rhetoric!

For *Modern Medicine* and its affiliated group of medical and dental publications, *The New York Times* was paying about two and one-half times to three times as much as what I paid three years earlier. The price was almost double what I would have paid had Cowles been willing to sell these properties to me, along with MFI—except that I would have paid all cash while the *Times* was paying 80 percent in stock. The *Times* assumed $15,000,000 in notes and would pay them over a long period. That made up the remaining 20 percent of the purchase price.

At least six business magazine publishers had been invited to bid for Magazines For Industry. They were very serious. If I did not proceed vigorously to buy back MFI, my company would be sold out from under me.

It was now Tuesday, and Mike was to give me his answer in "a day or two." I had to decide between Carl Marks and Diebold as my outside investor—I thought. But before the day was over, Dom Fitzpatrick of Diebold called me—to turn me down. He said we could reopen negotiations but he would need at least a 31 percent interest, instead of 25 percent, for the $350,000 he was to invest.

That simplified matters. Now I knew I would deal with Carl Marks, and I looked forward to a meeting to discuss contract details.

We had our meeting the next morning—and it was a fiasco!

I met Dave Regosin at his office and we walked over to keep our appointment at Carl Marks. Our meeting was supposed to be with Bob Davidoff. But when we got to the conference room, we found Harry Wise and another man, who was introduced to us as "one of the investors" in our deal. The name escaped me, and it did not seem important. Bob Davidoff came into the office, met Dave and left almost immediately. As the "investor" shuffled some papers while mumbling to himself, at the far side of the room, Harry Wise sat down with Dave and me to "review your deal." The review had little resemblance to the original proposition—first as outlined to me, and then as repeated slowly and simply to our eight insiders at the meeting on the Monday morning of the week previous.

"We will lend you $400,000 at nine percent, to be amortized over a six-year period. The loan will be collateralized by your 94,000 shares of Cowles stock and your house on 10th Street." As he talked, Harry appeared nervous. He kept banging his pencil on the conference table.

"Harry, this is not the deal Bob and you outlined to me originally, and that Bob repeated before our insiders a week ago Monday! The interest you were to charge was eight percent—not nine. And my house on 10th Street did not enter into the picture at all. You never even mentioned it . . ."

"You're wrong, the interest was always nine percent and, of course, it was understood that your house would be used as collateral. After all, the Cowles stock is selling at $3.50 a share, which means that the 94,000 shares are now worth less than $400,000—the amount of the loan. And it could go lower—even as low as $2."

"Harry, you never mentioned nine percent interest. It was always eight percent, a figure you used repeatedly. Remember, I have eight witnesses to prove this. And our house on 10th Street was not offered as collateral, and you never indicated that it would be required as collateral. The only reason you know about the house on 10th Street is that when you asked me to list all of my assets and those of my wife, the house was included. As a matter of fact, it is my wife who owns the house. As to the price of the Cowles stock, it has not changed much since you made me the original offer. And remember, you are getting seven year warrants which will give 25 percent of our company for $83,000. If you now want to change the deal—for whatever reason—then say so."

"Carl Marks will take only ten percent of the deal," Wise replied. "The rest will be divided among the other investors of our group. And we charge the investors five percent of their share for bringing the deal to them. The interest is nine percent and always was nine percent, and we must have the house on 10th Street as collateral

. . . That was understood . . ." And he kept banging the pencil as he talked.

Dave Regosin looked on in amazement. I felt both embarrassed and annoyed.

"I guess we don't have a deal," I finally said.

"Why don't you think it over, and let me know?" Harry asked.

We left and returned to Dave's office. Dave and I agreed that we could not consider a deal with Carl Marks in view of the new developments.

"I would not have minded it too much if he had said that he now found it necessary to change the deal . . . but to insist that this was the original deal is something else again. So I guess we have no deal with Carl Marks . . . and it seems we have no deal with Diebold either. . . . So, we have to start all over again."

I telephoned Henry Frommer at Irving Trust and told him what had happened. He, too, was shocked. I walked over to Irving Trust for a short meeting with Henry. He tried to soothe me: "Now, don't worry Don. We will get you another investor. I haven't exhausted our list. The only problem is that it will take time, maybe a week or longer, maybe a month . . ."

By the time I returned to the office I was completely spent. Utterly discouraged. I now felt very confident that Cowles would accept my offer, that I had put through the greatest piece of selling in my career. Except that I wouldn't have the $750,000 cash to make the buy-back a reality. I must find a way. There must be a way, I kept thinking, there must be a way.

With a blank piece of paper in front of me and a pencil in hand, I began to think as I looked out the window—over Turtle Bay and onto the East River. The Delacorte fountain on Welfare Island, billed as the highest fountain in the U.S.A., was shooting upwards . . . It was two o'clock.

Then a thought hit me: Why can't I do it myself?

Why do I need Carl Marks, Diebold or any outside investor? All I need is $750,000.

If I were to offer our insiders a better deal than the one outlined by Carl Marks, they might show greater enthusiasm.

Maybe I could increase the number of insiders by including some of our younger people. If I were to sell them forty percent of our company for $250,000, wouldn't they join forces in the buy-back? Forty percent for $250,000 means an evaluation of the company at $625,000. What a bargain! Especially since the appraiser had put a value of between $1,250,000 and $1,500,000 for MFI. Given two or three good, profitable years, MFI could well be worth two to three million dollars. Or more.

At any rate, $625,000 is still $125,000 less than the actual cash we would be paying Cowles to get our company back. So, no matter how you look at it, a $250,000 investment for a forty percent interest is really a great insider deal. They just cannot possibly lose, and the value of their stock could double or triple in a very short time.

But I still have to get $500,000 in cash. How? Where? Well, I could sell the Cowles stock which, at about $3.50 per share would give me about $300,000 to $350,000 before taxes. And I could sell our house on 10th Street for a net of approximately $150,000 to $175,000. But this would take time. I listed my other assets—our summer home on Monhegan, our condominium in St. Thomas, insurance, other stocks . . . and I came up with a figure in excess of $800,000 on a "rock bottom" basis. With assets of over $800,000, why shouldn't I be able to obtain a loan of $500,000? That's it. That's my plan. I will sell forty percent of MFI to our insiders for $250,000 and I will try to get a loan from Irving Trust for $500,000, offering all of my personal assets as collateral. Plus my personal signature guaranteeing the loan.

I called in Marv Toben, brought him up-to-date, and outlined my new plan. We went over it step by step, and we could not find any holes in it.

I then asked him to help me draw up a list of possible inside investors. He came up with twenty. And then we decided that the minimum single investment should be $7,500. Next to each prospect, we placed the amount we felt we could count on.

"I will call Bill Lyon at Irving Trust for a meeting, and in the meantime, you begin to get the $250,000," I said.

It was now 4:45. I got Bill Lyon on the telephone immediately and we made a date for ten thirty the next morning.

As I finished the telephone conversation, Jerry Stevens walked into my office and gave me a piece of news: "Don, the Dow Jones wire just said that Capital Cities Broadcasting Corporation had called off the deal to buy the *San Juan Star* from Cowles. Whatmore is quoted as saying that discussions are now under way to sell the newspaper to other buyers . . . Will this affect your buy-back of MFI?"

"I don't think so . . . but it might delay immediate action. With Whatmore, and probably Harding, busy with the new negotiations on the very critical sale to ease its serious liquidity problem, our deal is bound to be put aside for a while. We'll see."

I had expected to hear from Whatmore by Thursday, but now I was quite certain the call would not come. I called Gil Maurer and asked him what he thought.

"Don, you won't get that call. Marvin and Jack are working around the clock with the Number Two buyer for the *Star*. However, things look good with that purchase, and as a result, you'll probably hear from Marvin by Monday or Tuesday."

When I left my office for the two-block walk to Irving Trust on Thursday morning, I felt depressed, but by the time I entered the bank my mood had changed and I was ready for a strong, enthusiastic sales pitch.

When Bill Lyon greeted me, I said: "Hello, shall I call you Irving or Bill?" being very much aware of Irving Trust's corny advertising campaign which ends with the statement: "Call us Irving."

As we walked into his office, Bill asked the secretary to invite Sam Cunningham, the VP in charge of the branch, to join us. When Cunningham came in, Bill said: "Congratulations, Don, I see where you have a deal going with Carl Marks . . ."

I interposed: "I don't think I like the deal with Carl Marks—that is why I'm here. I have a completely different plan for our buy-back of MFI, and I'd like to tell you about it. My idea for the buy-back may come as a shock to you. I just thought I would warn you in advance—"

"Tell us what it is. Don't keep us in suspense," Bill said, smiling.

"We're going to do the financing ourselves and you will help us . . ."

"I *am* shocked," Bill said. "What is your plan?"

"It looks as if I can buy MFI on much better terms than I had thought were possible. I believe I can do it with only $750,000 cash and the rest on an open-end payout of ten percent of profit after taxes."

"You really think you can swing this kind of a deal, Don?"

"I feel confident I can. I presented this proposition to the executive committee of Cowles, with Gardner

Cowles in attendance, and I think that Cowles is going to buy my dream."

"That sounds marvelous," Bill said. "How do you propose to get the $750,000?"

"I have already gotten $250,000 from our employees —about fifteen of them, mostly top executives and including some of the up-and-coming younger men—for forty percent of our business. That makes it a very sweet, inside deal for them. And I'd like you to lend me the additional $500,000. I am prepared to pledge all of my assets, totaling close to $1,000,000, including my 94,000 shares of Cowles stock and our income-producing property on West 10th Street."

"Now I am really surprised! Will you be able to repay the loan within a year?"

"I think so . . . and here is how I propose to do it: After the buy-back, MFI will have about $500,000 in quick net assets—mostly in receivables and including at least $100,000 in cash. In addition, I am sure we can generate another $150,000 in cash in very short order. It will mean an aggressive collection program and I am ready to put this into action almost immediately. The other $250,000 will come from the sale of my Cowles stock."

"What is the price of the Cowles stock now?" Bill asked.

"It is selling at a very depressed price of between $3.50 and $4.00 a share. The liquidation value of the stock is about $20 a share."

"On stock selling at less than $10 a share, we never give a loan of more than fifty percent of the face value," Bill said.

"That's all right. Even if you figure the stock as collateral based on fifty percent of its value, my assets will exceed $500,000. Our house on 10th Street is worth between $250,000 and $300,000 and we have a mortgage of only $70,000. And then I have other securities, insurance totaling $250,000 with a cash value of at least $75,000, plus a few more items."

"Sam, if for some reason we cannot swing this loan here for Don, why can't we go upstate? You remember how we went all out for that terrible character and made a substantial loan available—just to accommodate our friends upstate. There is no reason that we cannot ask them to return the favor."

"I don't see any problems there," replied Sam. "Of course, the Federal Reserve frowns on loans made to buy businesses . . ."

"It's OK if we go upstate . . . Don, we want to do this for you. I can assure you that we'll try our best to get you the money. It looks as if you're getting a very good deal . . . Sam, why don't you have Don update his net worth statement? By the way, what is MFI's balance now?"

"At least $100,000 and it has been over $100,000 for some time," I said.

Sam Cunningham went outside and soon came back advising Bill that our present balance was $110,000. He also gave me some forms to take back and fill out.

"I have always liked to do business with Irving Trust . . . and you are proving again that it is a fine bank, that it is a bank with a heart. You consider the financials all right, as a bank should . . . but also the human element," I said and got up to leave.

"Don, you can be sure that we'll do all we can. We want to do this for you."

When I returned to the office, Marvin Toben, Nancy and I did a dance of joy . . . and for the first time in a long time, the cocktail hour with Betty that evening was a most spirited and pleasant one.

Marvin Toben and I devoted a good part of the rest of the week to signing up our insiders. There were a few surprises. Jack Mulligan came in for $50,000, but added: "Don, if you need more, you can count on me for another $25,000. Or, still better, I can let you have some of my stock, mostly Pfizer, to use as collateral for a short-term loan of about $150,000—the securities will be just as safe in the Irving Trust's vault as they are in mine." I was touched, but then, I was not really surprised. Jack could always be expected to come through in an emergency.

Our friendship went back to 1936, when I "trained" him as a space salesman for *International Confectioner,* one of the two trade magazines managed then by Tom Sullivan. On one busy morning when we were going to press, Tom brought the tall, smart-looking, stylishly dressed young man to my desk, and said: "Here is the great Mull I've been telling you about. He begins work for us today. Take him in hand and make a space salesman out of him."

I was then editor, publisher, production man, space salesman and just about everything else on the monthly magazine. My part-time assistant was ill and we were going to press. But, aware of Jack's possible long-range value to us, I tried to give him a short course in business magazine space selling, editing and publishing. I don't know what he learned from my top-speed briefing, but I wound up sending him out to sell space that day. He became a top salesman, a great performer, and eventually succeeded me as publisher of *International Confectioner*, when I went on to other things.

We remained friends—even when we were competitors—and four years after I launched *Candy Industry* Jack joined me as the advertising manager.

Another surprise was the amount of investment decided on by my brother, Robert, our purchasing director. At first, he said that he would invest $12,500; then he doubled that amount. Two others came in for

$25,000 each—Burt Gussow and Jay Sandler. Marv Toben finally made it $37,500; he sold his country place and borrowed from his family.

So, now we had $162,500. It would not be difficult to get the needed $250,000. We might even be over-subscribed. I left the job of obtaining the balance in the hands of Marvin who came through with flying colors.

The only unhappy surprise was the failure on the part of Jerry Stevens to come in for any amount—even the minimum of $7,500. However, as it turned out, we did not need Jerry's contribution. Before the week was over, we had sufficient pledges for the entire amount needed.

Now, for the call from Marvin Whatmore. After another "lost weekend" the call finally did come—on Monday morning: "OK, Don, you have a deal. Jack Harding is having Frank Barry draw up the contract. He will be calling your lawyer before the day is over."

Well, we finally had a deal—or did we? Someone had to draw the contract. And that someone turned out to be Frank Barry—Francis Barry, assistant secretary of the corporation, one of Cowles' four in-house law-yers: Seton Hall University, 1949; St. John's Law School, LLB degree, 1953; with Cowles' legal depart-ment since 1957; married; two children; long-time res-ident of Staten Island.

Since our merger with Cowles, Frank had been secretary of Magazines For Industry, Inc., and has also served as our attorney, replacing Dave Regosin. We seemed to have gotten along fairly well. He drew up our various divisional contracts and dealt with our not-too-numerous legal problems as they came up. Frank did not have the brilliance, the sophistication, or the back-ground of his boss, Harvard Man Jack Harding, but he was a good, hard-working journeyman corporation lawyer. He was a quiet, serious man with no apparent sense of humor. He was bogged down in work and rarely seemed to catch up. Whenever I gave him a job, it would require a letter and several follow-up telephone calls before I saw any action. Often, it would take a month before even a fairly routine legal matter was handled. Some weren't dealt with at all. I would just get tired of telephoning. If I really needed action I would call Jack Harding and the problem would be solved.

After more than a week Frank provided Dave Regosin with a draft of a contract. When Dave read it, he was thoroughly frustrated and patient Dave does not get frustrated often. He told me that the proposed contract was so one-sided, so restrictive that we just could not live with it.

"I could meet with Frank and try to go over it item by item, but from the several telephone conversations I had with him, I know that we would be wasting time," Dave said, "And I know that we can't afford to waste any time at all."

"What do you recommend?" I asked.

"I think it would be best if I set a meeting with Frank and have you join us at that meeting. Should we be unable to resolve our more serious problems with Frank, we will have no alternative but to bring Jack Harding directly into negotiations," Dave said. "We have to go through the motions with Frank before we talk to Jack. In the meantime, I am meeting with Ira."

Ira Sheinfeld was a bright young tax and contract expert from J. K. Lasser and Company, who was assigned to handle the accounting details of our buy-back. It was our plan to name Lasser, MFI's accountants prior to the sale to Cowles, as our auditors once again.

This was Tuesday, and the best Dave could do was to set a date with Frank for Friday morning. Promptly at ten, Dave and I were in Frank's office, a fairly small cubbyhole on the sixteenth floor. I had no idea he would turn out to be completely unwilling to yield even the slightest degree on the most minor question. Under the terms of the contract that Frank had drawn up, it would be impossible for us to buy or start a new magazine . . . We could hardly make any important decision relating to any form of expansion without requiring Cowles' approval. The salaries of our key personnel (including my own) were restricted beyond reason. These were just two of a long series of impossible restrictions.

Frank also wanted me to pay Cowles $56,000 in cash or lose the 15,000 shares of my CCI stock that were held in escrow at the Chemical Bank. This item had been in negotiation for over a year. It had annoyed me since the beginning of our merger. The stock was in escrow to provide for any possible unforeseen liability that might develop, or losses resulting from any possible failure to disclose or list any liabilities of MFI.

Following the signing of the contract, Jack Harding had volunteered the following comment: "Don, your operation was absolutely the cleanest and most organized that we have acquired, and all your papers and material data seemed to be in excellent order. I wish I could say the same for other companies that we bought or looked at during the past ten years or so."

Nevertheless, our lawyers and I (most reluctantly) agreed to let custom prevail and permitted 15,000 of my 101,000 shares of Cowles stock to be placed in escrow for three years—subject to a more detailed audit and/or examination by Cowles' internal auditors. Two years later, such an examination was completed—not by an outside auditing firm, but by Cowles' internal auditors. Marvin Whatmore thereupon invited me to have lunch with him and Jack Harding. The real reason for the luncheon was not disclosed to me, however, until we had discussed a number of things.

A raise of $5,000 was approved for Burt Cohen for his work on *Modern Medicine*, bringing him from $30,-000 when Cowles stepped into the picture to $45,000 a year. Since I was in charge of the entire operation, and my own salary was only $53,000, I reminded Marvin that he had pleaded with me to accept that amount and that he had told me I would be compensated "in other ways." I was still at $53,000, and my fine MFI pension program was out the window, and Cowles' dividends had been cut from 50 cents a share to 20 cents and would soon be zero.

Marvin Whatmore then told me his problem. He had paid an average of more than $10 a share for 120,000 shares of Cowles stock—contrary to my belief that, as a virtual founder, he had paid much less—and he had borrowed about $1,000,000 to buy the stock. His $60,000 in dividends just about paid the interest on the loan. Now the dividends had been cut and would soon probably stop. He had sold his estate in North Salem to get cash to meet calls by the bank. (At this point, I realized that if the president of the company controlling the investment of my life's work could do such a thing to himself, then my investment was no longer secure.)

"It's unbelievable!" I exclaimed.

Marvin looked sad and sheepish. "It's all true. So you see, Don, we have to do everything we can to maintain and increase the value of Cowles stock . . . and you must be patient."

Then came the real reason for the luncheon meeting.

"Don, when you placed 15,000 of your shares of CCI stock in escrow, the determination as to any possible liability had to await our audit of your books. Well, this was finally completed," Marvin said, "and I have a copy of the detailed report. Why don't you take it along and study it, and then let's have a meeting and resolve the matter?"

"How much do I owe—or rather how much does the report show that I owe?"

"Fifty-six thousand dollars," Jack said.

"You must be kidding. When we made the deal it was you, Jack, who said that our corporation was the cleanest that you acquired. That everything was in such good order . . ."

"I did say that, but this is what our internal audit found. I am as much surprised as you are."

"Not only was our own controller a CPA and an attorney," I interposed, "but we had three very competent attorneys on the job, and J. K. Lasser and Company, our auditors for over fifteen years, and recognized as the experts in the field of business magazine publishing, did a complete closing audit. This just couldn't be—"

"Let me say at the outset that I don't really think that you will owe us $56,000. I went over the figures and the contract and I have a feeling that it will be reduced by at least $25,000. Maybe more," Jack said.

"And speaking of the Lasser audit," Marvin said, "here is a real shocker. Ernst and Ernst, our auditors, also happened to be the auditors for *Modern Medicine*. We have just completed the audit of *Modern Medicine* and would you believe, Don, the Herzes and the Cohens owe us over $90,000 to cover the stock they placed in escrow?"

I looked at them in amazement.

"What can I say? It doesn't speak well for Ernst and Ernst, does it?"

"Anyway, Don, look over this report, check with Lasser and your old attorneys, and then let us review the whole thing and then let's have a meeting. I'm sure we can resolve it," Marvin said.

When Frank Barry brought up the matter of escrow and the $56,000 item, I saw red. I had gone over the internal audit report with Al Zuckerkorn, the Lasser partner who was in charge of our audits, and who directed the accounting work in connection with our merger with Cowles. Also, with Ed Singer and Dave Regosin. Everybody agreed that the Cowles' internal audit report was completely without merit. That was one reason for Jack Harding's willingness to "forgive" $25,000 immediately.

Among the biggest items in question were the salaries and commissions MFI paid Art Yohalem and Jerry Stevens on *Soft Drink Industry*. The contention of the internal auditor was that "no contracts for these men were listed among the existing employment contracts" and as a consequence, I was expected to cover their earnings for a certain period. This item alone amounted to about $26,000. When I tried to explain that Art and Jerry had no contracts but that they were being paid on a set formula that was consistent with the MFI custom of compensating executives of their class, the internal auditor kept mumbling: "But you did not list these contracts . . ."

From the tone of Frank's argument I knew we would not get very far with him. "Why are you worrying about such a small item as $56,000?" Frank said. "Look at the bargain you are getting in the buy-back to begin with. You're paying a lot less than we paid you. A lot less."

This was none of his business and was not germane to the contract. At this point I knew that we were wasting our time. Instead of arguing with him, trying to show him that I took stock selling at $3.50 per share against $15 when we made the deal, I just sat quietly, gritting my teeth—something I don't do normally. Dave tried to go over item after item with Frank, and Frank would not yield on any point.

"Dave, I have an important luncheon meeting. You don't need me any more. So, I will let you two lawyers go over the matter, item by item." And I left. I realized that we would have to meet with Jack Harding; otherwise, this would be the end of our buy-back.

Dave arranged a meeting with Harding for the following Tuesday. J. K. Lasser's Al Zuckerkorn would be there, as well as Cowles' internal auditor. Ed Singer would be there, and I hoped, in vain, that Frank Barry wouldn't.

The meeting was held in Jack Harding's office, but Frank Barry was sitting at Jack's desk. Jack kept leaving the office periodically. But I made certain that nothing specific and important was discussed unless Jack was in the room. Several times, I found it necessary to interrupt Ed Singer who seemed ready to negotiate with Frank Barry, who continued to be immovable.

However, when Jack came back, we went right to the nub of the problem. Although Jack's mind seemed to be on whatever had taken him out of his office, when we were able to bring him back on the track he proved to be reasonable and amenable. It was obvious that he wanted to make a deal and he wanted to end this meeting as quickly as possible. Obviously, something more important than $56,000 worried him.

Al Zuckerkorn was fully prepared with all sorts of documentations, refuting every item on the list that made up the $56,000, while Cowles' internal auditor was not prepared as well. Although Cowles' man had been in charge of the audit, the man who had actually done it had departed. I naturally kept insisting: "I think you'd better bring in the fellow who did the audit to explain." And since Al could refute every item we soon came close to a settlement, Jack finally gave in on the entire $56,000. By six o'clock we had a deal.

While all this was happening, we were working on the details of the agreement with Irving Trust for the $500,-000 loan. At that point—in August, 1970—the tight money situation was at its most critical stage and one "eager beaver" vice president, for some technical reason, tried to put a few roadblocks in the way. Fortunately, Peter Prestegaard, the young assistant VP who was in charge of our account, had just returned from his vacation and took over the loan application. Since he knew he had the backing of Bill Lyon and Doug McNamara, Peter went to work to clear all possible hurdles. Nevertheless, this took time and work, and it was not until the end of the month that he received both uptown and downtown approval of the loan—almost at the very moment that Jack Harding gave his sanction to the contract for the buy-back.

Now we had a deal that would work at both ends. The closing was set for Friday, September 4, at eleven o'clock.

"The loan and its terms are so unique that it has become 'the talk of the bank,'" Peter told me when he received final approval. "We have never made this type of loan before—but we feel quite good about it." That was mainly why the bank asked that the closing be held at its offices. However, on the afternoon preceding the morning of the closing, Dave telephoned me and asked that we change the locale for the closing to the Cowles offices.

"We haven't finished writing the contract," Dave said, "we will work late tonight and start again early the next morning. And, of course, we have all the papers in Frank's office."

"Do you think that you'll be ready to move with the closing by eleven o'clock?" I asked Dave.

"I believe we will. At any rate, I'd like you to be there at eleven and the rest could show up by eleven thirty. By noon, we should begin to sign the papers."

I was not the first to arrive on the sixteenth floor of 488 Madison. My wife, Betty, beat me by a few minutes.

Within the next half hour, our entire entourage arrived—Jack Mulligan, Beulah, Nancy, Marv and Jerry Epstein, our new controller, and my son, Paul, from the office. Then came my sons, Alan and Mel. Yet to arrive were Peter Prestegaard from the bank and the bank's two attorneys. I learned that they were busy drawing up the bank's contract for the loan. Dave Regosin came out to the reception room and said with his usual smile and reassuring manner: "It won't take long, Don."

Everyone except me went into the board room. I waited in the reception room for Dave's call. He was continuing the "finishing touches" on the contract in Jack Harding's office. Working with Dave, Frank Barry and Jack Harding were J. K. Lasser's Ira Sheinfeld, Dave's young assistant, Bob Stone, and Frank's and Jack's secretaries, plus four others enlisted to help type the numerous copies of a twenty-page contract.

It was an hour before Dave came out again and said: "I'm sorry but it seems to take us longer than we expected, Don, but everything is in order. It shouldn't be much longer now."

Peter Prestegaard and the two attorneys for the bank arrived, but they had not finished writing their contract. They took over an empty office to complete their work. Two secretaries were assigned to help them. There seemed to be plenty of empty offices on the Cowles executive floor today.

At two o'clock, sandwiches and coffee arrived and I joined the group in the board room. It was warm, and since the air-conditioning never did work too well in the board room, jackets were taken off and ties removed. Somehow the board room looked tired and wilted, too.

After a while Dave asked me to go over a number of items with him and Ira.

"It looks as if we got just about everything we asked for," Ira said.

"Jack seems to have stricken every major restriction Frank wanted to put in the contract," Dave said. Jack soon came in and exchanged greetings with me.

"I'm taking the weekend off," he said. "I really need it, and I must leave by four, but I believe everything will be cleared by then, Don. Let me extend my best wishes to you, in case I don't see you again by the time I leave." We shook hands warmly.

"By the way, Jack, there seem to be rumors that Cowles is selling the rest of its properties. Some sort of a deal is going on, isn't it?"

"This is what I was asked by the *Wall Street Journal* this morning. As of now, we have no deal of any kind . . . that's what I told them, and as of now, we have no deal."

"This means that some sort of deal is pending," I said. Jack smiled and walked away.

The deal that was under consideration and discussion was the sale of the rest of the profitable assets to *The New York Times*. As a matter of fact, discussions began on May 4. But from that time until October 28, when an agreement in principle was announced, the Cowles-New York Times deal continued to be in doubt.

Paralleling the "on again, off again" Times acquisition of the Cowles assets was the MFI buy-back. Thus, when everything was running smoothly and the Times deal was on, the MFI buy-back was on the track. But, when the Times negotiations seemed to have reached a stumbling block, the MFI buy-back began to falter. This on again, off again, yo-yo bouncing reached a high point on July 21 when I appeared before the Cowles executive committee to make the appeal for the buy-back. For the first time in several weeks, Chairman Gardner Cowles felt that the New York Times deal loomed as a reality. I had made it plain that I would not work for any other company. Under the terms of my contract, Cowles had no legal right to transfer my employment to anyone else—and that included the New York Times.

I learned later that Gardner Cowles was determined not to let anything stand in the way of the sale to the Times. The deal was so vital that Cowles could take no chances—and that turned out to be a break for me. I represented trouble. Letting me buy back MFI got me off his back. By the time we reached our closing on September 4, the New York Times situation was moving smoothly, so smoothly, in fact, that Jack Harding began to draw the first draft of the eventual 132-page printed proxy statement in consultation with SEC and IRS specialists of Lord, Day and Lord, special counsel for the Times. Jack's mind was on the crucial Times deal—not on the insignificant MFI buy-back. Of course, I did not know all this when we closed our deal, but I liked Jack's attitude and I sensed that something much more important than our buy-back was on his mind.

It was not until five o'clock that we began to sign "the papers." The contract with the bank needed some finishing touches. They were put into the agreement by the lawyers as preceding pages were being read. We signed and signed and signed. Sometimes papers were not quite ready for signature, but we signed anyway, with Pete taking the chance that "everything would be completed by attorneys" immediately after Labor Day. He was behaving more like a human being than a banker's representative because we all realized that we wanted to complete the buy-back on that day.

No one wanted to postpone the deal until after Labor Day because of a few unimportant technicalities. Pete, the bank's representative, had the $750,000 check in his hand. He was ready to release it as soon as every paper that needed to be signed was finally signed. Every now and then, Betty, Alan, Mel and Paul were called in to sign some papers. Also Jack Mulligan. At six thirty, the Irving Trust loan contract papers were fully signed and Peter delivered the check to Dave Regosin.

Dave then went to see whether Frank Barry and his secretarial staff had completed the work on the buy-back contract. It was not until ten minutes to seven that we were ready for the buy-back signings. And this took place in the board room—Frank's preference.

What were we buying back from Cowles? What were we getting for the $750,000 in cash and over $500,000 in contingent liability?

The Magazines For Industry, Inc. that we were buying back was now larger—by at least $1,000,000 in sales and potentially much greater in earnings. In addition to the magazines that we had sold to Cowles in 1966, we were getting the Bettendorf operation. Specifically our buy-back included:

1. Seven magazines: *Food and Drug Packaging, Soft Drink Industry, Candy and Snack Industry, Glass Industry, Paperboard Packaging, Candy Marketer* and *Dairy and Ice Cream Field.*

2. Six directories: *Candy and Snack Industry Buyers Guide, Candy Marketer's Almanac, Soft Drink Industry Annual Manual, Glass Industry Directory, Dairy Industry Catalog* and the *Official Container Directory.*

3. Two domestic newsletters: *Official Board Markets* and *Inside Industry.*

4. An international division that included one maga-

zine, *Paperboard Packaging International*, and two newsletters, *European Board Markets* and *Agricultural Supply Industry*.

5. Our balance sheet would show that we had net quick assets of close to $500,000 which would give us an opportunity to pay off our newly incurred debts quickly and put us on the road to a new expansion program.

We were buying back a bigger and potentially much more profitable business that we had sold four years earlier. And now we were ready for a new beginning.

Throughout the day, we saw no sign of Marvin Whatmore or Gardner Cowles and I did not know whether they were in their offices. I concluded that they must have been away from New York or taken the day off for a longer Labor Day weekend. I just could not believe that Marvin Whatmore would not come out to make some sort of comment, had he been in his office. This, despite the fact that he left the details of the closing to Jack Harding.

Shortly after seven, however, as we finished signing the last of the papers and were leaving the board room, both Marvin Whatmore and Gardner Cowles appeared. As we shook hands with Marv, the old charmer, I noticed that he looked more tired and older than ever before. He also appeared high. He bowed and kissed Betty. He wished me luck: "Don, I hope everything will turn out for you for the best . . . and I want you to know that I wish you the best." Gardner Cowles just looked at us in a detached sort of way and said nothing. They left. We followed in a minute or two. I had not known that Marvin and Gardner had been having a long, quiet drink in the executive lunchroom to celebrate the upcoming deal with the New York Times.

I turned around to take a last look before leaving. The sixteenth floor reception room which once seemed so bright, cheerful and which had been the entrance to so much promise—not only for me but for many others, including Gardner Cowles and Marvin Whatmore— now looked dark and bleak. It had the odor of death— the untimely death of a budding communications empire.

In the weeks that followed, Jack and the attorneys of Lord, Day and Lord completed one of the most complex proxies ever put on paper. It required many days and nights of consultation, negotiation, reading, writing and rewriting. Thousands of pages were written and typed before the huge mass of paperwork was condensed to a 132-page printed proxy on February 27, 1971.

The New York Times deal was put in simplistic terms in a Cowles release dated October 28, 1970, and in a front-page story (with pictures of the printed properties to be acquired) in *Times Talk*, the New York Times internal house organ of November, 1970.

Briefly, the New York Times acquisition included: the *Modern Medicine* group of eight domestic and international professional magazines in the medical and dental field, headquartered in Minneapolis; the Cambridge Book Company, which specializes in educational reading material, largely high school textbooks; *Family Circle*, a monthly women's service magazine, distributed through supermarkets; WREC–TV, a CBS affiliate in Memphis, Tennessee; and three daily newspapers—*The Lakeland Ledger*, the *Gainesville Sun* and the *Ocala Star-Banner*, all profitable.

For this, the New York Times was paying Cowles 2.6 million shares or 25.1 percent of the Times Class A Common (equal to 23.3 percent of the total combined shares of the Times Class A Common and Class B Common). The Times also agreed to assume Cowles' $15,000,000 debt to Investors Diversified Services, Minneapolis, due in annual installments of $1,500,000 for ten years, beginning May 1, 1971. In assuming the notes, the Times agreed to pay an annual interest rate of 6½ percent instead of the 4⅞ percent on the original notes. As a result of the change, IDS agreed to a reduction of the required working capital for Cowles from $23,000,000 to $17,000,000, thus eliminating a technical default and making it possible for Gardner Cowles and Marvin Whatmore to breathe easier.

While Cowles Communications, with Gardner Cowles in control, would own a 23 percent interest in the New York Times Company, the control of the Times would not change very much, since the Times Class A stock elects only 30 percent of the board of directors of the Times, while the Times Class B stock elects the remaining 70 percent. Inasmuch as the Sulzberger family owned over 65 percent of the Times B stock and apparently would continue to own approximately this percentage after the Cowles deal, it could continue to control the Times by virtue of electing at least 70 percent of the Times directors. Of course, the Sulzberger family would continue to own a big chunk of the Times Class A stock, too, giving it a directorship control of better than 85 percent. Gardner Cowles would become one of nine directors—the only one representing the Cowles interests on the board.

Ivan Veit, executive vice president of the New York Times, who is in charge of the company's development programs, said in *Times Talk*: "This is a deal that is highly advantageous to both parties. Punch Sulzberger and Mike Cowles have been personal friends for years and have discussed this as friends. It was all worked out in a friendly manner."

The New York Times deal saved Gardner Cowles' financial neck, but what it would do for the other Cowles stockholders, including President Marvin Whatmore, continued to be an interesting question.

The answer would depend on what the chairman decided to do with the Times stock, worth more than $50,000,000 at that time. Should Gardner Cowles decide to continue to operate *Look* magazine, it would become necessary to sell off part of the Times stock to cover losses and to make a needed promotional effort. Explorations to dispose of *Look* had been fruitless.

Of course, Cowles had the option to suspend publication. However, this could cost as much as $25,000,-000. Cowles Communications had accumulated about $45,000,000 in "deferred income" which would become taxable at the point of *Look's* suspension. This deferred income was money from subscriptions and newsstand sales of the magazine which, consistent with accepted accounting procedure and IRS regulations, is declared "deferred" until the subscriptions are fulfilled. Additionally, Cowles would be required to return money paid by subscribers for unfulfilled portions of subscriptions to *Look*, unless subscribers were willing to accept substitute subscriptions to other magazines such as *Life,* or *McCall's*—and only if satisfactory arrangements for substitutions could be made. Then there was the hefty cost of severance pay for *Look* employees. Obviously, the suspension of *Look* represented a costly and complicated situation and would be undertaken only as "a last resort."

In an interview with *Newsweek* magazine (September 14, 1970), Gardner Cowles was quoted as saying: "My heart is in *Look*—it's my baby. I founded it 33 years ago. I'd sell everything to keep it going." Gardner Cowles' strong emotional attachment to his "baby" could prove a very costly affair—for the chairman, for Marvin Whatmore and for the other Cowles Communications stockholders. It was not to be an easy choice.

Insofar as Marvin Whatmore was concerned, the price of Cowles stock had to reach $10 a share before he would "break even." The price would have to hit $15 before he would realize a capital gain of about a half million dollars—for a lifetime of work. But there appeared to be little likelihood of the stock reaching a price much beyond $12 a share. Besides, as an "insider," Marvin Whatmore could not sell his stock freely, probably no more than several thousand shares a month. The only way he could really get his half million would be in the event of a public secondary sale of the stock, and that possibility appeared remote.

In the meantime, the SEC was eyeing Cowles Communications. Was it becoming an investment company rather than an operating company? Just as long as *Look* was part of it, CCI could go on as an operating company. However, if *Look* were eliminated through sale or suspension, the SEC would undoubtedly look upon Cowles as an investment operation subject to a new set of rules and regulations.

Should *Look* be disposed of, the earnings of CCI would come almost entirely from dividends paid by the New York Times—$1,560,000 a year on 2,600,000 shares at the rate of 60 cents per share. With earnings of about 40 cents per share on its 4,000,000 shares, Cowles would pay a dividend of about 25 cents a share. Cowles stock would be worth from $4 to $8 a share—ten or twenty times earnings.

For Cowles stock to be worth $12 a share, earnings would have to be increased substantially, either through dividends from the Times or other profitable investments. Since the Times–Cowles deal might not be consummated, I decided to begin selling my 94,000 shares of CCI stock on the upswing, slowly. I sold a few shares in the $4 to $6 range. I sold most of them in the $8 to $9 range. My final batch brought $12.50. (I kept 100 shares for sentimental reasons.) A few weeks after I got out of it, Cowles stock touched a high of 12⅞ and then began to decline. At mid-1971 it was selling for 10½ cents per share.

As the Times–Cowles deal began to unfold, I began to wonder what would have happened to me if I had not bought back Magazines For Industry. For one thing, my seven year contract with Cowles as president and chief executive officer of Cowles Business and Professional Magazine Division did not expire until November 30, 1973, or more than three years after our closing. The Cowles management may or may not have thought of selling MFI—as an entity or its magazines piecemeal. It could also have moved to buy out the remaining portion of my contract. It could not transfer my contract to the Times unless I agreed and unless the Times management also agreed. I would have contested both a sale of MFI and an attempt by Cowles to buy out my contract. On the other hand, I might not have objected too strenuously to the transfer of my contract to the Times as long as it was clearly understood that I would have full autonomy to run the Business and Professional Magazine Division, including *Modern Medicine* and MFI, under ownership and direction of the Times.

The *Times* had a special psychological attraction for me. My son, Mel, was a drama critic. I had applied for an editorial job there—unsuccessfully—back in 1929. But the dream of working for *The New York Times* had long faded. I could not imagine enjoying a more rewarding and satisfying career than as a business magazine editor and publisher.

While the average person knows little or nothing about trade papers (or business magazines, as they are known today), just about every one identified with business, industry and the professions at any sort of executive level has some kind of involvement with this unique but very practical and valuable medium. Many executives in a long list of industries would be lost without their favorite business magazines.

Trade journals or business magazines provide news and information about a particular business, industry, profession or function. While the medical field is the largest, with over 350 different periodicals and with an annual advertising volume in excess of $100,000,000, just about every trade, industry or profession has at least one or two of its very own specialized magazines. And some have many more. For example, the computer field has twenty different publications, the electronic industry has more than a dozen and the chemical, food, metal and other basic industries have numerous magazines. But there are trade journals for plumbers, funeral directors, bakers, candy manufacturers, soft drink bottlers, machine tool people, pet shop operators, accountants, lawyers, teachers and insurance men. About 2,500 business and professional magazines are published in the United States, and thousands more throughout the world. It is a big, unusual, highly specialized business with an annual advertising revenue approaching one billion dollars in the United States alone.

While subscribers pay for many trade journals and a small group of business magazines can be had only on a subscription basis, most trade magazines are now distributed on a "controlled" basis. This means that the publisher of the magazine selects his readers on a highly scientific basis, providing advertisers with complete or nearly complete coverage of an industry, trade or profession, or a segment of it. Most of the better magazines have their circulation audited—usually by the Business Publications Audit of Circulations or the Audit Bureau of Circulations. One of the requirements for membership in the American Business Press is a circulation audited by either of these bureaus.

The writer, editor or publisher of a trade paper or business magazine must be a professional. He must have detailed, working knowledge of the trade, industry or profession which his magazine serves. Often he has to be a jack-of-all-trades, since his magazine may deal with many facets of a complicated industry. During my years in the business magazine field, I have learned the uses of thousands of products, I have seen many unusual marketing approaches in various industries but, most important of all, I have made hundreds of personal friends and thousands of interesting acquaintances in many parts of the world. I travel a lot and wherever I go I meet old friends and discover new acquaintances in fields covered by our magazines.

The opportunities in business magazines go much beyond the basic job of publishing a magazine. Often the trade paper editor and publisher serves as a one-man confidential employment agency, as a merger marriage broker and confidant—all without pay. His basic source of revenue is advertising and, to a much lesser degree, subscriptions.

Some business magazine companies—ours included —are beginning to expand into other forms of communications such as running and managing seminars and trade shows, producing cassettes (sound now, video soon), running special-purpose tours and, of course, supplying direct mail and creative services on various levels.

Publishing business magazines has provided me with a most satisfying, rewarding, exciting career. I feel that I have fulfilled myself. I can't imagine a career as satisfying anywhere else, including the *New York Times*!

During the past few years, I have even had the interesting vicarious experience of "working" for the *Times* through my son Mel who, after ten years with

Newsweek as its entertainment specialist, joined the *Times* in 1969 as drama reviewer and cultural reporter. It has been a great joy to read Mel's interviews and reviews in my favorite newspaper. Of course, I know that Mel's reviews are better than Clive Barnes'!

Epilogue

The life of a magazine has a beginning and an end. The lifespan of a magazine can be one issue—a week, two weeks or a month—or it can be a hundred years of issues.

But one thing is certain. Unless a magazine continues to renew itself periodically, unless it serves the ever-changing needs of readers, providing news, information and/or entertainment of a unique and timely nature, it cannot long endure.

And so it came to pass that the lifespan of *Look*, the flagship property of Cowles Communications, in its thirty-fifth year of existence, was coming to an end. After an illness of at least five years, perhaps longer. Some were aware of the symptoms earlier than others, but it was not easy for them to face up to the reality of its terminal phase. Especially for Gardner Cowles who created it, nourished and nursed it along for almost fifteen years before it was strong enough to stand on its own feet. Finally, it began to dawn on its maker that the last days of his beloved magazine were approaching.

It was disturbing and it was sad, but Gardner Cowles at last realized that he had to face reality and permit the patient to die quietly and peacefully.

The last days before *Look*'s demise were very painful for its founder—especially during the early hours of Saturday morning, September 4, 1971, just ten days before the magazine's death throes.

This was during the long Labor Day weekend. Time began to drag shortly after Cowles reached home—his lush, spacious, shockingly modern and newly furnished apartment on Fifth Avenue. It had taken almost two years and about two million dollars to complete the job under the direction of Paul Rudolf, famous mod architect, with the assistance of interior designers François Catroux of Paris and Mark Hampton of New York.

Cowles was downcast. His head was bowed, his tall frame stooped, as he walked through the long, wide entrance hall of the apartment, for the first time failing to admire Picasso's 1964 *Femme Couchée au Chat*, the Gaston Lachaise 1927 bronze or the paintings by his brother, Russell, or the one by Rufino Tamayo, all of which gave the entrance to the Cowles apartment a gallery- or museum-like feeling.

Jan greeted him with a kiss and a smile. They had their predinner drink in the large and very colorful living room, strikingly furnished with an assortment of white, deep-cushioned sofas, interspersed with a collection of white and plum rose pillows, the latter to match the bright rose carpeting. A huge rainbow-like Frank Stella painting on one wall gave contrast and accent to a dark and moody Dan Christensen painting, *Antila*, 1968, on the wall on the left. Cowles passed the serene Henry Moore sculpture, *The Queen*, a dark, seated figure on a large white base, next to a plastic mirrored window. Jan and he sat down on a sofa facing a fireplace with a marble hearth, over which was a Cy

Twombly painting that looked like a child's chalk scribbling on a schoolroom blackboard. On the side of the fireplace were groupings of multicolored flowers and plants.

Jan could sense that she had a tired, weary and worried husband on her hands. But knowing that there were times when this very private man wanted to be alone, she left him to his thoughts. She knew that the hour of decision on *Look* was near.

After dinner—which he ate sparingly—he went to the library and sat down in one of the two rose leather captain's chairs, surrounded by a huge curving wall of books and with more modern paintings and sculpture throughout this unique and spectacular publisher's rendezvous, complete with a carpet specially designed by Guccione in Black Angus hide. At first he tried to read, then began to make some notes, doodling with figures. Then he just sat and began to think—of *Look*.

Rumors of the impending folding of *Look* had been widespread for over a year. More than any other periodical, *Look* had been a target of *The Gallagher Report*. Barnie Gallagher had been pounding away at Cowles and his company's growing problems—particularly the problems of *Look*. In its July 28, 1970 issue, *The Gallagher Report* had devoted its lead story to Cowles and *Look* under the headline: "Cowles Communications—A Race to the Grave." The story began: "Chairman 'Mike' Cowles can't postpone decision on ailing flagship *Look*—six-months revenue down $4,859,338, ad pages off 12.9 percent. Attempt to sell *San Juan Star* underscores desperation. January time to fold magazine. After fat fourth quarter. Before lean first quarter."

On August 18, it followed up with this item: "Desperation Effort to Save *Look*. 'Mike' Cowles gives himself one year to turn *Look* around. Orders bloodbath to cut costs. 60 people fired."

On September 9, the *Report* said: "Sick Image Aggravates *Look*'s Problems. Sale of Magazines For Industry back to Don Gussow, loss of Cowles Communications Editor-in-Chief Bill Attwood, exit of *Look* Executive Editor, Pat Carbine, confirms judgments of sinking ship. Don Gussow resigns from Cowles board, pays estimated $2 million to regain properties sold to Cowles in 1966. Don opposed 'Mike' Cowles' plan to keep *Look* alive, complained of flagship's drain on corporate profits."

At a board meeting late in 1968, the future of *Look* came up for discussion. This was the first time since I had been elected to the board, two years earlier, that a question relating to the magazine's well-being was raised. Until then, the only concern expressed about major Cowles properties dealt with the *Suffolk Sun* where problems had begun to mount, and *Family Circle*, which "suddenly" acquired very special problems.

But *Look*? Why, that was bigger than *Life*. It was a great property. In 1966, gross advertising revenue hit a new record—over $80,000,000—although advertising pages had been slipping from the high of 1,641 in 1960. Increased page rates made the difference, and *Look* accounted for over $4,000,000 of the corporation's pretax profits of $6,623,000 for that year. By 1967, *Look*'s pages slipped a little more and so did revenue. *Look*'s profits were cut by more than half and the entire corporation reported a loss of $3,434,000.

By 1968, it was apparent that *Look* would show a marginal profit at best, since both pages and revenue continued to slip, particularly the former. And there was a limit to rate increases. The big hope was now placed in *Look*'s new Top/Spot marketing plan which meant a much higher page rate for advertising to about

1,000,000 of *Look*'s group of special "higher earner" readers classified according to zip code or area. Hopes were also on *Look*'s MagaMarket 75 (which meant the publication of seventy-five different regional editions of the magazine, with a special advertising rate card for each).

The circulation guarantee of *Look* had been increased by two percent, and advertising rates increased five percent. Additionally, the basic annual subscription price was raised from four to five dollars a year and the newsstand price from 35 to 50 cents. But none of these palliatives helped.

Improve the editorial product? Why? *Look* was a great general-interest magazine—much better than *Life* or *Reader's Digest*. So what was there to change?

Look's editorial staff, including the top editors, were basically liberal, and *Look* carried features that expressed the liberal view, on a variety of subjects. But *Look* made it a matter of policy to try to please readers of all shades of opinion. Thus, an article with a liberal view on a current subject was usually matched with one of a more conservative viewpoint—in the same issue or in the following issue. Thus, if *Look* dealt with a feature on "Vietnam—An Obviously Insane Adventure," it also carried an article on "Vietnam: The Costs . . . Make Sense" by none other than "Hawk" Walt Rostow.

Of course, *Look* published some "in" material, catering to today's generation. But that was always balanced with "love thy mother, love thy father in the old-fashioned way, my dear" stuff. During my almost four-year tenure with Cowles, the only two really controversial pieces published that made headlines in newspapers across the nation were excerpts from the book *The Death of a President* by William Manchester, and a feature on San Francisco's Mayor Joseph Alioto, which called attention to his alleged associations

with members of the Mafia. The latter involved
Cowles in a $12,000,000 libel suit, which has not been
fully resolved, although Cowles has won the first
round as a result of a "hung jury" at the first trial. A
retrial is on the court calendar.

Thus, when the future of *Look* came up for discussion at the November 1968 board meeting, no one
seemed to have any clear answer to the magazine's
declining fortunes. They were beginning to cut into
the earnings of the profitable properties, particularly
those of the growing and increasingly profitable Business and Professional Magazine Division, of which I
was president. So, I was shocked to listen to a diatribe
dribble-mouthed by *Look*'s publisher, Tom Shephard. I
was appalled by the inert rhetoric of *Look*'s division
president, Vern Myers, especially since I knew that in-
wardly Vern was terribly pessimistic about *Look*'s
future. (As a matter of fact, when the Time, Inc., stock
reached a low of $26 a share, he bought a bundle,
which meant, according to some of his associates, that
he was betting against himself—against *Look*.)

I wasn't lulled by Marvin Whatmore's pious view
that "tomorrow would be better" or by Gardner Cowles'
story that: "We have had our ups and downs on *Look*
over the years and we were always able to weather the
storm and come through with flying colors . . . We'll do
it again . . ."

I thought it was time for me to ask some questions
and to make some suggestions.

"Mike," I said, "I believe that we must do something
dramatic, something special to stop the deterioration of
Look's ad revenue and profits—and we must do it
now . . ."

"What do you suggest, Don?" the chairman asked in
a tired, half-annoyed manner, as if to say, "You're a

trade paper man; what do you know about the big-league consumer magazine business?"

"I do have a suggestion, Mike," I said. "While my professional expertise is in the business and professional magazine field, I have been studying the consumer publishing picture very intensely during the past year and a half. As you know, I have a very important investment in it. I've come to the conclusion that we cannot go on with *Look* on a more or less status quo basis.

"For one thing, I don't see any real value in continuing in our circulation war with *Life*. It is a forced circulation to begin with, since our newsstand sales are less than 500,000 per issue, sometimes much less. Even the great Manchester PR has not helped us very much. Circulation has been declining. The only way we can increase it is through high-pressure very costly subscription campaigns. It makes no sense.

"And the cost of running a mass-circulation, general-interest, large-size biweekly is becoming prohibitive. I suggest that we seriously consider changing *Look* to a special interest monthly for today's readers—the young and young-in-heart readers, on the order of *Esquire*—with a circulation of 1,000,000 instead of 8,000,000, and we ought to go to standard size. . . ."

As I finished talking, I looked around at a sea of annoyed faces.

Deliberately, and in a low voice, Cowles said: "Don, I don't want to say that we are a bit ahead of you, but I can assure you that we have been considering changes in *Look* . . . over the years, and some of the suggestions you have made were among those considered. We have turned them down because none of them were practical."

I replied: "This is probably no place to discuss the practicality of the changes I propose—or the ones you have considered—but I have a gut feeling that it is the beginning of the end of general-interest magazines . . . and I mean for *Life* and the *Reader's Digest* just as much as for *Look*. The only difference is that they have more money than we have, but they are doomed, just as *Look* is doomed."

Marvin Whatmore broke in: "Don, even if we wanted to cut the circulation of *Look* sharply—and there are some of us who have been thinking in this direction—we can't to it, because the cost would be prohibitive. We would have to make refunds to subscribers in the millions. What we did not refund would become taxable income. It could cost us more than $20,000,000."

I asked: "Don't we have enough tax experts and can't we obtain the best tax advice to solve this problem?"

"We've tried, Don. So far we have not found any answers."

"Then this means that, even if we wanted to suspend the publication of *Look*, we would be faced with the same problem?" I asked.

"I'm afraid this is the case . . . this is it," Whatmore said.

"What about changing *Look* to a standard-size monthly in the meantime?" I asked.

"We have considered that, too," Whatmore said. "As a matter of fact, I have a standard-size dummy of *Look* in my office, and I will be glad to show it to you . . . but we can't do that either. Our printers, R. R. Donnelley, told us that they would need at least three years to set up the necessary presses for the changeover in size."

It seemed strange, unconvincingly strange to me that, with all of the talent available to us, both internally and externally, we could not find the answers to our problems. But I felt that I had asked enough questions for one meeting. I could sense the great reluctance of

Gardner Cowles and his team to deal with the problem head-on.

At the next board meeting—in February, 1969—the subject of *Look*'s future came up again. This time, *Look*'s viability was even more in doubt, and the overall problems of the corporation had mounted, particularly in the face of a $15,000,000 loss in the *Suffolk Sun,* soon to be dropped. At a previous meeting I had suggested that the *Suffolk Sun* be spun off from the corporation and that outside funds be used for its development. That would shelter Cowles Communications, Inc., from the continuing losses of the Long Island daily newspaper.

Jack Harding had responded: "We can't do it, Don. To spin off a property or division, it must be at least five years old."

Since Jack knew his law, I did not pursue this matter. However, at the February, 1969 meeting, when the future of *Look* was under discussion once more, I reminded the board of my previous suggestion to spin off the *Sun,* and Harding's response.

Then I said: "*Look* is more than five years old. Have we considered spinning off *Look* into a separate corporation?"

"It wouldn't work, Don," Whatmore said, and he did not explain.

Before the end of the year, when a decision to suspend the *Suffolk Sun* was finally made, a step in the direction I had recommended on *Look* was finally taken. But it was too little and too late. The decision was to cut the circulation from 7,750,000 to 6,500,000, reduce rates, and emphasize to advertisers that the smaller circulation would be concentrated in central, major urban markets with high buying power.

When this decision was announced—and it was strictly a management and not a board decision—I countered with: "This is an interesting approach, but why don't we go further and cut circulation to 2,500,-000 or 3,000,000 and then make *Look* a smart, urban magazine—a truly modern product?"

"We are thinking in this direction, Don," Cowles said. "What we are doing now is just 'a first step'. Eventually, we will cut the circulation to 5,000,000 and then to 3,000,000 . . . and I can assure you that it is our intention to make *Look* more of an urban-oriented magazine that it is today."

None of these plans came to pass. It was not until April, 1970, that *Look*'s circulation was cut from 7,750,000 to 6,500,000 and it was announced that "over 80 percent of this circulation is being concentrated in the top sixty metropolitan markets." It was explained further that "the reduction in circulation is expected to reduce production and circulation expenses proportionately, and the concomitant reduction in advertising page rates together with the improved matching of circulation to advertisers' marketing plans is expected to enhance *Look*'s value as an advertising medium."

Apparently, the advertiser and advertising agency communities were not impressed. *Look* wound up 1970 with another sharp loss—both in pages and dollars. *Look* accounted for a pretax loss of $8,000,000 for the year. My division's profit was almost $2,500,000 and the broadcasting and newspaper divisions showed slightly higher earnings. But they were not sufficient to overcome the drain of *Look* (together with other losses). The end result was that the company had a loss from operations of $3,061,000.

In the first quarter of 1971, *Look*'s advertising volume did increase by almost twenty-five pages—mostly from cigarettes, since the advertising of cigarettes was banned from television. Then the advertising volume began to decline and by mid-year *Look* had carried fewer pages than in the very depressed year of 1970 and at lower rates that meant subsantially lower dollar volume.

While all this took place, the editorial product began to deteriorate. The editorial staff was emasculated. Outside writer interest was waning. The pressure on cost reduction was mounting. A good part of the material published was from standing manuscripts, long-written and paid for. In the normal course of events, most of it would have remained peacefully buried. *Look* also ran "reruns", like reruns of old movies.

By mid-1971 it was clear (to those who wanted to see) that *Look* was doomed. It was being "phased out."

The New York Times deal was ready to be consummated and Gardner Cowles' mind was now on the over fifty million dollars in Times stock soon to be added to the Cowles exchequer. He was also thinking about his new image resulting from his upcoming directorship of the New York Times Company.

Cowles, Whatmore and Harding began to confer on the eventuality of dropping *Look*. The major problem they faced was to reduce to a minimum the liability of the "deferred income" resulting from *Look*'s unfulfilled subscriptions. In January, 1971, they had reduced *Look*'s subscription price from $5 to $3 per year and the newsstand single copy price from 50 cents to 35 cents. *Look*'s "deferred income" liability was reduced from $43,000,000 in 1969 to $35,000,000 in 1971. Part of this reduction, of course, was due to the drop in *Look*'s circulation from 7,750,000 to 6,500,000. Obviously, this liability could have been cut to a much greater extent if Cowles had acted on my suggestion of reducing circulation to 1,000,000, or at least to 2,500,000—and to begin to do it in 1968 or 1969. I wondered, but shouldn't have, why no one at Cowles thought about this in the mid-sixties when management should have anticipated the upcoming problems instead of flying into the storm head-on.

Between conferences, Cowles, Whatmore and Harding moved to find a buyer or buyers for *Look* or some of its assets. The New York Times management had been approached on the subject. The Times people were ready and willing to buy most of Cowles' remaining profitable assets and *Look* was no longer profitable. On top of the whopping loss of $8,000,000 in 1970, the loss for 1971 was expected to be in the neighborhood of $5,000,000 to $6,000,000. The Times was ready to save Gardner Cowles' financial neck but it was not going to stick its own neck in the noose now being tightened around *Look*. Time, Inc., Reader's Digest, CBS, NBC, the Times-Mirror and a host of others were contacted. No one was interested in buying *Look* under almost any terms. Cowles couldn't give it away.

Despite the sharp competition between them, Gardner Cowles and Andrew Heiskell had a long-standing friendship. Heiskell was chairman of the board of Time, Inc. Although Time, Inc., could not possibly buy or take over *Look,* Heiskell agreed to purchase the real estate which housed *Look*'s subscription facilities in Des Moines. The price was $2,900,000. Cowles had paid upwards of $20,000,000 over a period of years for them. To sweeten the deal, Time, Inc. would agree to accept (for free, of course) 20 percent of *Look*'s current subscriptions. Upon suspension of *Look,* Time, Inc. would offer *Look* readers substitute subscriptions to *Life* (up to 800,000), to *Time* (up to 400,000), to *Sports Illustrated* (up to 50,000) and to *Fortune* (up to 15,000).

It was a good deal.

If subscribers agreed to accept substitute subscriptions instead of cash—and experience indicated that from 50 percent to 80 percent of them would—then Cowles' "deferred income" liability would be reduced substantially. Instead of having to pay out $20,000,000 to $25,000,000 in cash, Cowles would have to pay out only $10,000,000—and perhaps only $8,000,000. Yet, when I had made the suggestion to move in this direction in 1968 and in 1969, I was told that it couldn't be done.

This step would mean the death of Gardner Cowles' thirty-four year old "baby," but it would save Marvin Whatmore's financial neck and, to a lesser degree, it would help other stockholders—and Gardner Cowles personally, of course, since he was the biggest stockholder of them all. It would save Whatmore's neck because he had bought his 120,000 shares of Cowles stock at an average price of $10 a share. With the announcement of *Look*'s demise and the end of its drain on profits, the price of Cowles' stock was expected to rise. My guess was that it would not go much higher than $12.50 a share and this was the price at which I sold the last batch of Cowles' shares in my portfolio.

When Gardner Cowles went to sleep around midnight on Friday, September 3, he was still thinking about suspending *Look*. He was tired, and by one o'clock he had dozed off. He slept for the next few hours, but it was not a restful sleep. He tossed and tossed. And he snored. He woke up at three, propped himself up a bit higher on the pillow, lit a cigarette and began to think. He was thirty-three when his dream of owning his own magazine—a new kind of magazine, a picture magazine—had become a reality. He was sixty-eight now. How those thirty-five eventful years had gone by! . . . How many years had he left? Ten? Maybe fifteen? His father had died at eighty-four, his older brother was eighty-three . . . Well, the years ahead didn't look so bad. The directorship on the Times, on the board of half a dozen other corporations . . .

After breakfast, he called Marvin Whatmore and Jack Harding and asked that they meet him in his office. He had made his decision. Now it was a matter of timing.

With the subscription substitution problem cleared away, it was really just a matter of going through a few required motions. Key people on *Look* had to be notified. Somebody had to tell *Look*'s 1,000 employees. "Official" board sanction was required.

While the actual decision to suspend *Look* had been made by Gardner Cowles on Saturday, September 4, a board meeting was called for 10 A.M. on Thursday, September 16, to get the "official" sanction for the action. After all, Cowles was a public company and everything had to be done according to the book of corporate rules. It was one of the most depressing board meetings ever held by Cowles, even more depressing than when the board met to suspend the *Suffolk Sun*.

The board now had only ten members, seven of whom attended. In addition to Cowles, Whatmore and Harding, the three decision-makers, the meeting was attended by Vern Myers, Tom Shephard, Bill Arthur and John Weinberg. Merrill Clough was seriously ill. John Fischer was too busy with registration matters at Teachers College, and John Perry was in one of his submarines in Florida and did not want to be disturbed. All seven present, with the exception of John Weinberg, were Cowles employees.

Gone from the Cowles board were:

• Don Perkins, formerly executive vice president of sales, who retired at fifty-nine. He took a trip to Africa to get away from it all. Upon his return, he tended the rose bushes at his comfortable Connecticut house

- Shap Shapiro, who was busy with many lucrative projects that included a good share of fun and games

- Lester Suhler, who was tending his bulls (or were they heifers?) on his Westchester estate

- Larry Hanson, the space salesman extraordinary, who continued to enjoy his share of daily martinis with his advertising friends, although he did not have any magazine in which to sell space—but that would come eventually

- William Attwood, the one-time ambassador-at-large, now firmly ensconced in his publishers chair at *Newsday* in Garden City, Long Island

- Palmer K. Leberman, the former chairman of *Family Circle,* quietly enjoying his fortune on his pleasant estate on Long Island

- Carl Schaeffer, P.K.'s sidekick on *FC*, who was now consulting with other publishers, but missing his nap at Cowles board meetings

- Gilbert C. Maurer, who unexpectedly left his post as vice president of corporate planning and first assistant to the president, when it dawned on him (and on the president) that there would not be much corporate planning for a while. Shortly after his departure, Gil became vice president of planning for FAS, Inc., the public company that was once known as the Famous Artists School. Almost two months later, FAS' corporate problems broke into the newspapers and major personnel changes followed. The corporation's already much depressed stock went from $60 a share to $7 to $4 when the SEC ordered trading in it stopped on the New York Stock Exchange.

And, finally, yours truly.

In a halting voice, appearing extremely tired, Chairman Cowles explained the purpose of the meeting, although this was hardly necessary since everyone in attendance knew why he was there.

"Gentlemen, this is one of the saddest days in my life . . . but we have no choice. We have tried everything we could, and until a few months ago, we thought that we might be able to save it. *Look* has to be suspended. I am going to ask Tom Shephard to explain the more current problems of *Look* and to tell you in more detail why we no longer have a choice . . . Tom . . ."

Tom Shephard was ashen. The rings around his eyes were now deeper and his salt-and-pepper hair seemed to have more salt than pepper. Slowly, catching a deep breath now and then, Tom went into details of the efforts made during the past few months to save *Look*: "Even this morning our men are out selling space— Gentlemen, you have seen our annual automobile issue, dated September 21, and on the newsstands on the seventh. It carried only three pages of auto ads . . . a real disaster. Normally we publish at least twenty to thirty pages of auto ads, including spreads and pullouts. *Look* is a great magazine, now better than ever, but we have not been able to get the needed linage, and without the needed advertising we have no magazine. Ironically, as of today, our space tally is almost equal to the space we carried last year . . . but the final quarter does not look good and if we continue through the year, we will wind up with less than 1,100 pages of advertising, perhaps much less, and you know that we need 1,500 pages to break even . . . It just isn't there . . ." His voice broke and he had a difficult time continuing.

A resolution was read to suspend *Look*. It was quickly seconded. There was no discussion, no questions. The chairman called for a vote. The ayes were hardly audible. There were no nays.

"The motion is carried unanimously," Gardner Cowles said. The meeting was over.

Gardner Cowles then said to Bill Arthur, the editor: "Bill, now you and I have to perform the most unpleasant rite of all—to tell your staff that *Look* is dead. Bill, let's go and get it over with . . . I don't know how or what I will say . . ."

"Mike, I know how you feel—almost thirty-five years of your life . . . twenty-five and a half years of mine . . . The staff has been alerted. I have a feeling they know, although most of them don't want to know . . . I have scheduled the meeting for 10:30 A.M. It is now 10:35."

When Gardner Cowles and Bill Arthur reached the eleventh floor and the staff members became aware of their presence, everything came to a halt. About thirty-five or forty of the reduced editorial staff, together with a dozen or more secretaries, had gathered to hear the momentous decision from the mouth of Chairman Cowles and some word from Editor Bill Arthur.

The rumor mill had ground vigorously, of course: "*Life* will call it a day and will be merged with *Look*" . . . "I think we're being taken over by *Reader's Digest*" . . . "Gardner Cowles killing his own baby? I don't dig it" . . . "Baby, nothing! It's an old bag . . . it deserves to die . . . we haven't done a damn thing new in years. It needed rejuvenation a long time ago. It's dying from old age . . . from arteriosclerosis . . ."

Bill Arthur called for attention. "Ladies and gentlemen . . . fellow staff members . . . Mr. Gardner Cowles has an announcement."

"Men and women of *Look*," Cowles began, "I do not know how to tell you this, but at a meeting of the board of directors of Cowles Communications, Inc., this morn-

ing, it was unanimously decided . . ." . . . his voice
broke, and for a moment he could not continue . . .
". . . to suspend *Look,* effective with the October 19
issue."

There were ahs and ohs and sobs . . . as Cowles began to cry, Bill put his arm around him and Bill, too,
broke out into uncontrolled sobbing.

An hour and one half later, in the ballroom of the
New York Hilton, Gardner Cowles walked briskly to
the dais for a hastily arranged press conference. He was
followed by five of his executives—all members of the
board of directors: Marvin Whatmore, Jack Harding,
Vernon Myers, Tom Shephard and Bill Arthur.

Cowles said: "Good afternoon. I am Gardner Cowles,
Chairman of the Board and Editor-in-Chief of Cowles
Communications . . . With me here on the dais are . . ."
His voice faltered as he began the introductions. It
quavered when he said: "As you know, the Directors
of our company voted this morning to cease publication
of *Look* after its October 19 issue. I founded *Look* in
1937 and have been a part of all the fine and exciting
things it has done during the last thirty-five years . . . I
am proud of the men and women of *Look* who have
worked so tirelessly and loyally in what has now proved
to be a losing cause . . . Why did we fail? For a
variety of reasons . . . The economy went sour, and
Look, after twenty-one consecutive years of profitability, became unprofitable. As the recession worsened, so
did *Look*'s troubles. The economy is not the whole answer. Television cut deeply into our advertising revenues. We could not compensate for lower advertising
volume by increasing rates because of the competitive
situation. Major costs are out of our control. Postal
rates have risen dramatically, and they are due to go
still higher.

"Is there any longer a need for large circulation magazines? My answer and the answers of the 28,000,000 adult readers of *Look* will differ from that of many people in the advertising community—and apparently the Postal Service. Readership surveys and the response to *Look*'s subscription and renewal offers have never been better. As the educational level of America increased, *Look* became more and more challenging and intellectually stimulating. Now, at the end, we have the most interested and best educated audience.

"And this makes the decision to stop publishing even more painful. As we considered this action, my heart said, 'keep it going' but my head said, 'suspend it.' Despite our commercial failure, other publications will continue to inform, educate and entertain America. I deeply regret that *Look* will not be able to share with them any longer this rewarding and satisfying task . . . thanks . . . thanks from the bottom of my heart, to my associates here on the platform and to all the other people at *Look* and at Cowles Communications . . . thanks for everything you did to bring *Look* alive, make it wanted and desired and, on occasion, even loved . . . and thanks for everything you did to try to keep it alive . . . thanks."

His voice broke again. When he composed himself, he asked: "Are there any questions?"

Up went the hands. During Cowles' reading of his formal statement television cameras ground away and still cameras clicked. The room was jam packed—with men and women and equipment, mostly TV equipment.

Did he really believe that there was a future for general-interest magazines?

"The future for *Life* is very, very good . . . it is too bad that the country can only support one quality photo journalism magazine."

Did Cowles Communications plan to liquidate the rest of its business?

"We have no intention of liquidating Cowles Communications. The corporation is in sound condition and we have many options open to us for the future."

Gardner Cowles now looked very tired. The wrinkles in his forehead had deepened. His jowls lengthened and had more creases. His eyes were bloodshot . . . But there were more question, he had to answer.

Is there a chance that *Look,* like the *Saturday Evening Post,* might eventually be revived, in less ambitious form?

"Our company wouldn't do it," he replied. *"Look* is dead." His voice broke again, he sighed . . . and turned away. . . . *Look* was dead, and that was that.

On the eleventh floor of the *Look* building, a kind of carnival spirit took over. Someone brought pitchers full of Bloody Marys, and as they drank and talked, there was banter . . . kisses . . . handshakes . . . and tears . . . No one seemed surprised.

"Yesterday I was in shock," Editor Bill Arthur told me over the telephone the next day, "today, I am sad. Now I know that *Look* has died. It's terribly sad. I expect to remain here until the end of the year, to try to find jobs for my staff. They are great people—we have some fine talent."

During the next few days, Cowles Communications turned into a very active employment agency. The secretaries could find jobs easily. Despite a depressed job situation in New York, the demand for secretarial help was still greater than the supply. So, *Look* secretaries found that they had a choice of jobs but they were not rushing to take any. After all, they were promised severance pay; in some cases, that could be a substantial amount. Besides, the excitement following the announcement of *Look*'s demise was contagious. The top editors, particularly Editor Bill Arthur and Managing Editor David Maxey, were beginning to get offers

and they, too, did not rush to accept the initial propositions. Like ships' captains, they were first concerned
with finding jobs for their staff members. Time, Inc.
people came and talked to some of the *Look* editors.
And representatives of other publishing companies followed suit. "It's cold outside," David Maxey told me,
"but not that cold . . . I believe we'll be able to place
quite a few of our staff members. We have some very
talented people here."

What were the options open to Cowles Communications that the chairman had alluded to, at the press
conference? There were at least five: (1) to operate
Cowles as an investment company (technically it became an investment company at noon on September 16,
actually it was to assume that status on October 20, the
day after the date of *Look*'s last issue); (2) to acquire
another communications company; (3) to merge into
another company; (4) to liquidate and give its share-
holders their proportionate shares of the New York
Times stock; or (5) to do nothing.

I rule out options One, Two and Five. Eventually, Cowles is bound to do something. It is not likely
to acquire another communications company. The
"loser" image is much too strong for any communications operation of merit to want to merge into Cowles.

Liquidation is possible and even probable, despite
the chairman's well-intentioned protestations. It is a fair
way to deal with the stockholders.

Merge into another publishing company? That is also
quite possible. Especially for a privately held communications firm of size and profit that may have a
yen to become public and have its shares listed on the
New York Stock Exchange automatically. It would
seem to be a good thing for a firm like the *Reader's
Digest*. In the bargain, that firm would also capture

2,600,000 shares, or about 25 percent of The New York Times A stock.

Thus, I opt for Options Three and Four as the most probable of the five.

Another, remote, possibility remains—that the New York Times would move to acquire Cowles Communications, Inc. Certainly, the New York Times management would not like to see the Los Angeles Times, or any other company of that type, acquire Cowles Communications and its 2,600,000 shares of Times stock. Which means that the New York Times will be watching activities in that direction very carefully. As a director, Gardner Cowles is bound to keep the Times informed of any such moves.

Several days after the press conference, I telephoned Gardner Cowles and expressed a wish to see him to check on some facts for my book and to discuss the last days of *Look*. He was receptive and we made a date for three in the afternoon of Tuesday, September 28.

When I approached 488 Madison Avenue on a gray, drizzly afternoon, I saw that the "Look Building" sign was still up on top of the twenty-three floor structure. To me it looked dirty, shoddy—as if ready to be taken down any minute. I entered the lobby where once brightly lit enlargements of front covers of *Look, Venture* and *Family Circle* greeted you from all sides. The walls were gray, bare, in need of a paint job.

On the sixteenth floor, a receptionist I had not seen before looked up at me. She left to announce me and on her return she said, "Mr. Cowles will see you in a few minutes."

The huge reception room seemed cold, empty, impersonal. Mounted pages from the last issue of *Look* were still on display. A copy of the last issue of *Look* was on a glass table. It felt even thinner than it looked. No longer on display were copies of the four daily newspapers once published by Cowles or copies of the thirty-two periodicals published by my division. Eighteen were now published by me under the buy-back, the rest by the New York Times, which now also owned three of the dailies.

Martha Stephens, Gardner Cowles' long-time secretary, came out to escort me to Cowles' office. As she led me in, she said, "Mr. Cowles . . . Mr. Gussow here . . ." Did I need an introduction? I took a seat facing his desk. He said nothing, just looked at me. I started the conversation.

Briefly, I explained that while my book dealt with my four years with Cowles Communications and the details of the buy-back, it also included his biography and those of others "because you can't view the present without relating it to the past." He smiled and nodded his head as if agreeing with what I had said. He still looked tired, but somewhat better than he had looked at the press conference. He wore a dark blue suit and a maroon bow tie that I had seen him wearing on previous occasions. I added that I wanted to check some facts with him. Then I said: "Thursday, September 16, must have been the saddest day in your life . . . . Which was the happiest?"

He looked at me and smiled, but said nothing, thinking, perhaps, that I was just talking for the sake of saying something.

"I am serious, Mike, if September 16 was the saddest day for you, which was your happiest?"

He took a puff on his cigarette, sat back, thought for a moment, then said: "I presume you mean in relation to *Look* . . ."

"Not necessarily," I said.

"Well, there is no one day that I would call '*the* happiest'. There were a few . . . When *Look*'s circulation topped that of *Life,* that was a very happy day.

And when we began to carry more advertising per issue than *Life* published per issue, that was a very happy day . . . and the happiest time in my life was the around-the-world trip that I took with Wendell Willkie in the fall of 1942. I had campaigned first for Willkie in 1940 . . . and *Look* went all out for him, we were heartbroken when he lost. But two years later I was with the Office of War Information. Roosevelt had taken a liking to Willkie and arranged for us to make the month-long world-wide trip—to show the world that both major U.S. political parties were united, and to meet with world leaders as his unofficial representatives, and express the President's good will and good wishes . . . We flew to Brazil, to Dakar, then to Accra in Ghana . . . then to Khartoum in the Sudan . . . and from there to the battle scene in Africa . . ."

The highlight of this trip, he said, was his visit with Joseph Stalin.

"Stalin was very angry with Roosevelt because supplies were not coming in fast enough . . . Stalin said he joined forces with Hitler because Russia had not been ready for a war with Germany, with or without the help of the allies. He felt that he needed three years of intensive preparation, and now the United States was not supplying the arms that he needed so badly fast enough. He took me up the parapet of the Kremlin where he pointed out the artillery shelling by the Germans of the outskirts of Moscow . . . that was shortly before the Hitler troops began the siege of Leningrad."

Then he proceeded to describe the rest of the Willkie "one world" trip—in detail, with names and dates . . . as if it had all happened only the other day.

"Some years later . . . quite a few years later, about ten years ago, I went to Russia again, and this time I visited Khrushchev. He was entirely different from Stalin. He was a natural extrovert, friendly and talkative. He loved to talk, and ask questions. If Khrushchev had been brought to the United States as a child, he would have become an American quickly, and in my opinion, he would have wound up as president of a large corporation. He was tough, but down-to-earth, a realist . . ."

I redirected the subject to *Look* . . . but it was apparent that he preferred to discuss the past, the "happier days."

I reminded him that at the press conference he said that *"Life* had a very, very good future."

"You didn't really mean that, did you, Mike?" I asked.

"For the immediate future, *Life* will be OK but not long range, I'm afraid. Their problems are the same that we faced on *Look* . . . the lack of real interest on the part of advertisers and agencies in mass-circulation, general-interest magazines. *Life* salesmen are out on Madison Avenue trying to scoop up the ad pages scheduled in *Look* for the rest of 1971. I'm afraid that they will not get many of those pages. They will sell some—but not many. When the *Saturday Evening Post* folded, *Life* and *Look* thought that each of us would get a good share of the *Post* business—We didn't—Both magazines continued to lose linage . . ."

"Financially, I guess you have come out well . . . but what about emotionally?" I asked.

"The financial analysts down on Wall Street said that Cowles Communications would be worth more with *Look* dead than alive. We tried to prove them wrong . . . you know this, Don . . . we went through this when you were still on the board. But I am afraid they're right. Yes, financially, we have done all right. Our 2,600,000 shares of New York Times stock are now worth approximately $60,000,000. The TV and radio stations we own have a value of about $12,000,000—

which makes it a total of $72,000,000. The suspension of *Look* will cost us about $10,000,000. Our severance pay needs of about $3,000,000 will be covered by the amount we will receive from Time, Inc. for our subscription fulfillment facilities and real estate in Des Moines. This means that Cowles Communications will have a value of $60,000,000—more, if the price of the Times stock goes up. Not bad when you realize that the Cowles family invested only $5,000,000 in Cowles Communications and when we went public, stockholders invested another $5,000,000. That is a total investment of $10,000,000—and we are now worth six to seven times that."

He said nothing about the emotional values involved. So I asked the question, again, putting it in another way: "I suppose, from the emotional point of view you feel satisfied with your substantial ownership in the New York Times and with your directorship of the Times?"

"Yes, that's right . . ."

My questions that followed dealt with dates and places and Gardner Cowles answered most of them. The interview was over and we parted. I had seen no visitors during my short wait in the reception room and I saw none as I left.

As I waited for the elevator, I wondered what would happen to the twelve floors of space Cowles had on lease, what use would be made of Gardner Cowles' own lunchroom on the sixteenth floor and the three other lunchrooms located on the other floors in the building. The elevator came: no one was in it. It stopped on the eleventh floor but no one entered. I saw one person—the moustached young man who usually picks up the intracompany memorandums. He just stood there.

As I walked back to my office, I wondered what the $5,000,000 originally invested by the Cowles family since 1936 would have been worth if the amount had been placed in a savings bank, bearing compound interest of five percent. When I returned, our controller gave me the answer: $23,000,000. Inasmuch as the Cowles family now owns approximately 25 percent of Cowles Communications, Inc., it will mean a value of approximately $15,000,000. In other words, Gardner Cowles and members of his family would have done better financially if they had put the $5,000,000 in a savings account.

The final issue of *Look,* dated October 19, 1971, did not have the appearance or "feel" of a last issue. It was a "fat cat." It had a folio (number of pages) of 94 and an additional 28 pages of regional or demographic pages, for a total of 122. Of these, 65 pages were advertising (45 national, 20 regional or demographic). This meant an advertising revenue in excess of $3,000,-000. This issue carried a considerable volume of automobile advertising pages. And it was loaded with cigarette advertising. It should have been a profitable issue.

Editorially, it was one of *Look*'s better issues—probably the best published in 1971. The feature was a six-page excerpt from Allen Drury's new book, *Inside the White House 1971*. This was displayed on the cover in big, red and white (on black) type under a picture of the White House. It promised "An unforgettable portrait of the 'shy, lonely, much wounded, ambitious, courageous and deeply patriotic President' and those who surround him, by the Pulitzer Prize-winning author of *Advise and Consent.*" A big order, and exciting to contemplate. While this promise was only partially fulfilled, either the result of an ineffectual job of excerpting, or because the book itself was not that good, it was an interesting and readable feature. Other quality features in this issue were: "The Power and the Glory Are

Passing," by *Look*'s Senior Editor Joseph Roddy, which dealt with the "declining power of the Vatican," and an avid piece on Peggy Lee, the great singer (which appeared in the New York issue and several other regional issues only). This was written by Charles Mangel, also a *Look* Senior Editor. The rest of the issue was filled out with "filler," but generally good filler.

With the exception of the Drury excerpt, the entire issue was staff written.

The issue should have sold well, but it didn't. Almost two weeks after it reached the stands, large piles of copies were still there. This was a shame, since copies of this edition will become collector's items—ultimately.

Look's demise turned out to be front page news in the *New York Times* and other newspapers across the country, on network television news programs, in the publishing and advertising business press which quoted competitors and non-competitive publishing executives. And advertisers. As in the case of a deceased person, even those who had no particular brief for *Look* or Cowles proved to be most charitable, and had only "nice" things to say to the bereaved.

Curtis Judge, president of P. Lorillard, division of Loew's Corporation, was among the major advertisers, particularly those of cigarettes and liquor, who were especially disturbed by *Look*'s closing. He said: "'I hated to see *Look*'s demise. If the financial pressures on magazines continue, then *Life* could be in trouble, and then where are you going to get the attributes of those great big pages and the broad reach?"

Charles McCarty, director of marketing at Brown & Williamson Tobacco Corporation, expressed his feeling in this way: "*Look*'s folding means less opportunity, less flexibility in the use of media. It keeps coming down to specialized publications with smaller circulations."

Gail Smith, director of advertising and sales promotion of General Motors, had this to say: "We've lost what's been an important outlet for us in the automobile business, with its good circulation, it's too damn bad, just like it was with the others. This cuts us down in the general audience magazines to just one that's out with more frequency than monthly. We've always thought highly of the magazine, as evidenced by the fact that we've been one of the major advertisers—in the corporation and the industry."

George Simko, media director of Benton and Bowles, said he was disturbed about *Look*'s folding, adding: "Anybody in the advertising business has to be, when a major medium goes out of business. It has to tell you something about the problems facing the whole industry. The root problem is the cost of producing a major magazine."

Said Time, Inc. Board Chairman Andrew Heiskell: "It is always bad news for this country when a responsible journal is forced to close down. It is particularly bad news when that development is in part engendered by an arm of the government—in this case, the Postal Service, which has already taken the first step in raising second-class mail rates to irresponsibly high levels."

Said Bill Attwood, publisher of *Newsday* and former editor-in-chief of Cowles Communications: "*Look*'s death is a real tragedy. . . . The government is making it harder and harder for magazines to survive."

It was Magazine Week in New York when *Look* decided to call it a day. Steve Kelly, president of the Magazine Publishers Association, and others of the group who met at the Plaza Hotel, expressed "regret" and "sadness" over the Cowles announcement.

There was one exception. John Mack Carter, president of Downe Publishing, a division of Downe Communications, Inc., publishers of the *Ladies Home Journal* and the *American Home,* was quoted in *Advertising Age* to the effect that the decision to fold *Look* was an unnecessary one and could have been avoided, primarily because of the magazine's "great potential." *Look*'s problems, Carter felt, had been with it for a long time, and most of them were shared by every other publishing enterprise. He said that the management of *Look* "tended to postpone correction of their problems to a point where it seemed that dissolution of the magazine was the best course." Up to a year ago, the financial troubles that had beset *Look* in its final period "could have been brought to manageable proportions," Carter said. The fact that Cowles' top management opted to cease publication was more a reflection of their determination to get out of the publishing business than of the potential of the magazine itself, he pointed out, adding: "Cowles' dedication to publishing evaporated and no magazine could exist in that atmosphere."

Chris Welles, a former editor of *Life*, in a publishing commentary in the *New York Times* on September 17, said: "Neither *Life* nor *Look* attempted to alter its traditionally free-wheeling, wide-ranging editorial policy, which many Madison Avenue media experts found inconsistent with the new era of special interests. Magazines such as *Playboy* and *Cosmopolitan* were successful, these experts felt, because they fulfilled the specific needs of a specific audience. Even such large circulation publications as *Reader's Digest* and *TV Guide* served a clearly defined function. Readers were thus 'involved,' the theory went, and more receptive to the magazine's advertising. What function did *Life* and *Look* serve, the media men wondered. Who really needed them? If their readers subscribed only from habit or the low subscription rates, they probably didn't pay that much attention to the advertising."

Time devoted a full page to *Look*'s demise, *Newsweek,* slightly less. The headline of each story was the same: "The Last Look."

About The Author

A product of the East Side of New York, DON GUSSOW was educated in the New York City public schools and at the University of Vermont where he majored in Education and minored in Journalism.

Deciding on a career in journalism, he served as editor of several food magazines before he launched his own company, Magazines For Industry, Inc., in 1944. With 18 periodicals, covering 8 industries, it has grown to be one of the larger and more important of the 250 multiple business magazine publishing companies.

Mr. Gussow is a founder of the American Association of Candy Technologists and the creator of the annual "Kettle Award," the "Oscar" of the candy industry. Until last year he was a member of the board of directors of the American Business Press and he has been actively identified with many committees in the industries served by his magazines. For 25 years he was a contributing editor of the *Encyclopedia Britannica* and he has authored numerous business editorials and articles. Last year he was a nominee for the Leading Business Magazine Publisher of the Year Award, conducted by The Gallagher Report.

Mr. Gussow and his wife, Betty, reside in New York. They have three sons, Alan, a landscape painter, author and conservationist; Mel, drama critic of *The New York Times* and author, and Paul, who is associated with Magazines For Industry, Inc.